You Don't
Have to Be
Rich

PORTFOLIO

Jean Chatzky

You Don't Have to Be Rich

Comfort, Happiness, and
Financial Security on
Your Own Terms

PORTFOLIO

PORTFOLIO
Published by the Penguin Group
Penguin Group (USA) Inc., 375 Hudson Street,
New York, New York 10014, U.S.A.
Penguin Books Ltd, 80 Strand, London WC2R 0RL, England
Penguin Books Australia Ltd, 250 Camberwell Road, Camberwell,
Victoria 3124, Australia
Penguin Books Canada Ltd, 10 Alcorn Avenue,
Toronto, Ontario, Canada M4V 3B2
Penguin Books India (P) Ltd, 11 Community Centre, Panchsheel Park,
New Delhi – 110 017, India
Penguin Books (N.Z.) Ltd, Cnr Rosedale and Airborne Roads, Albany,
Auckland, New Zealand
Penguin Books (South Africa) (Pty) Ltd, 24 Sturdee Avenue,
Rosebank, Johannesburg 2196, South Africa

Penguin Books Ltd, Registered Offices:
80 Strand, London WC2R 0RL, England

First published in 2003 by Portfolio,
a member of Penguin Group (USA) Inc.

3   5   7   9   10   8   6   4   2

Money and Happiness Survey TM and © 2003 Time Inc. Used by permission.

Publisher's Note: This publication is designed to provide accurate and authoritative information in regard to the subject matter covered. It is sold with the understanding that the publisher is not engaged in rendering legal, accounting, or other professional services. If you require legal advice or other expert assistance, you should seek the services of a competent professional.

LIBRARY OF CONGRESS CATALOGING-IN-PUBLICATION DATA
Chatzky, Jean Sherman, 1964–
You don't have to be rich : comfort, happiness, and financial security
on your own terms / by Jean Chatzky.
p.   cm.
Includes index.
ISBN 1-59184-012-0
1. Finance, Personal.   I. Title.
HG179.C5363 2003
332.024'01—dc21   2003050677

This book is printed on acid-free paper. ∞

Printed in the United States of America
Set in Giovanni Book
Charts and graphs created by Mark Stein Studios

For Jake and Julia

Acknowledgments

This project could not have come together without the efforts of some seriously talented and incredibly supportive individuals. I am particularly grateful to:

—Bob Safian, managing editor of *Money* magazine and the best boss on the planet, who backs me at every turn. Thank you for giving me free rein on this one.

—Literary agent Richard Pine, who coerced a proposal from me when I didn't think I had one to write, then shepherded this project through to completion (and who taught me to think big).

—Publisher Adrian Zackheim and the rest of the team at Portfolio, particularly Will Weisser and Stephanie Land, for lending form to this idea, then massaging the manuscript into shape—and making the process a pleasure.

—Sheryl Tucker, Andy Borinstein, and Douglas King at *Money* magazine and Annie Weber, Vanessa Downing, and Cathy Butler at RoperASW, who helped design and conduct the research and then analyze the findings. I never knew numbers could tell such a great story.

—Denise Martin, Patricia Luchsinger, Betsy Alexander, Nellie Huang, Nick Pachetti, Amy Wilson, Jonah Freedman, and Connie Kurz, my colleagues at *Money*, *Today*, and *USA Weekend*, for their support and guidance along the way.

—The two Amys (Wolfcale and Mahfouz), publicity mavens extraordinaire. Thank you for the amazing effort.

—Nancy Kay and Richard Liebner at N.S. Blenstock, for their ongoing support with this project and so many others.

—The wonderful and generous sources who shared with me their own happiness findings: Daniel Gilbert at Harvard University, Ed Diener at the University of Illinois, Richard Easterlin of the University of Southern California, Robert Lane at Yale University, Andrew Oswald at Warwick University, David G. Myers at Hope College, Tim Kasser at Knox College, *Affluenza* editor John De Graaf, Manfred Garhammer at the University of Bamberg, Jon and Eileen Gallo of the Gallo Institute, and particularly my *Money* magazine colleague Jason Zweig, who not only opened up his own meticulous files but was always willing to talk about happiness despite having his own book to finish.

—The financial experts who helped pull together the rest of the picture: Steve Norwitz at T. Rowe Price, Eric Jacobson at Morningstar, Harold Evensky of the Evensky Group, Ross Levin of Accredited Investors, Bruce Tulgan of Rainmaker Thinking, Jim Ball of The Goals Institute, Keith Gumbinger of HSH Associates, Jim Doyle of Upromise.com, Susan Beacham of Money Savvy Generation, and Feng Shui practitioner Sandra Goodall.

—Reporter Brian B. Reid, who did great work finding real people willing to talk on this topic—and all of those people who shared their stories with him and with me.

—Norm Pearlstine, John Huey, Dan Goodgame, Leah Rozen, Andy Serwer, David Handelman, Wally Konrad, Elaine Sherman, Steven Levitsky, Jeri Kronen, Diane Adler, Laura Mogil, Debi Epstein, Roberta Socolof, and Jan Fisher, who read chapters and proposed titles, for their helpful suggestions and additions to the manuscript (you'll find many of your potential titles are now chapter headings).

—Finally, my family—the Shermans, the Chatzkys, and especially my husband, the Mayor—I wish you all happiness on your own terms.

Contents

Introduction   1

1. **Sophie Tucker Was Wrong.**   12
   Why being rich is not necessarily better.

2. **Enough Is Enough.**   34
   Wanting breeds . . . more wanting. And it can be toxic.
   How to learn to be happy with what you have.

3. **Feng Shui Finance.**   58
   If you're in control of your money, you're in control of your life.
   Here are the keys to control.

4. **What Do You *Really* Want?**   81
   Setting financial goals that are meaningful for your life.

5. **Making It Happen.**   108
   How to turn those goals into your reality.

6. **Living Within Your Means.**   129
   It's impossible to save much—if anything—until you stop
   spending more than you make. Here's how.

7. **Go with the "Flow."**   157
   On-the-job happiness is an important piece of lifetime
   happiness. You can find it if you know where to look.

8. **It's Not Just About the Money.**   179

    Taking the proper precautions for your family and loved ones
    makes you feel happier and more content. So does volunteering.

9. **Don't Dictate, Communicate.**   207

    When does money breed the most unhappiness?
    When you're fighting about it. If you can learn to
    communicate—with your spouse, your kids, your parents—
    you can stop squabbling.

10. **The Ten Commandments of Financial Happiness.**   226

    Living by four—just four—of these commandments
    can be like earning an extra 50 percent a year.

Index   235

Introduction

It was shortly after September 11—a time of turmoil in the markets, when it was impossible to read the newspapers, turn on the television, or even listen to the radio without feeling out of control financially—that I started to think about the effects money has on the happiness of individuals. The shenanigans of corporate executives in far-flung locales from Texas to Connecticut to Mississippi had sent stock prices plummeting. Wall Street analysts—those supposedly neutral parties who tell us what to buy, hold, and (all too rarely) sell—could no longer be trusted. Neither could the accounting firms that were supposed to keep companies on the straight and narrow. The measures that usually moved stocks in a positive direction—from cost-saving layoffs to corporate stock buybacks—had stopped working their magic. Even speeches from the President of the United States and (can you believe it!) Alan Greenspan couldn't seem to turn the indexes around.

And we—you and I—the individual investors and consumers sitting at home, pouring money into our 401(k)s, putting money into college savings accounts for our kids, counting on these companies to continue to employ us—we couldn't do a *thing* about any of it.

We had no way of knowing whether more corporations would fess up to creative accounting, no crystal balls to tell us if more CFOs were cooking the books. All we knew was that the tried-and-true wisdom—"buy and hold," "buy the dips"—wasn't doing the trick this time around. And although we had past history to fall back on—the history that tells us that markets do, over the long term, come back—we could only hope that would prove to be the case once again. But whether or not it actually happened was clearly beyond our control.

There were a lot of us sitting in that rocky boat. Some 100 million Americans had bought individual stocks by the turn of the new century. And every one of them had the distinct impression (not to mention the correct impression) that their world had been rocked.

You know this. You were there with me trying to get a clear sense of what was down that uncertain road. You knew you wanted to buy that first house (or trade up from the one you were living in now). You wanted to send those kids off to a great college, without saddling them with an unimaginable amount of debt. You wanted to be able to retire someday, or at least slow the pace a bit. And when you left this earth, you thought it might be nice to leave at least a little something behind for the next generation. All of those things that seemed so possible, so feasible, so *easy* a scant few years ago now seemed out of reach.

I know that's how you've been feeling the past couple of years. I know you've been sitting up nights, sweating your future, pondering your losses, worrying that you're going to have to give up that comfortable home, or that keeping it means you'll never be able to stop working—and even dreading the thought that when your health goes, you're going to end up being something you never wanted to be: a burden to your adult kids. I know that your financial situation has become a big drain on your happiness.

I know because you've been telling me. You've been writing me, filling my e-mail box (and occasionally my snail-mail one) with the details of your financial lives and how complicated they've become—and the drain on your overall happiness that can be.

Some of you were looking for an easy fix. Florence from Philadelphia wrote: "I have 75 percent of my money tied up in stocks. Should I leave what's in my portfolio there and see what happens—or sell to preserve what I have left?" R.C. from Albuquerque was in similar straits: "Would you please give some basic suggestions to us shopaholics with no budgeting skills? Must I go cold turkey?"

But many others, like Peter in Colorado, just wanted to commiserate. "I have had to defer my retirement, even though I've been saving and investing in stocks and mutual funds that I felt were relatively secure. Now, with companies like Enron and Worldcom losing value, coupled with the Nasdaq and Dow plunging, a fair percentage of my portfolio has disappeared. As a result, I expect to work a couple of years longer."

How We Embraced the Market—and Lost Our Way

How did we get here? How did we allow this to happen to us? These are the kinds of overarching questions investors and, to a lesser extent, consumers were asking themselves in the beginning of 2003.

To understand the transformation from the arm's-length-from-the-market bystanders we used to be to the in-the-game-at-all-times participants we've become, you have to revisit the longest bull market in history, starting with the crash of 1987. To most people 1987 was the year the Dow dropped 400 points and lost 22 percent of its value in a single trading session. I was working as an assistant business editor at *Working Woman* magazine at the time and vividly remember spending the day talking to distraught traders and investment bankers in lower Manhattan. The shaky voices, tears, and disbelief told me none of them had seen anything like this in their careers. For many, it was their own little taste of the Great Depression.

Yet the crash of '29 wasn't at all like the crash of '87 if you measure by speed of the rebound. In 1987 the Dow Jones Industrial Average posted an overall gain for the year. That fact was pounded on tables for the next decade—and more. The lesson was: If you'd used the crash as a buying opportunity—you would have come out ahead. All of a sudden, buying the dips was the clever thing to do.

Not only that, it was fun! It was a kick to sink your free cash into a stock like Microsoft, then watch it double and split, double and split. If you were smart enough to buy Citigroup when it dropped to $13, or IBM in the teens in '93, you were rewarded as both soared into triple digits. And, because this strategy worked so often and for so long, we stopped asking ourselves, But is this a company worth its share price? Or does it have such deep-seated fundamental problems that it will never recover?

The market became a game. And it had to be played. If you opted out, you left good money on the table. Worse, you had no stories to tell your friends over drinks, no tall tales for Saturday night's dinner party. As Walter Kirn wrote in *The New York Times Magazine* in mid-2002: "It's as if the whole country put up an 'Out to Lunch' sign sometime around mid-1997, except that we didn't really go to lunch; we logged onto the Motley Fool Web site behind closed doors and screened our calls while quietly tracking Intel."

It was hotter than Trivial Pursuit. Better than Pictionary. Compelling. Addictive. Who needed to tune into *Who Wants to Be a Millionnaire*? We could play the real-life version by watching CNBC on cable and making our own bets on e*trade at home. No surprise, then, that we all knew people who took the market to the extreme, giving up decent-paying jobs to try their hot little hands at day trading. Even if you didn't go quite that far, you could still be a player. By the early '90s many of us had the next best thing: a 401(k).

And 401(k)s changed everything. I am not exaggerating when I say it's impossible to overstate the impact that 401(k)s, invented just twenty years ago, have had on our financial lives. By replacing the pension as the retirement vehicle of choice, 401(k)s took the responsibility for paying for our retirements off the shoulders of America's corporations and put it squarely on your shoulders and mine. And while in the very beginning we were reticent to accept such a shift, as soon as the markets took off we embraced it.

And why wouldn't we? Our 401(k)s were giving us the opportunity to snare a much more lavish retirement than we had ever thought possible. We could rack up beaucoup bucks in these accounts during our working years and then, when we slowed down, use the money to summer in Nantucket and winter in Telluride, to send our grandkids to Princeton, to retire at fifty if that was the goal. We knew it was possible. And we had gurus like Jim Cramer and Joe

Battapaglia and books like *The 401(k) Millionaire* and *Dow 36,000* to tell us how.

And Then We Got Ahead of Ourselves

As our paper riches started to accumulate faster and faster, it began to seem okay, natural, even deserving, to spend some of that money. After all, if our brilliance as investors had made us this much money, it would certainly make us much more. But rather than cashing out our positions in order to do it—which would leave potential profits on the table (our shares of Amazon.com, after all, were still climbing toward analyst Henry Blodgett's $400 price target)—we borrowed. We floated trips to Europe and the Caribbean on our Visas and MasterCards. We didn't put much money down on that new car or second home. Instead, we leveraged up. Debt seemed to make sense when the money was flowing this freely.

We didn't even stop spending when the dot bomb blew. Consumer debt continued to rise through the 1990s and into the new millennium. Personal bankruptcies hit new highs every year. But instead of scaling back and taking a break from living large, we began to raid the equity in our homes to support our new lifestyles. With mortgage and home equity rates scraping the bottom of the barrel, we refinanced and took on lines of credit, not just to renovate and add value to our homes, but to consolidate credit card debts that we then allowed to ratchet right back up. A Louis Uchitelle piece in *The New York Times* in 2001 reported that despite the trillions in new wealth generated by the bull market, we owned less of the equity in our homes than any previous generation had.

There seemed to be no going back. By continuing to borrow during the late '90s, we were able to continue to spend more than we were actually earning. In November 2002—three years into the market's steady decline—our personal incomes climbed by only 3 percent. Personal spending grew a full 5 percent.

When the Worry Finally Caught Up

What finally stopped us in our tracks? What finally brought us back to reality? Not three consecutive down years in the stock market. Not rising unemployment. Not the threat of war overseas. No single one of these factors was enough to burst our bubble of glee. It wasn't until a perfect storm of all of these factors hit at precisely the same time that we started to worry.

Unfortunately—besides worrying—we didn't know what to *do*.

An NBC News/*Wall Street Journal* poll released in July 2002, after the Dow Jones Industrial Average lost 1,300 points in ten consecutive trading days, showed that 70 percent of individuals—*nearly three-quarters of us*—have little or no faith in the information that comes out of brokerage houses and investment banks. And yet many of us continue to rely on those institutions to manage our money for us. Shortly thereafter, a *New York* magazine piece focused on a woman who "vowed" not to open her 401(k) statements for the next two years. And there are plenty more where she came from.

As all of this distressing evidence poured in, I started looking for answers. I wasn't certain of what I might find, but I was certain of this: Turning the other cheek wasn't the answer. Nor was sitting around feeling sorry for ourselves, as if we were the minions in a market-run dictatorship that could do with us (and our money) as it wished.

Taking Back Your Financial Life

The conclusion I came to was this: It's time to take back our lives. And in order to do that we need to take back our money. Not just the manner in which we manage it by learning, once again, to live within our means, however modest or expansive those means happen to be. We need to regain our financial power if we feel we've ceded it. Or to grab hold of that power, even if we've never paid much attention before. And we need to do it in a way that will allow us to feel good—*not* compromised, not guilty, not second-rate—but good, happy, smart, and confident about our choices.

But how? If you've watched me on television or read my columns, you know I'm all about the tactical and practical. I look for real solutions to all sorts of money problems, and then I want to see data that prove to me that the solutions work.

Where money and happiness were concerned, useful data didn't exist. There was a bounty of research showing that, indeed, money wasn't the key to lifetime happiness (although it did have a role to play). But when I started looking for lists of behaviors and habits, things you could actually alter in your lives that would positively impact your relationship with money, I found nothing.

So I went looking for those answers myself. At the end of 2002, with the help and support of *Money* magazine, extensive proprietary research was conducted for this book by RoperASW. The goal was to figure out, first, what influence money has over an individual's overall happiness; second, what habits, attitudes, behaviors, and knowledge separate those people who are satisfied with their financial lives from those who are not; and third, what effect changing those habits, attitudes, behaviors, and knowledge might have on a person's life.

The results were staggering. Of course, money plays a role in the happiness equation. To try to deny that link would be disingenuous, not to mention unbelievable. But it's not as strong a link—as big a contributing factor—in your happiness as you might think. Moreover, money can be a bigger cause of *un*happiness than many other factors in your life. Let me say that again. *Even when it's working in your favor, money can't make you completely happy. But it can—without a doubt—make you miserable.*

Our study examined nine factors that contribute to a person's general happiness: things like a marriage or other important personal relationship, good friends, children, job, and lifestyle. Of all of these, money, it turns out, is the biggest contributing factor to a person's *un*happiness. It is the factor we worry most about—the one we feel is furthest from our control.

Then we dug deeper. We delved into the lives of people for whom money was not a roadblock to happiness. These were people who said they felt in control of their money, who didn't spend nights staring at the ceiling worrying about it. And we were able to isolate their habits, attitudes, and behaviors.

The links between those people—the habits, attitudes, and behaviors that separate them from those who are unhappy—form the basis of an astounding new way to manage your money. Follow the prescription, adopt the habits, by which these people live and it will lead you directly to a happier life. You will reduce money-related stress. You will start making financial decisions that truly make you happy—and that aren't based on someone else's definition of satisfaction.

And I have the research to prove: *It's not about how much you have.* You don't have to be a Rockefeller. You don't even have to be rich. That's right. Whether you pull in $50,000 a year or $500,000 a year, you have the same shot at achieving this sort of financial satisfaction.

In fact, adopting these habits, my research shows, is worth an extra $25,000 a year. Picture this. You have two American families. The first earns less than $50,000 a year but is in control of their money. They're not anal with a capital *A,* but they've adopted a handful of the good habits I'll outline for you in the pages that follow. The second family earns at least 50 percent more—upward of $75,000 a year—but they're less in control. They're not financial fiascoes across the board, but they've picked up a couple of not-so-good habits.

Who's happier with their finances? Neither one. Roughly six out of ten families like the first will say they're financially happy. Roughly six out of ten families like the second will say they're financially happy. Good money management—taking ownership of your money rather than letting it ride roughshod over you—makes the difference.

In other words, adopting good money management habits rather than poor ones is like earning another $25,000 a year.

What are you waiting for?

Money and Happiness Evaluation: Part 1

While you are reading this book, you will have an opportunity to ask yourself a series of questions that will help you to better understand how you handle money. In order to get the most out of taking the survey—the same survey used in the new research conducted for this book—you will need to know how to score your own answers. For some questions it will be obvious, since the answers are simple words such as agree "a lot" or "sometimes." However, for other questions the possible answers are numbered from 1 to 7, where 1 stands for "not important at all" and 7 stands for "very important." When you score your own answers on these number scales, an answer of 5, 6, or 7 is agreement that something is important. An answer of 1, 2, or 3 is disagreement, that is, saying that something is unimportant. Answering 4, in the middle of the scale, means something is neither important nor unimportant. That's the way the analysis of people's responses on these number scales was handled for discussion in the book. You should score your own answers this way too, so you can both compare yourself to other people and learn about your own money mindset.

1. Thinking about all aspects of your life, in general, how *happy* are you these days? (Circle one letter.)

   a. Very happy
   b. Somewhat happy
   c. Not too happy
   d. Not at all happy
   e. Don't know

2. On the whole, how *happy* are you with the following aspects of your life? (Check one box for each.)

	VERY HAPPY	SOMEWHAT HAPPY	NOT TOO HAPPY	NOT AT ALL HAPPY	DON'T KNOW OR N/A
a. Your job	❑	❑	❑	❑	❑

Methodology: This mail study was conducted for Jean Chatzky and *Money* magazine by RoperASW among a national sample of 1,505 adults 18 years or older. The surveys were collected from November 14 through December 10, 2002.

The sample was weighted by demographic factors including age, gender, education, and geographic region to ensure reliable and accurate representation of adults in U.S. households.

Results based on the entire sample of 1,505 adults are projectable to the entire adult population in the United States, with a sampling error of ±2.7 percentage points. Results based on subgroups have a larger sampling error.

	VERY HAPPY	SOMEWHAT HAPPY	NOT TOO HAPPY	NOT AT ALL HAPPY	DON'T KNOW OR N/A
b. Your marriage/ serious personal relationship	❏	❏	❏	❏	❏
c. Your health	❏	❏	❏	❏	❏
d. Your friendships	❏	❏	❏	❏	❏
e. Your appearance/ weight	❏	❏	❏	❏	❏
f. Your self-esteem	❏	❏	❏	❏	❏
g. Your financial situation	❏	❏	❏	❏	❏
h. Your children	❏	❏	❏	❏	❏
i. Your lifestyle (standard of living)	❏	❏	❏	❏	❏

3. How often, if at all, do you *worry* about the following? (Check one box for each.)

	A LOT	SOMETIMES	NOT TOO MUCH	NOT AT ALL	DON'T KNOW OR N/A
a. Your job	❏	❏	❏	❏	❏
b. Your marriage/ serious personal relationship	❏	❏	❏	❏	❏
c. Your health	❏	❏	❏	❏	❏
d. Your friendships	❏	❏	❏	❏	❏
e. Your appearance/ weight	❏	❏	❏	❏	❏
f. Your self-esteem	❏	❏	❏	❏	❏
g. Your financial situation	❏	❏	❏	❏	❏
h. Your children	❏	❏	❏	❏	❏
i. Your lifestyle (standard of living)	❏	❏	❏	❏	❏

4. How often, if at all, do you feel in *control* of the following? (Check one box for each.)

	A LOT	SOMETIMES	NOT TOO MUCH	NOT AT ALL	DON'T KNOW OR N/A
a. Your job	❑	❑	❑	❑	❑
b. Your marriage/ serious personal relationship	❑	❑	❑	❑	❑
c. Your health	❑	❑	❑	❑	❑
d. Your friendships	❑	❑	❑	❑	❑
e. Your appearance/ weight	❑	❑	❑	❑	❑
f. Your self-esteem	❑	❑	❑	❑	❑
g. Your financial situation	❑	❑	❑	❑	❑
h. Your children	❑	❑	❑	❑	❑
	A LOT	SOMETIMES	NOT TOO MUCH	NOT AT ALL	DON'T KNOW OR N/A
i. Your lifestyle/ standard of living	❑	❑	❑	❑	❑

5. In the past 30 days, about how often did you feel each of the following? (Check one box for each.)

	A LOT	SOMETIMES	NOT TOO MUCH	NOT AT ALL	DON'T KNOW
a. Restless	❑	❑	❑	❑	❑
b. Useful	❑	❑	❑	❑	❑
c. Stressed	❑	❑	❑	❑	❑
d. Content	❑	❑	❑	❑	❑
e. Hopeless	❑	❑	❑	❑	❑
f. Confident	❑	❑	❑	❑	❑

1. Sophie Tucker Was Wrong

I've been rich and I've been poor. Believe me, honey, rich is better.
—Sophie Tucker

No disrespect intended to the Last of the Red Hot Mamas. Not only was Sophie Tucker (who also wrote a song called "I'm Living Alone and I Like It") a brilliant vaudevillian, she was an independent woman ahead of her time. But when she made this whopper of a statement, she was off her game.

Being rich doesn't guarantee your happiness. Being poor doesn't rob you of it.

Want proof? Meet Nancy and Lloyd. They're a two-career couple living outside Chicago. They have two beautiful daughters, live in a cozy house in a nicely wooded suburb, and, like many of us, pursued '90s style living with a vengeance.

Nancy spent two decades building up her corporate résumé— and her salary. By the late '90s, as an investment banker and money manager, she was bringing in a decent six figures. As a consultant with a major accounting firm, Lloyd was doing the same. They took two vacations a year to fabulous places like Puerto Rico and Belize, had a sizable cushion in cash and stocks, no credit card debt, and knew that when college for their two girls rolled around, paying for it wouldn't be a problem.

In fact, they were so comfortable—so secure—that in late 1999,

Nancy decided to quit banking and start her own business. She had developed a product, an educational toy, that she felt passionate about, and she wanted to see if she could make a go of it. Lloyd was as supportive as you could ask a spouse to be. They sat down together, ran the numbers, and figured that if she just broke even, they could more than manage on the salary he was earning. Even if she lost a little money, they'd be okay. Their portfolio was fat enough to get them through. *Do it,* Lloyd encouraged.

Their ambitions were right on target. But their timing couldn't have been worse. Just as Nancy geared up, the market shut down. She was ready to deal with a bit of a roller coaster, but not primed for companies slashing their budgets and having little to spend on an unproven product like hers. By the time 2001 rolled around, the market had decimated their fat portfolio. Then Lloyd lost his job. And when, more than a year later, he was still unable to find a new one, he settled in to work with Nancy in her business.

So how are they doing? In fact, they're doing pretty well. Much better than you'd probably imagine. For the first time in years, Nancy says, they both feel fulfilled by the work they're doing. They're spending more—and better, more satisfying—time with the kids. Their marriage is stronger than it's been in years because they're communicating more honestly.

All of which is not to say that making the transition to live on less hasn't been a bit of an adjustment. Nancy had little trouble cutting out vacations and dinners out for her and Lloyd. But when it came to weighing extras for their daughters—things like the Irish dance lessons that are the highlight of their week, but that run $1,200 a year—it was a hard call.

The surprising reward is that Nancy and Lloyd feel more in control of their spending than ever before. Things last longer. Fewer things are wasted. "When you have a big paycheck coming in every two or three weeks, very few people can tell you what they're spending. They figure, if they go a little over, it's okay because they have a paycheck coming in. That's how we were. But now, every transaction is well thought out. They're all pure," Nancy says. What's more important, she and Lloyd are "at peace" on issues they weren't able to confront before—things like the importance of family, of friends, of feeling fulfilled by your work. "We're happier," she says.

It makes her wonder, "Do you have to be rich to be happy? I don't think so." Nancy shrugs. "I certainly haven't felt rich the last couple of years, and yet I've had more great moments in the last few years than I had in the previous twenty. Maybe it wasn't supposed to happen to me until I was old enough, experienced enough, to actually get it."

What We Know for Sure

It's an interesting—and tough—series of questions: Do you have to be rich to be happy? Would being richer make you happier? Does money buy happiness?

If you're like most people, you came up with some very strong gut answers.

You either thought, *Of course I'd be happier if I was richer. If someone handed me $10,000 on a street corner, I'd be delighted. Wouldn't you?*

Or you thought, *Don't be ridiculous. I have a spouse (significant other) and kids I love. I have a challenging job that I really enjoy. I have great friends. Money can't buy any of these things.*

In both cases, you'd be right. And you'd be wrong. Why? Because, it turns out, these are not simple yes or no questions. Rather, they are very complicated issues that some of the world's top economists, sociologists, and psychologists have spent decades studying. They've debated, tested, researched, butted heads, written papers, gotten those papers published, stomached the feedback, and started all over again.

And at the end of the day, this is what we know for sure: Money can't buy the sort of happiness you and I are looking for.

To persons in a developing country, a little extra money absolutely can bring happiness. An extra $100 or $1,000 means they can eat every day. It means they can afford a warm place to sleep or an electric fan to drive off the heat. Money brings a huge happiness boost in these circumstances because it can provide basic comforts. Existing without these comforts means living with great *dis*comfort, and that leads to unhappiness.

But in wealthier, developed countries like the United States, that extra $100 or $1,000—even $10,000—isn't going to vastly improve your life. Maybe it will buy you that new pair of shoes you saw in the window at Bloomingdale's. Maybe it will cover a plane ticket to somewhere warmer and sunnier than you happen to be right this minute. It might put a short-lived smile on your face. But will it buy you lasting happiness? Not a chance.

Once you've achieved life's basic comforts and necessities, more money doesn't necessarily buy more happiness. In part that's because we make poor choices about how to spend that extra $100 or $1,000. All too often, we spend $5 here and $10 there rather than do something significant or meaningful with it. But happiness is also a product of things that can't be bought. To people who live in the sort of places where electric fans long ago gave way to air conditioners, happiness is what your husband or wife said to you this morning. It's how you're getting along with your children. It's the pat on the back you get on the job.

Which is why on a national level, it's not surprising that the average happiness of people in the United States hasn't grown over the years, despite the fact that our cumulative wealth has shot up since World War II. The same has been proved in Great Britain. In fact, there's been shown to be very little relationship between income and happiness among most of the world's well-off countries.

Consider: Americans are twice as likely today to own cars, clothes dryers, and air conditioners as we were in the 1960s. In the '70s the average house was 1,700 square feet with three bedrooms and one-and-a-half baths. Today our average home is more than 3,200 square feet. We have islands in the kitchen, televisions the size of small cars, and master bedroom suites you could land a plane in. Yet the divorce rate has doubled and teen suicide is on the rise.

But that doesn't mean money has no role at all in determining your happiness. It does.

Where Money Fits into the Picture

It helps if you can imagine your overall happiness as a pie. First, understand there is a genetic component to your happiness. Academic research says this accounts for about 25 to 40 percent of your overall well-being. Your genetic predisposition toward happiness is a little like your cholesterol level. It can be influenced by good habits (exercise and regular sleeping) and bad habits (poor eating, overindulging in drugs or alcohol), as well as by prescription medication (like Prozac). But part of it is simply your chemical makeup.

Then there are a number of other controllable factors that affect your happiness. Some of these, not surprisingly, are much more important than others. (We know this from my study as well as many academic ones.) And, as you'll see in the coming list, some of them—a marriage, for example—don't apply across the board. Let's take a look at them in order of their significance.

Marriage or another significant personal relationship accounts for about the biggest chunk of your overall happiness. People who are married are more likely to be very happy than those who are single, divorced, or widowed. Those who are living with another person or in a serious long-term relationship get almost all of the beneficial effects. Why is this the case? Married people not only enjoy continued company, but also stay in better physical and mental condition, arguably because they take care of one another. They're also happier with their financial situation than singles, perhaps because they have one another's income (or ability to earn an income) to fall back on.

Lifestyle. Merriam-Webster's Collegiate Dictionary defines lifestyle as "the typical way of life of an individual, group, or culture." The world *typical* is the important one here. If you're happy with the pace, structure, process of your life typically, on a daily basis, you're more likely to be happy overall. Note that this term is also broader than the others on the list. Many of the items below play into it.

Self-esteem. People who feel good about themselves are able to weather ups and downs in all of the other categories. If you feel good about yourself, you'll come through a divorce or loss of a job thinking clearer and feeling more optimistic—and you'll rebound more quickly as a result.

Finances. People with a little more green in their pockets are a little happier because they can afford more of life's basic comforts as well as a few extras. But, despite what you may think, they are not that much happier.

Job satisfaction. People employed full-time are much happier not only than people who are unemployed because they were forced out of the workforce or haven't been able to find jobs, but also than those who don't work by choice. There are a couple of reasons for this. First, people who are employed usually don't have to worry about paying the mortgage or putting food on the table.

More important, though, a job you enjoy can be a terrific source of satisfaction and self-esteem. It can be a place to enhance your life well beyond your résumé and retirement portfolio: Long-lasting friendships are forged on the job, and many people marry someone they work with.

(Note: Staying home to raise your kids, if you're doing it by choice, seems to qualify as a job of this type. Women not out in the workforce in the 18–45 age group, which these days qualifies as the childbearing years, have happiness scores nearly as high as those of women *in* the workforce. They feel just as useful, confident, and content. Their self-esteem is just as high. They are, admittedly, a little more stressed, but I can't say I find that surprising. I'm fortunate to spend a day a week at home caring for my children, and I *know* it's much tougher than going to work.)

Unemployed people, on the other hand, are more often bored and depressed. They more often turn to drugs and alcohol and are more likely to commit suicide. And the longer they're out of work, the worse the situation gets. Retired people are an interesting mix. They tend to be happier than working people as long as they can maintain their standard of living.

Friendships. For the same reason that marriages add happiness to life, friendships do, too. Everything—from eating in a restaurant, to watching a movie, to going for a jog—is more pleasant when you have others to share it with.

Health. I think of Ally McBeal, frustrated in yet another of her long line of disastrous dating attempts, banging her head against the wall. "I have my health. I have my health. I have my health," she is repeating to herself over and over again. And it's true. If you have your health you can get to that job each day, you can enjoy time with your spouse, you can take your kids sledding, and you can get an endorphin jolt as good as any low-fat grande cappuccino will provide.

My research took a look at a group of people representative—in terms of age, gender, locale, profession, and income—of the general population of the United States. The results show an increase in happiness—a happiness pop if you will—between people who earn $25,000 or less a year and those earning $50,000. Surprisingly, though, there is no discernible difference in the overall happiness of those with incomes over $50,000 and those with incomes over $100,000.

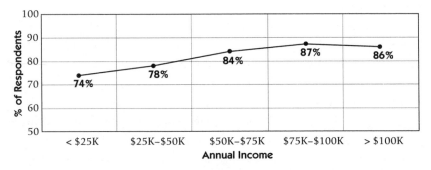

Income matters, but it isn't everything. Graph shows percentage of respondents who are "very or somewhat happy" overall.

As you can see, only 74 percent of those earning less than $25,000 said they were somewhat or very happy with their lives compared with 84 percent of the higher earners. But once you reach that $50,000 level, overall happiness levels off. In addition, people who earn around $50,000 a year are just as happy with their friendships, standard of living, marriage, children, and appearance as those who earn more than $100,000 a year.

The very good news is that in terms of income, most of us are either at that $50,000 level of household income already—or very, very close. Median household income in this country is just over $42,000. And if you're slowly creeping up to those levels, the financial advice that begins in the next chapter will help you feel as if you're there even faster.

What this means is that earning more is no guarantee of happiness. And if you think about your circle of friends, that makes sense. Chances are you know people who make $100,000 a year who are miserable, just as you probably know people who earn $25,000 who are perfectly content. There are plenty of people with six-figure stock portfolios or multiple pieces of real estate who feel their lives are missing that little extra something. And there are those with five-year-old cars in their garages who walk around with smiles on their faces every day.

But Money Can Make You Very *Un*happy

Okay. So money can't buy the sort of happiness you and I are looking for. But it can rob you of it. Studies over the years have shown that money bears the ultimate responsibility for many of life's problems.

Divorce? Money is the number one cause of splits.

Fights in a marriage? Even during the first year of marriage money spats are the number one cause of strife. (In-laws run a distant second.)

Health problems like depression? Alcoholism? Addictions to drugs and gambling? Check, check, and check. Financial woes are known triggers of all these problems. They're even a known motive for suicide. Not only did the number of deaths from suicide peak during the Great Depression, but unemployed people take their lives twelve times more often than people with jobs. Even out-of-control shopping is now considered by some to be a medical disorder, worthy of treatment with antidepressants.

How is it that while money is responsible for only a relatively small piece of your overall happiness, it can rob you of happiness so completely? Two reasons.

The first is that these five top variables involved in happiness—relationships, self-esteem, job satisfaction, health, and money—are highly interrelated. And money, when it's working against you, can set up a particularly large roadblock to achieving a feeling of well-being in any of the other areas. For example, if fighting about money drains the joy from your marriage, there goes a whopping chunk of your overall happiness. If you forgo important medical treatments because they're not covered by your HMO (and you therefore can't afford them) it robs you of another piece of the pie. If you feel that you're working too hard for too little financial reward, it's pretty difficult to plaster a smile on your face each day at your job.

The second—and probably more important—reason is that, despite the fact that income can produce only a small piece of happiness, most of us *believe* it has the power to do much more. My research shows that nearly one-third of Americans believe in some deep-seated, long-lasting, fundamental way that money represents happiness. (Another 20 percent are on the fence.)

So what do we do? We go after the money. We chase it like there's no tomorrow. And as we do that, we lose time that we could spend having a leisurely dinner or taking a long walk with the love of our life; we lose time we could spend hitting the StairMaster or making a sandwich rather than driving through a fast-food joint for a grease-fest; we lose time we could spend taking classes that might lead us to a career we'd truly enjoy. In other words, when we chase money, we lose the opportunity to focus on the relationships, health, and work satisfaction that could reward us with a huge upward swing in happiness.

If and when we actually get the money, are we any happier? Not necessarily. Look at lottery winners and people who've inherited large sums of money. There have been conflicting studies on the impact of such windfalls on the recipients. One showed that an extra $1.5 million in your coffers could make a marked and lasting difference in your happiness. But let's get real. Most of us will never get our hands on anywhere near that much money. And most of the evidence goes in the other direction, showing that lottery winners and other windfall recipients are in fact no happier a few years down the road. Why? Because once they have the extra money they abandon the things that made them truly happy: the job that made them feel valued, the decidedly nongourmet but never disappointing first-Sunday-of-the-month potluck with friends, the satisfaction they got from saving enough to take the kids for five full days in Disney World.

The bottom line: Wealth is a little like health. The total absence of it can make you absolutely miserable. But having it is no guarantee of bliss.

So Stop Chasing the Buck—and Live

If you bought this book because you can see yourself in these examples, you've come to the right place. It's time to stop chasing the buck—and live. And in order to do that, you have to put money back in its proper place and perspective.

It's kind of like having a new puppy. You bring that cute little eight-pound bundle of fur into your house. It's tempting to give him free rein. You want him to sleep at the foot of your bed, to cozy up under your desk as you work from home during the day. Why shouldn't you give him the rest of your hamburger? If you're not going to eat it, it shouldn't go to waste. But give that new puppy an inch and he'll take a mile. All of a sudden you have an 85-pound *dog* that chews your furniture, sheds on your couch, licks the dishes before you can shut the dishwasher, piddles on the floor when you're fifteen minutes late getting home, and jumps exuberantly to greet your friends.

In order to transform that malleable pup into the kind of dog those same friends will volunteer to care for while you're away for the weekend, you have to lay down the law. You must be the master. That dog needs to know that he has his own bed, his own food, and a bladder that can make it for eight hours at a stretch. He has to learn that jumping is unacceptable. And that if his tongue gets near the dishwasher there's a fairly good chance it'll come in contact with a dash of Tabasco. Put that pup in his place for the first couple of months of his life and you'll be rewarded with a dog that provides you with immeasurable happiness—and very little on the downside.

Money is precisely the same. If money is the master and you're the slave, it becomes a big drain on your overall life. Unfortunately, our research shows one in five of you feels precisely that way. But if you're the alpha dog in this relationship—if you're at the controls— then you can use your money to your best advantage, to add to your happiness and quality of life.

Want Proof? Meet the Financially Happy

Let's back up a second and talk about what happiness is. It's not something you can buy or own or hold. The best explanation I've heard—and it comes from Ed Diener, a psychology professor at the University of Illinois who has written extensively on the subject—is that happiness is the *process* of enjoying what you're doing: your relationships; your job; your free time; your life.

One thing my research clearly demonstrates is that people who have found a happy middle ground with their money are happier overall with their lives. Of people who are very happy with their financial situation, more than six in ten say they are very happy overall, compared to four in ten of those who are somewhat happy with their finances and just 15 percent of Americans whose money is making them miserable.

People who are happier with their finances are more likely to be happy with their jobs, relationships, health, friendships, appearance, self-esteem, children (if they have them), and lifestyle. They are less likely to worry about all of these aspects of their lives. People who are happier with their financial situation are more likely to feel useful, confident, and content.

And when they do feel stressed (these days, everybody feels stressed sometimes), they are more likely to work those feelings out by doing something positive, like exercising. People who are dissatisfied with their finances are more likely to deal with stress by doing something that's not good for them—eating (more Doritos than broccoli, I'd imagine), smoking, or doing drugs.

What do these people look like demographically? Fortunately, or unfortunately, you can't see them. As I noted earlier, they're a little wealthier, with a little more in the bank (this gives men an edge over women). They're somewhat likely to be older, married, have a college degree, and own their own homes. And although they have similar debt loads overall to those of people who are not as happy with their finances, they have significantly less credit card debt.

But demographics aren't the dividing line. It's what these people are *doing* that makes the difference. They are distinctly different from the financially unhappy in their habits and behavior. They have a different take on

- financial organization
- bill paying
- record keeping
- saving
- spending
- setting goals

Over the next nine chapters, you'll learn to follow in their productive footsteps. And I just want to remind you, once again, that it's possible to be part of this happy group, no matter how much money you have.

Money and Happiness Results: Part 1

But before I can get you there, I need to figure out where you stand.

In the Introduction, I talked a bit about research undertaken for this book. An eight-page written survey of 1,500 individuals was conducted by RoperASW. At the very beginning of each chapter—as you were at the start of this one—you'll be asked to answer some of the same questions they were. The questions correlate with the information in each chapter. By answering them, you'll be able to see where your attitudes, habits, skills, and ideals square with those of the population at large. But more important, you'll be able to see where those same attitudes, habits, skills, and ideas are getting in the way of your personal happiness. You'll get a valuable sense of where the control you're trying to exercise over your money is impeding the control you have over your life. And you'll learn what changes you can make—and how they will make a difference.

Let's go!

1. Thinking about all aspects of your life, in general, how *happy* are you these days? (Circle one letter.)

 a. Very happy
 b. Somewhat happy
 c. Not too happy
 d. Not at all happy
 e. Don't know

About your response: Of the 1,500-plus people we surveyed at the end of 2002, almost one-third said they were very happy these days. Half were somewhat happy, and the rest ranged from not too happy to not at all happy.

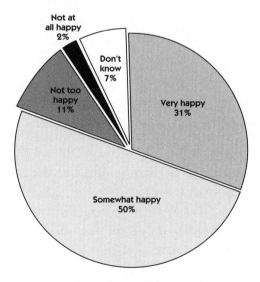

Are Americans happy? Generally, yes.

The generally high happiness scores are, I believe, an affirmation of the strength of American optimism. Despite a pending war and a weak economy, despite being just a year clear from the dust of September 11, four out of five Americans continued to look for—and find—the bright side in late 2002.

2. On the whole, how *happy* are you with the following aspects of your life? (Check one box for each.)

	VERY HAPPY	SOMEWHAT HAPPY	NOT TOO HAPPY	NOT AT ALL HAPPY	DON'T KNOW OR N/A
a. Your job	❏	❏	❏	❏	❏
b. Your marriage/ serious personal relationship	❏	❏	❏	❏	❏
c. Your health	❏	❏	❏	❏	❏
d. Your friendships	❏	❏	❏	❏	❏
e. Your appearance/ weight	❏	❏	❏	❏	❏
f. Your self-esteem	❏	❏	❏	❏	❏
g. Your financial situation	❏	❏	❏	❏	❏
h. Your children	❏	❏	❏	❏	❏
i. Your lifestyle (standard of living)	❏	❏	❏	❏	❏

About your responses: Americans are most happy with their marriages/ relationships (among those living with a partner) and their friends. We are least happy about our financial situations and jobs. The rest of the factors fell somewhere in the middle.

How does income play into this equation? If you don't have enough money to live comfortably, you're more likely to be unhappy with every aspect of your life. As household income increases to $50,000 annually, happiness in each of these categories grows. Beyond that, though, it levels off. The conclusion: Income contributes to your happiness to the extent that it makes you comfortable. Once you've achieved those basic comforts, your happiness has to come from another place.

3. How often, if at all, do you *worry* about the following? (Check one box for each.)

	A LOT	SOMETIMES HAPPY	NOT TOO MUCH	NOT AT ALL	DON'T KNOW OR N/A
a. Your job	❑	❑	❑	❑	❑
b. Your marriage/ serious personal relationship	❑	❑	❑	❑	❑
c. Your health	❑	❑	❑	❑	❑
d. Your friendships	❑	❑	❑	❑	❑
e. Your appearance/ weight	❑	❑	❑	❑	❑
f. Your self-esteem	❑	❑	❑	❑	❑
g. Your financial situation	❑	❑	❑	❑	❑
h. Your children	❑	❑	❑	❑	❑
i. Your lifestyle (standard of living)	❑	❑	❑	❑	❑

About your responses: Cartoonist Cathy Guisewite has referred to food, Mom, love, and work as the "four guilt groups." And she has a point. A quick look at the line items on the list above reveals that Americans have a lot to worry about. Who hasn't struggled with the fact that their eight-year-old was having a difficult time in school, that they weren't communicating with their spouse the way they did when they were first married, that they found a lump somewhere on their body?

Yet among all of these potential causes of worry, what do we worry about most: money!

Six in ten Americans worry a lot or sometimes about their financial situation, about twice as many as worry about self-esteem, jobs, marriage, and friendship. Women are more likely to feel this way than men. If you're among the chronic worriers, your anxiety is likely blocking you from setting—and then achieving—your financial goals. But there is a silver lining: Worrying seems to slow with age.

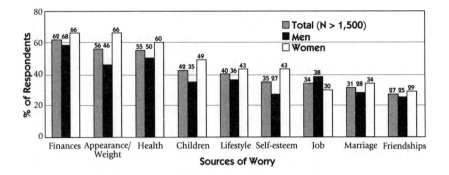

What do we worry about? Money! Graph shows percentage of respondents who worry "a lot or sometimes" about the aspects shown.

4. How often, if at all, do you feel in *control* of the following? (Check one box for each.)

	A LOT	SOMETIMES	NOT TOO MUCH	NOT AT ALL	DON'T KNOW OR N/A
a. Your job	❏	❏	❏	❏	❏
b. Your marriage/ serious personal relationship	❏	❏	❏	❏	❏
c. Your health	❏	❏	❏	❏	❏
d. Your friendships	❏	❏	❏	❏	❏
e. Your appearance/ weight	❏	❏	❏	❏	❏
f. Your self-esteem	❏	❏	❏	❏	❏
g. Your financial situation	❏	❏	❏	❏	❏
h. Your children	❏	❏	❏	❏	❏
i. Your lifestyle/ standard of living	❏	❏	❏	❏	❏

5. In the past 30 days, about how often did you feel each of the following? (Check one box for each.)

	A LOT	SOMETIMES	NOT TOO MUCH	NOT AT ALL	DON'T KNOW
a. Restless	❑	❑	❑	❑	❑
b. Useful	❑	❑	❑	❑	❑
c. Stressed	❑	❑	❑	❑	❑
d. Content	❑	❑	❑	❑	❑
e. Hopeless	❑	❑	❑	❑	❑
f. Confident	❑	❑	❑	❑	❑

About your responses: If finances topped your lack-of-control list, you're once again in good company. More people say they have less control over their finances than any other item on the list, ahead, once again, of weight, health, and children (and anyone with a teenager in the house knows that's saying something). In general, men are a bit more likely to feel financial control than women (and parents a little less likely than nonparents, perhaps because they don't have college bills to contend with).

And again, age makes a difference. Seniors feel significantly more control over their finances than younger people. It may be that once they leave the working world, they have time to manage their money and that brings a sense of control. But income doesn't, even once you cross that $50,000 earnings line. About one-quarter of people earning more than that say they feel little or no control as well.

If you're feeling out of control about your money, chances are you're also feeling inadequate as an investor and money manager. But if you can grab hold, chances are good you'll be happier both in general and with the specific aspects of your life we examined, and you are likely to feel less worried and more useful, content, and confident. In other words, seizing control over your finances seems to be a stepping stone to gaining control over your life and achieving happiness. It's worth striving for.

The Upshot?

Harnessing your financial happiness—and therefore your overall happiness—has excellent implications for your life. If you're happy, you're less likely to have coronary artery disease, quit a job in frustration, or routinely be out of work. If they ever lose their jobs, happy people are likely to find new ones faster and therefore spend less time twiddling their thumbs. They're also more productive. They can derive pleasure and satisfaction from accomplishing even small tasks that they've accomplished many times before (unhappy people find routine boring and frustrating). They're likelier to get married and stay married. They also live longer.

Get a grip on your financial happiness—and therefore your overall happiness—and you're also likely to be the recipient of a little chicken-and-egg reward. Over the course of their lives, people who are financially happy are more likely to be more successful financially. That's right. You don't *have* to be rich. But you may end up richer anyway, in more ways than one.

The rest of this book is dedicated to helping you do just that.

Money and Happiness Evaluation: Part 2

1. Money means different things to different people. I'd like to find out what money means to you personally. Take a look at the list of items below. Then rate each item using a scale ranging from 1 to 7, with 1 meaning money does not at all represent this to you, 7 meaning money completely represents this to you, and the other numbers representing levels in between.

a. Achievement
b. Comfort
c. Control
d. Happiness
e. Independence
f. Power
g. Security
h. Social status
i. Enjoyment

2. Different things are important to different people when it comes to enjoying life. Using a scale ranging from 1 to 7, with 1 meaning "not important at all to you," 7 meaning "very important to you," and the other numbers representing levels in between, indicate how important each of the following is to you personally.

a. Living in a beautifully decorated home
b. Owning a new car
c. Wearing the latest style in clothing
d. Being good-looking
e. Having a good-looking spouse/partner
f. Having the latest technology/gadgets
g. Taking really nice vacations
h. Living in an upscale neighborhood
i. Owning a luxury car

3. When you look at the following two statements, choose the one that comes closer to your own personal behavior.

a. When I was 18, I expected that I'd be better off financially than I actually am today.
b. When I was 18, I didn't expect I'd be doing as well financially as I actually am today.

4. How much do you agree or disagree with each of the following statements? Use a scale ranging from 1 to 7, where 1 means you completely disagree with the statement, 7 means you completely agree with the statement, and the other numbers represent levels in between.

a. I am sometimes frustrated that I do not have as much money as others my age.
b. I am sometimes frustrated that I do not manage my money as well as others I know.

5. How much do you agree or disagree with each of the following statements? Use a scale ranging from 1 to 7, where 1 means you completely disagree with the statement, and 7 means you completely agree with the statement, and the other numbers represent levels in between.

a. I have found that the more money I make, the more money I need.
b. Splurging makes me feel good.
c. I often find myself purchasing things I don't really need.

6. Different people have different ways of coping with stress. Tell me how often, if at all, you personally do each of the following to cope with stress. (Check one box for each.)

	A LOT	SOMETIMES	NOT TOO MUCH	NOT AT ALL	DON'T KNOW
a. Eat	❏	❏	❏	❏	❏
b. Exercise	❏	❏	❏	❏	❏
c. Shop	❏	❏	❏	❏	❏
d. Listen to or play music	❏	❏	❏	❏	❏
e. Have sex	❏	❏	❏	❏	❏

	A LOT	SOMETIMES	NOT TOO MUCH	NOT AT ALL	DON'T KNOW
f. Drink alcohol	❑	❑	❑	❑	❑
g. Smoke	❑	❑	❑	❑	❑
h. Take drugs	❑	❑	❑	❑	❑
i. Sleep	❑	❑	❑	❑	❑
j. Go to therapy/ counseling	❑	❑	❑	❑	❑

2. Enough Is Enough

Money has never made a man happy yet, nor will it. The more a man has, the more he wants.

—Ben Franklin

Take a minute and think back to high school. In your graduating class, there were probably two groups of students: those who went to college to further their education and boost their earning power, and those for whom senior year was the end of the educational road. Overall, research shows, the higher-earning college grads start adult life on a slightly higher happiness rung than those on the high school track. Why? Life is easier for them. They don't have to jump through as many hoops to afford basic comforts and necessities. And as a result, they're happier on average.

But then an interesting thing happens. Over the years, while both the high school and college grads earn more, the earnings of the college grads increase faster and farther. You would think that would mean the happiness of the college grads would outpace that of the high school ones as well. It doesn't. Academic research conducted in this country and around the world shows that the happiness of both groups plateaus and stays about the same.

How is that possible? It's possible because the reality is that it doesn't take a heck of a lot of income to buy happiness. And because there are two other factors hard at work here as well: expectations and aspirations.

Wanting Gets in the Way

Higher expectations and greater aspirations are the big differences between the high school grads and the college grads. People who pursue a college education expect that they'll earn more, live in larger houses, and see more of the world. If they don't measure up to those standards they've set for themselves, many are extremely disappointed.

Higher-earning college grads, in general, also want more. Their quest for material possessions—nice homes, nice cars, nice clothes—seems to increase in proportion to their income. Take the once-a-year raise you typically receive in the working world. That extra padding to your income may bring a short-term happiness jolt. But it's only a matter of weeks before you're spending to match the new level of your income. A few months down the road and you can no longer remember how you possibly lived on less. Which brings you right back to the same level of happiness you started with.

The derogatory label we hear bandied about in this context is "materialism." Let's take a minute to talk about what that means. When I say materialism, I don't mean having a lot of stuff. This book is not a missive on the simplification movement or a diatribe on paring down. And though I, personally, get a huge rush from cleaning out a closet, I also think having stuff is fine as long as you can truly afford it (more on that in Chapter 6). What I mean by materialism is placing a higher value on material possessions and income than you do on your personal relationships, your free time, and your health.

People who want this way—who *over*want—tend to believe that money equals happiness. And my research shows that they are the very same people for whom money gets in the way of ever achieving the happiness they seek.

Do You Believe?

If you believe money equals happiness, you're in good company. Nearly one-third of Americans do, and they're substantially less happy as a result. People who believe money can buy their happiness are less satisfied with their self-esteem, their friendships, and their life overall. A greater number of them worry about their lifestyles, their jobs, and their financial situations. And half of them feel they don't measure up, financially, to others their age.

Feelings of stress, restlessness, and hopelessness are more prevalent in their lives, and a greater percentage of "believers" than "nonbelievers" cope with these feelings by doing things (like shopping and drinking) that aren't necessarily good for them or their financial situation. These are my findings, but earlier studies back them up. Other research has shown that "overwanting" produces anxiety, insecurity, and depression.

Who are these overwanters, these people who believe money equals happiness? You can't spot them by looking. Other than gender (men are a bit more likely to be believers than women), there are no significant demographic differences between believers and nonbelievers. Their ages and educational levels parallel those of the general population. They are similarly likely to have full-time jobs, own their own homes, and be married.

What differentiates them are their attitudes and beliefs about money. Almost all of the people who believe money represents happiness also think it represents independence, security, comfort, and enjoyment. Three-quarters say money represents control, while two-thirds say achievement and power. Far fewer nonbelievers see money in those terms. People who see money as happiness are also more likely to say it's important to own new cars, wear the latest clothes, have the latest gadgets, and be good-looking.

Not surprisingly, believers are also more likely to say they need more money in the bank to feel happy. They say they'd need close to a half million dollars to put a smile on their faces. Nonbelievers would be happy with half that amount.

The irony is that the financial habits of people who believe money equals happiness stand in the way of achieving that happiness. Believers are less likely to balance their checkbooks, less likely to remember to pay their bills on time, and more likely to say their finances are disorganized. They are more spontaneous with their spending. They are more likely to enjoy splurging. Getting a bargain can make their day.

Unfortunately, it can also ruin their months or their years. One-quarter of believers often purchase things they don't need. Just as many are surprised when they open their credit card bills at the end of the month. The end result? People who believe money equals happiness are no likelier to have a higher income or net worth than nonbelievers.

Why We Want

In order to conquer this problem—and if your goal in life is to be happy, then it *is* a problem—you need to understand why you want so many possessions.

Often, material possessions are substitutes for other, nontangible, things. Psychologists turn to "attachment theory" as one explanation for this phenomenon. In animals, this is why ducklings and geese bond to the first moving objects they see. In humans, it's an indication of how secure infants and children feel in their relationships with their parents, primarily their mothers. By age two, children who are securely attached tend to be enthusiastic, outgoing, curious, and socially competent. They will try to solve problems on their own, but ask their mothers for problems that prove too tough. And they're more likely to be leaders.

Children who are insecurely attached tend to be more whiny and needy. They aren't as able to play on their own or to solve their own problems and conflicts. In later years, they often suffer from low self-esteem. They may seem completely in control, even domineering to the outside world, but they are easily disappointed, let down, and hurt. They rarely believe themselves to be good enough for their parents to begin with, and in later years, this conviction extends to friends, employers, would-be spouses, and the world at large.

As they mature, insecurely attached children try in a variety of ways to fill the void left by the lack of parental bonds. They're looking for something to make them feel good about themselves. Some turn to food, others to sex, others to drugs or alcohol. Still others turn to things—material possessions—and shop with abandon. And there are quite a few of these people; experts estimate that 30 to 35 percent of children are insecurely attached.

Attachment problems represent one school of thought in answering questions of materialism. (And while adhering to it may seem to give you license to blame your money troubles on your parents, it's no excuse not to tackle your issues as adults.)

Another theory is that we're powerless to resist. We live in a culture that bombards us with messages about things that will make us better people if we're able to own them. There's no subtlety about it. Advertisers want us to believe that if we had the right pair of jeans we could dance like that hot guy in the Gap ad (or, better yet, he'd dance his way right over to us). They want us to think that a little L'Oréal will make us look as good at forty as Andie MacDowell and that waking up to a cup of Folgers coffee means we'll have a better day.

The messages are inescapable. Turn off the television and you'll see them in magazines and newspapers. They pop up uninvited when we troll the Web. They leave us messages on our voice mail and send us faxes. Even Mr. Moviephone can't help himself. He won't give us the running time for that next showing of *Harry Potter* until we've listened to a preview for, say, *The Lord of the Rings*.

As a result, many people are never satisfied. According to Harvard economist Juliet Schor, author of *The Overspent American,* only half the population of the richest country in the world say they can afford everything they really need. Earning more only exacerbates the situation. While 40 percent of households making $50,000 to $100,000 a year say they can afford to buy what they need, only one-third of those making more than $100,000 concur.

Status for Sale

The question is: What are we really buying? To the extent that we're buying food to eat, a coat to wear, heating oil or new windows for our house to keep us warm at night, even a cell phone to use in emergencies (or as our primary phone because it's become cheaper and easier than a landline), we're buying utility. But when we start to spend more than necessary in any of those categories, we're trying to buy something else: status. Do we *need* status? The answer's not as much of a clear-cut no as you might think.

Status is not necessarily a bad thing. Over the years, medical researchers have found that higher status translates into a healthier and longer life. That makes sense. Status-seekers not only want to wear the trendiest clothes and drink the latest vodka, but also want to see the best doctors. They're more likely to have bought into the latest diets or exercise regimens.

But that's the exception, not the rule. Take your cell phone as an example. Sure, you may use it. But the ability to communicate isn't what you get when you spend $300 on a teeny-tiny phone with a full-color screen. No more than keeping your tootsies warm is what you get when you buy a pair of $300 bone-crushing stilettos. When you make purchases like these you're trying to better your position in life through shopping.

This happens constantly. It happens every time you buy into a trend or succumb to a fad. And it happens every time you make an impulse purchase not driven by your sudden recollection that you ripped your last pair of black panty hose or used up the roll of tinfoil. Andrew Oswald, an economist at the University of Warwick in England, believes that 80 percent of all spending is an attempt to buy status. The goal is to purchase not something that actually makes your life better or easier, but something that makes you feel superior to friends, neighbors, relatives, or colleagues—and that simultaneously makes them pale in comparison.

Hardwired to Measure Up

The curse of human beings—Americans, in particular—is that we must keep looking over our shoulders before we can decide how we feel. We can't know how we're doing until we know how others around us are doing. If we pale in comparison, we tend to feel inferior. The wider the gap, the bigger the blow to our ego.

Take income, for example. Income discrepancies between men and women have been studied on a state-by-state basis. The results indicate that in those states where the wage gap is largest—with women earning less than men—overall happiness for women is lower. This holds true on an individual level as well. Couples in which women outearn their husbands are more likely to divorce than couples in which the man is the primary breadwinner. Why? If you're a person who attaches value to the size of a paycheck, it may be tough to stick with a relationship in which you feel you (or your spouse) doesn't measure up.

Keeping Up with Ross and Rachel

This urge to compete is nothing new. The phrase "Keeping Up with the Joneses" was introduced into the popular culture in 1913 by Arthur R. ("Pop") Momand, a cartoonist from Cedarhurst, Long Island, who turned his experiences living among the affluent into a daily comic strip that ran for 28 years. America took the title of the strip literally. For decades, keeping up with the Joneses was precisely what we tried to do. If our neighbors got a color TV, we could put the same make and model in our living room and level the playing field.

By the 1990s, however, maintaining the status quo was no longer good enough. Instead, we had to outdo our neighbors. If the Joneses redid their basement to include a big-screen TV and an exercise bike, ours needed a home theater and fully equipped gym.

Today, making matters worse, it's no longer just the Joneses on our backs. Many of us feel we have to compete with celebrities we don't even know. Magazines from *People* and *InStyle* to *US* tell us that Jennifer Love Hewitt shops at Fred Segal, Jennifer Aniston has her hair cut by Chris McMillan, and Jennifer Lopez's most recent engagement ring came from Harry Winston. Lucky us! Now we can go out and get those things too. Or at least we can buy the reasonable cheaper facsimiles—"Lust? Or Must?"—these glossies juxtapose on the same page.

Celebrities don't even have to be real for us to aspire to be like them. We make as much money as struggling interior designer Grace Adler on *Will & Grace* or often-out-of-work actor Joey Tribbiani on *Friends*. So it figures that our apartments should be as large, well furnished, and centrally located as theirs. Doesn't it?

C'mon. Studies have shown that the apparent average income of people on fictional television is way above the median income of the American family. Yet when this is your point of reference—and for Americans who spend the average equivalent of fifty-two days in front of the television each year it often is—it's tough not to compare. And when you measure yourself against celebrities who have personal trainers, personal chefs, and personal shoppers on their payrolls, who spend hours each week in salons and gyms making sure they look good *because it's their job,* guess who loses? Right.

(Besides, if you think they pay retail for those designer clothes and jewels and the rest of that stuff, you've been drinking Kool-Aid. Often they don't pay for them at all. Publicists, chomping at the bit to get celebrities to try the latest in their line of makeup, skin care, or home furnishings, hand freebies out like Gummi Bears. Why? Because then they can place a small item about it in a glossy.)

My point is this: If you can afford those trendy items, there's nothing wrong with marching right out and getting them. But wanting more than you can afford rarely translates into happiness and contentment. In fact, it can actually rob you of them. Such wanting, says Ed Diener, a happiness expert from the University of Illinois, can be "toxic."

How do you wise up? Age may do the trick. Seniors are far less likely than Generation Xers and baby boomers to covet. Unfortunately, by the time you get your AARP card, you may have compromised your chances of saving enough to put your kids through college or affording the retirement you want. You'll be better served if you can escape your materialistic urges in your earlier years.

Recipe for Satisfaction: Three Kids, No Student Loans

At the start of their marriage more than thirty years ago, Yvette, a teacher in the Boston suburbs, and her husband, Brian, a dentist, had grandiose dreams chock full of acquisitions. How nice it would be, they thought, to have a family getaway on a lake or a beach house near the ocean. How much fun it would be to travel—first class and nonstop. But along the way, as they had three kids and went through the process of raising them, their priorities shifted. Education for those three children jumped to the head of the list.

"We wanted to see our children emerge from college educated, employable, and debt free," Yvette explains, "and most of our resources have been spent meeting that goal." Resources that—particularly in triplicate—could easily have provided a down payment on that second home or bought several trips around the globe. But for Yvette, knowing that her children would be able to contribute to society in their jobs as a journalist, a dentist, and a speech therapist was just a matter of putting first things first.

In the beginning, she acknowledges, it seemed to be a sacrifice—albeit one they were willing to make, just as their parents had sacrificed to make life easier for them. But as she and Brian grew older, it became apparent that expensive belongings weren't what mattered to them. "All we've ever wanted was a clean home where we could comfortably entertain both our friends and ourselves," she says. "Even though we have at times packed people around our table, somehow we made it work. We always figured that we had a nice house, cars that ran, clothes, and plenty of food."

In fact, Yvette notes, more money might have made life more complicated rather than easier. "If we had more money, all we would have would be a bigger house (which would mean more work), bigger cars (which would guzzle more gas), more clothes (and everyone knows you can wear just one pair of pants at a time), and more food (which none of us need—definitely)." It's not that she's a penny-pincher, a charter subscriber to the "Tightwad Gazette," or even a meticulous coupon clipper. "We're not scrupulously frugal like some of our friends," she says. "We do indulge in free pursuits like long bike rides on nearby country roads and hikes on the mountains that abound in New England. But we also enjoy meals out at least twice a week."

A quick check of the couple's cash flow statement would attest to that. It's balanced. They enjoy a night on the town and travel at least a couple of times a year. But they buy airline tickets and book hotels on Web sites that discount. They've been longtime members of a gorgeous and well-maintained golf club, but because it's in a rural area, the dues are comparatively low. They ski all winter long but buy season passes before the first snowfall to take advantage of a sizable discount. And while, no, they've never managed to eke out a lake house, they can trailer their twenty-year-old boat to the river any day in the summer and pretend they're far, far away.

Ask Yvette if she feels she's missing out and she laughs. "I think what makes us the happiest is that we tend not to compare ourselves to other people, because we realize everyone has different priorities for their resources. We keep asking ourselves, 'What makes us happy?' Money doesn't make anyone happy. Possessions don't make us happy. Relationships are better than money. Family is better than money. Education is better than money. Exercise and a good diet are better than money. Even when we had a lot less money than we have now, we always had those things. It's interesting that none of those things—except education—cost money and I can't 'possess' any of them. But they all make me feel like the richest person in the world."

Money and Happiness Results: Part 2

So where do you stack up on all these issues of wants and needs? Let's take a look at how you answered the questions posed at the beginning of this chapter.

1. Money means different things to different people. We'd like to find out what money means to you personally. Take a look at the list of items below. Then rate each item using a scale ranging from 1 to 7 with 1 meaning money does not at all represent this to

you, 7 meaning money completely represents this to you, and the other numbers representing levels in between.

a. Achievement
b. Comfort
c. Control
d. Happiness
e. Independence
f. Power
g. Security
h. Social status
i. Enjoyment

About your responses: For three-quarters of Americans money means security. For two-thirds it means independence and comfort. And for one-third it actually means happiness. What sort of people tend to share these feelings? People who worry more about their financial situation are likely to believe money represents a wide range of things from security to enjoyment to power, as are people who believe that being in control of your money means that you are in control of your life. Those who say they are happy because they are successful—not successful because they are happy—are also likely to say that money means more to them.

2. Different things are important to different people when it comes to enjoying life. Using a scale ranging from 1 to 7, with 1 meaning "not important at all to you," 7 meaning "very important to you," and the other numbers representing levels in between, indicate how important each of the following is to you personally.

a. Living in a beautifully decorated home
b. Owning a new car
c. Wearing the latest style in clothing
d. Being good-looking
e. Having a good-looking spouse/partner
f. Having the latest technology/gadgets
g. Taking really nice vacations

h. Living in an upscale neighborhood
i. Owning a luxury car

About your responses: The majority of people do not consider any of these important to enjoying their lives. Still, that leaves a not-insignificant third of Americans who do place a large value on having some of these things.

Which ones? Family-oriented purchases, such as homes, vacations, and cars, rank highest. Trendy clothes, cars, and gadgets rank lowest. And good looks—for ourselves and our significant others—fall somewhere in between. Younger, single folks are more likely to value disposable items than those who are married (and may be saving for a house) and those who have advanced degrees. Men are more likely than women to say that owning a new car, having a good-looking spouse, living in an upscale neighborhood, and having the latest technology are important to enjoying their lives. Women, on the other hand, tend to value wearing the latest clothing and being good-looking themselves.

But does wanting these things lead to a happier life? No. It leads to more wanting.

3. When you look at the following two statements, choose the one that comes closer to your own personal behavior.

a. When I was 18, I expected that I'd be better off financially than I actually am today.
b. When I was 18, I didn't expect to be doing as well financially as I actually am today.

4. How much do you agree or disagree with each of the following statements? Use a scale ranging from 1 to 7, where 1 means you completely disagree with the statement, 7 means you completely agree with the statement, and the other numbers represent levels in between.

a. I am sometimes frustrated that I do not have as much money as others my age.
b. I am sometimes frustrated that I do not manage my money as well as others I know.

About your responses: Fully half of Americans thought they'd be doing better financially than they are today. Younger adults are more likely to say they expected to be better off, suggesting they may need more time for their reality to catch up with their expectations (or for them to get a clue). Those with less education and who are not married are also more likely to be disappointed. Finally, those who don't describe themselves as knowledgeable investors or good money managers expected—when they were eighteen—to be doing better than they are today. Perhaps they feel the bull market let them down, or left them behind.

Nearly as many Americans are frustrated with the amount of money they have compared with their peers. A significant number also feel that their money management skills don't measure up. For some, these feelings may be surmountable. Money management, as you'll see in the coming chapters, can be learned, and people who regularly keep budgets and manage their spending are likely to report less frustration in this department.

5. How much do you agree or disagree with each of the following statements? Use a scale ranging from 1 to 7, where 1 means you completely disagree with the statement, 7 means you completely agree with the statement, and the other numbers represent levels in between.

a. I have found that the more money I make, the more money I need.
b. Splurging makes me feel good.
c. I often find myself purchasing things I don't really need.

About your responses: Unfortunately, for other people learning the new money management skills that follow in this and subsequent chapters may not be enough. If you're among the people for whom having some money only makes you yearn for more, frustration may be inevitable. Why? Because no amount of money will ever be enough. You need to adjust your attitudes. We'll discuss how to do that in the coming pages as well.

6. Different people have different ways of coping with stress. Please tell me how often, if at all, you personally do each of the following to cope with stress. (Check one box for each.)

	A LOT	SOMETIMES	NOT TOO MUCH	NOT AT ALL	DON'T KNOW
a. Eat	❏	❏	❏	❏	❏
b. Exercise	❏	❏	❏	❏	❏
c. Shop	❏	❏	❏	❏	❏
d. Listen to or play music	❏	❏	❏	❏	❏
e. Have sex	❏	❏	❏	❏	❏
f. Drink alcohol	❏	❏	❏	❏	❏
g. Smoke	❏	❏	❏	❏	❏
h. Take drugs	❏	❏	❏	❏	❏
i. Sleep	❏	❏	❏	❏	❏
j. Go to therapy/ counseling	❏	❏	❏	❏	❏

About your responses: As you see, shopping falls right in the middle of our hierarchy of stress behaviors.

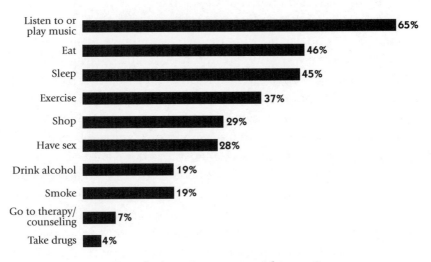

How do Americans cope with stress?

Women are significantly more likely than men to shop when stressed (nearly half of women do). But there aren't huge differences between age groups (only those age sixty-five and older are less likely to be "stress shop-

pers") or income groups (those with the lowest household incomes are just as likely as those with the highest incomes to shop to deal with stress). The bigger difference lies in attitudes: People who view money as happiness are more likely to shop when stressed, which makes sense. They apparently think money can buy them relief from tension and a better mood.

More troubling is this: Americans who are worried about their finances are more likely to shop to deal with stress than those who aren't worried. What they get as a result is a shopping high—but not a lasting one. It ends as soon as the credit card bill arrives in the mail.

Downside Protection: The Emotional Immune System

Is there anything you can do if you don't like the person your responses make you out to be? While it's eminently possible to change your habits and behaviors (we'll work on that more in the coming chapters), it's tougher to change your attitudes and beliefs. And those are the factors that drive your wants.

It's tougher. But it's not impossible.

First, try to understand what happens if and when you don't get the things you want. I want you to think about something you absolutely value. Now, imagine what would happen if that something were taken away from you. (If you're having trouble, think about your spouse or partner. Now imagine what your reaction might be if you came home one day to find that person in bed with the UPS driver.)

Dan Gilbert, a Harvard psychologist, has done a lot of work on this subject, and he knows that you believe your life would be completely ruined, that you'd be totally devastated. And maybe you would, for a while. But over the long haul, you'd rebound and eventually be just fine. Likewise, just as losing the things we value may cause a temporary downer, *getting* the things we want may provide a temporary happiness boost. But it doesn't make us happy for as long as we believe it will. And *not* getting those things we covet doesn't result in permanent unhappiness.

Why? Two reasons. First, just as your body has an immune system to fight off disease, Gilbert's research shows that your psyche has an immune system to stem disappointment. That's why, when that cute girl (or guy) from Chem Lab breaks up with you, you can immediately come up with a dozen reasons why you didn't like her (or him) anyway. In other words, when you don't get what you want or when something is taken away from you, you adapt. Similarly, if the cute girl (or guy) agrees to a date after months of pursuit, you may be delighted for a few days or a few weeks. But for many people the fact that the chase is over means the thrill is about to vanish as well.

It's not unlike your reaction to changing temperatures. Each year, as summer transitions to fall, a drop on the thermometer from 60°F to 50°F is likely to send you running back into the house for a long-sleeved T-shirt or fleece pullover. It feels cold because you've gotten used to the warmth of summer. But when winter is giving way to spring, you can't wait—on that first 50° day—to shed your layers and feel the mild air. It feels warm by comparison. Changes in income and professional status and the belongings we're able to afford work the same way. Each new raise, promotion, or acquisition brings a new thrill. But as we adapt to that level of attainment, the special feelings dissipate.

There's also a second reason we're able to rebound emotionally: We're not particularly good at knowing what will—and what won't—make us truly happy. You know how you obsess when you really want something, whether it's a promotion, a date with your co-worker in the next cubicle, or a new car. You think about it in great detail. If it's a car, you know precisely what you want it to look like. You know, let's say, that it *must* be an Acura MDX. It must be black with a caramel-colored leather interior. It must have a sunroof and CD changer, heated seats and a GPX navigational system. You won't be able to live without them.

Now think about what would happen if you and your spouse were to sit down and decide that the MDX is beyond the budget. What you can afford is a Honda Pilot with a CD player (not a changer), plush upholstery (not leather), and no navigational system (a four-figure option). The dealership is out of black but can order it; however, silver is available today. The price is right, and you can drive it off the lot.

You probably think you'll be disappointed for as long as you own the car. Every time you flip on the garage light and see that silver Pilot, you figure you'll be overwhelmed with the feeling that you should have held out for the MDX. At the very least, you should have held out for black. Yet that's not what happens at all.

Not only do you find you like driving the Pilot, you start to appreciate the very attributes you thought you didn't want. In the summer, you thank your lucky stars for plush upholstery that doesn't get hot and sticky like leather. You proclaim to enjoy the fact that you can switch CDs at will, rather than having to run back and forth to the trunk to exchange six at a time. You pat yourself on the back for not spending two grand on a GPX system, particularly when you hear from friends that following a computer's directions turned what should have been a one-and-a-half-hour road trip from Westchester County to Long Island into a three-hour nightmare. And that silver color? It shows much less dirt.

What would have happened if you had gotten the MDX you craved? It would have felt good for a while. But that feeling—just like the feeling that follows every other purchase—would have been temporary. A year down the road, when the MDX had been unable (as most *things* are) to make you as happy as you thought it would, you might even have started thinking you'd made a mistake and purchased the wrong car. So you'd have started imagining your next one. Maybe you're more of a convertible person. That new Thunderbird looks pretty nice. . . .

Happiness Happens

It's a common human misconception: We suffer from the delusion that happiness is a property of things, like mass and weight are properties of cars. All we have to do is get those things and we can suck down the happiness like so many calories. It doesn't work that way. Why? Because happiness isn't a property of that car, coat, house, pair of boots, or any other thing. Happiness is, as psychologist Ed Diener says, the *process* of what we go through when we do or don't get to experience those things. It's our *reaction* to that experience. Complicating matters even more—that reaction is temporary.

An example: I was at a birthday lunch recently with eight of my girlfriends for our friend Elisa's birthday. Birthday lunches are something of a ritual with my crowd. We take a break from work and carpooling to sit down for sandwiches, salads, a decadent midday glass of wine, and some conversation. On this particular day, Susan was sitting across the table from me. She's the one we can usually count on to be first out of the gate with a funny story about her kids or her husband, or some outrageous news about what's happening in the very, very small town in which we live. But on this day, she looked completely spent.

"I hate my house," she said. "It's too much. Too big. Too overwhelming."

"But you built that house," Debbie pointed out.

"I know." Susan shrugged. "When we first moved here, I was probably thirty-five, all I wanted was a big, gorgeous house. I wanted to furnish it. I was going to entertain nonstop. But it's too much. It eats up all my time. Moving the groceries from the garage to the kitchen is a big production. We've been there seven years and we still aren't completely furnished, which doesn't seem to matter all that much because when we do entertain no one leaves the kitchen anyway. But still, I have all that extra space to clean. Plus the yard to take care of. The driveway to clear. Remember when we had that freezing rain last week? My daughter and I had to slide down to the bus stop on our rear ends! We cried the entire way."

She paused. "You know that new development of cluster houses that's going up near the golf course? No land. No maintenance. No enormous kitchen. I think I'm going to talk my husband into moving there."

Would that smaller, low-hassle house make Susan happy? It's hard to tell. Two things are working in her favor: Chances are she knows herself a little better than she did seven years ago, and spending less to buy less work for yourself and more time with your family is generally a good bet.

Although it's tough to generalize, there are other good bets you can make on acquisitions. One is that purchases you *experience* (vacations or theater tickets, for example) bring more happiness than tangible items. Many people assume that things—belongings—will make you happier because you'll have them longer. Nope.

Academics who've studied this believe experiences make you happier because you can relive them in your mind. You can even embellish a bit to make yourself feel still better. Experiences also give you more to talk about; they provide the sort of cocktail party fodder that makes you a frequently invited guest. And they tend to be more a part of who we are (or who we like to believe we are) than the coat or immersion blender we bought at Bloomie's (no matter how wonderful that blender happens to be).

Learning to Want Less

From 1957 through 1963, a sociologist named Hadley Cantril conducted a remarkable study entitled "The Pattern of Human Concerns." He asked people around the world two basic questions: What do you think would make for the best of all possible worlds? And what do you think would make for the worst of all possible worlds? Unlike many earlier and later studies, this study did not involve a list of items to select from. Rather, Cantril took the time to ask open-ended questions and then listen to—and try to classify—the answers.

What he found was that people only reached so high. People in very poor, underdeveloped areas of the world didn't wish for fancy cars and high-tech appliances. They wanted electric fans. Those with sick children wanted good medical care. In wealthy countries like the United States, however, the more people had, the more they tended to want. Nothing has changed.

But, like Yvette from Boston, you can train yourself to want fewer—and different—things. Listen again to what she said:

Relationships are better than money.

Family is better than money.

Exercise and a good diet are better than money.

A major reason that we give in to our materialistic urges is that we're creatures of habit. It might take some thought and effort, but habits can be broken. So, if you find it difficult to walk past your favorite store without going in, try crossing to the other side of the street. If you can't resist buying something every time the Williams-Sonoma catalog arrives in the mail, have yourself removed from the mailing list. Here are a few other suggestions:

Remember the difference between a want and a need. How many times have you carted a five-year-old through the grocery store and had an exchange like this one?

Child: "We need Fruit Roll-Ups."
Parent: "No we don't. We have grapes. They're better for you."
Child: "We need the kind of color-changing Oreos."
Parent: "No we don't. We already have the regular kind at home. They taste the same."
Child: "I need a new Barbie."
Parent (frustrated that they actually sell Barbies in the supermarket): "No you *really* don't. You *want* a new Barbie. But you don't *need* one. Anyway, your birthday is next month. If you still *want* a new Barbie then, we'll put it on your wish list."
Child: "Well, if I can't have the new Barbie, can I at least have the Fruit Roll-Ups?"

You understand the difference between a want and a need enough to explain it to your five-year-old. The key is remembering that difference—and conducting a similar internal dialogue—when you're facing a tempting purchase for yourself.

Teach yourself to compare down, not up. It makes complete sense that you'll be disappointed if you're constantly comparing your wardrobe to that of your boss (who earns twice as much as you do) or your colleague (whose spouse created the latest reality-TV smash). Instead, if you need to compare at all—and most of us do—try to do it in a way in which you come out feeling good.

This tends to work no matter what you're comparing—wardrobes, homes, salaries, whatever. David G. Myers, professor of psychology at Hope College, recalls the year he spent living in Scotland. His income didn't change, but that part of the world was relatively poor by American standards. Fewer than half the people owned cars. He and his wife felt rich by comparison. On the other hand, when vacationing with his parents in affluent Rancho Mirage, California—the so-called playground of presidents, where shopping includes Escada, St. John, Saks Fifth Avenue, and an Oilily for the kids—they felt comparatively poor.

Remember, you can choose the people you surround yourself with just as you can choose the town in which you live. There are people in my community who moved from a neighboring town where they felt parents were too competitive and materialistic. Similarly, you can regain perspective by vacationing with Habitat for Humanity, spending Thanksgiving morning serving in a soup kitchen, or doing volunteer service in the Third World.

Seek a devoted social network. Interestingly, research has found that religious people want less, perhaps because most religions encourage you to enjoy what you have ("Thou shalt not covet . . .") rather than reach for more. But I think it's more likely that the deep social ties of a congregation make you comfortable enough in your own skin that you don't feel compelled to compete on the basis of possessions.

Monitor your reactions to things. The next time you buy something you're hankering for, whether it's a new outfit, new car, or dinner in a restaurant, take note of how the purchase makes you feel and how long the feeling lasts. You may decide it's not worth it to spend the time away from friends, family, and children that's necessary to earn the money your purchase cost.

Keep your experiences fresh. As we know that experiences can provide a happiness boost, it makes sense to try to remember them well. So don't just take pictures; put those pictures in albums that are easily accessible to you and your family. If you spend the better part of your life online, create a trip Web site. Or keep a journal. My husband and I did that on our honeymoon: A friend gave me a blank book as a shower gift, and we used it to track what we ate as we traveled through Italy. It's been twelve years, and I still refer to it each time I want to send people to that terrific place for *bistecca fiorentina* but can't remember the name, and occasionally just for fun. (If you're ever in Florence, it's Il Latini.)

Get general, not specific. You may think you want one particular item rather than several others: one model of car, one make of computer, one breed of dog. But if all satisfy your underlying need—for transportation, Internet access, or companionship—all will eventually satisfy your wants as well. The difference between outcomes is never as great as you think it will be. (Dan Gilbert, the aforementioned Harvard psychologist, even suggests that you try not to dwell so much on the particulars. In *Hamlet* Shakespeare said, "There is nothing either good or bad, but thinking makes it so." Gilbert, with apologies to the Bard, would amend that to say: "Nothing is as good or bad as it appears to be, but thinking makes the difference.")

If all else fails, count your friends. And try to act your age (or better yet, your mother's or father's age). As we retire from the workforce with all its associated daily comparisons (promotions, wardrobes, office space), our need to measure ourselves against others starts to diminish. And that is a very good thing.

Money and Happiness Evaluation: Part 3

1. How much do you agree or disagree with each of the following statements? Use a scale ranging from 1 to 7, where 1 means you completely disagree with the statement, 7 means you completely agree with the statement, and the other numbers represent levels in between.

a. I spend a lot of time and energy managing my finances and making financial decisions.
b. Managing money is too complicated and time-consuming.

2. Choose the statement that comes closer to your own personal behavior.

a. My finances are somewhat disorganized and I have to scramble to find what I need.
b. My finances are pretty well organized and I can find what I need quickly.

3. How much do you agree or disagree with the following statement? Use a scale ranging from 1 to 7, where 1 means you completely disagree with the statement, 7 means you completely agree with the statement, and the other numbers represent levels in between.

I balance my checkbook at least once a month.

4. Choose the statement that comes closer to your own personal behavior.

a. I pay my bills as they come in.
b. I wait until all my bills have come in for the month and then I pay them all at once.

5. How much do you agree or disagree with the following statement? Use a scale ranging from 1 to 7, where 1 means you completely disagree with the statement, 7 means you completely agree with the statement, and the other numbers represent levels in between.

Sometimes, frankly, I forget to pay my bills on time.

3. Feng Shui Finance

What the world really needs is more love and less paperwork.
—Pearl Bailey

Pearl Bailey may have uttered that sentiment, but few people would agree more than Emily, a television producer in the Midwest. For decades, she felt overwhelmed by paperwork (and unloved to boot).

Emily wasn't the primary breadwinner, but she wasn't an insignificant contributor either. Year in and year out, she took home a high five figures. Yet she had absolutely no control over her own—or her family's—money.

That control sat in the lap of her husband. As an accountant, he brought home a salary double the size of hers. Early in their marriage, she thought that also earned him control of the financial reins (and truth be told, in the early years her energies were so focused on getting promoted at work, she was glad to be rid of what she viewed as financial chores). But as the years dragged on, despite her increasing willingness to participate in the process—even to take it on once in a while so that he could, say, play a round of golf—the degree to which she was excluded grew. And it drained her.

For many years, for example, Emily's husband wouldn't allow her to write in their joint checkbook. Why? Her writing wasn't "neat" enough. He himself would write in the checkbook only in blue ink. "He was a total control freak," she admits.

Except where it came to his spending. While Emily was tabulating unit prices on detergent and Ziploc bags to get the best deal at the local Walgreen's, her husband wouldn't shop around when he needed suits. He'd buy the first two that fit, no matter how pricey they were. How did it make her feel? "Frustrated!" she says. And not only that, she felt robbed and ripped off. Her finances were so far out of her control it was as if they belonged to another person, on another continent.

Then, in 2000, Emily and her husband separated. They eventually divorced, and Emily was forced to take hold of her own financial life. It wasn't an easy process to go through, particularly after so many years of not paying attention. In fact, early on, she was so frightened of making the wrong decisions that she made no decisions at all. "While we were getting divorced—which took about two years—he asked me to get my own credit card." Then he asked again. "It took me several weeks just to make the call," she admits.

Doing so was a much needed step in the right direction. Once she had that Visa application under her belt, she was able to take a hard look at their joint accounts and realized the $4,000-a-month apartment he rented when he moved out of the house was draining their savings. That was something she couldn't afford if she expected to buy something decent on her own. So she took a deep breath, called him, and suggested that they sell their house and each buy something smaller.

Emily then went out and bought a condo on her own. And that's not all. She shopped around for car insurance and long-distance service. She moved her oldest child off the family cell phone plan (because he was running up the bills) and onto a bare-bones one of his own (any overages were his responsibility). She hired a financial adviser for a consult. And after she'd been in that new condo a scant few months, she refinanced, saving herself $590 dollars a month.

What did she do next? She got HBO! "Because I was saving all that money, I decided I was going to get HBO, which I'd always denied myself. I want to watch *Sex and the City*, okay?" she asks.

Okay? More than okay. Fine. Great. Terrific. The newfound control Emily has over her money is not only allowing her to make her own choices about what she wants to spend it on and what she doesn't, but also making her feel free. It's making her feel secure and content. It's making her feel that she can be more generous; she's currently dating a man who earns very little, and she didn't mind footing a little more than her share when they recently traveled to Mexico. Why? Because she knew what she had in the bank and what was coming in, and she knew she could afford it. "I'm much more comfortable with my financial situation now than I was when I was married," she says, "even though I have less disposable income."

Without even realizing it, Emily tapped into an overriding truth about money. The more control you have over your finances—no matter how much you earn, no matter how much you've saved—the less money stresses you out. And less stress translates, across the board, into more happiness.

You Can't Control Everything About Money

One belief many of us hold tight—too tight—about money is that it is beyond our control. And to some degree that is true. You and I can't control the markets. Despite the fact that individual investors continued to pour in their hard-earned capital during 2000 and 2001, the markets continued their slide. Then when investors learned their lesson, reversed that behavior, and pulled out in 2002—the first year that stock mutual fund redemptions exceeded stock mutual fund investments since 1988—what happened? The markets went down even further.

We can't control corporate America either. Unless you work at a particular company, sit on its board of directors, or are the sort of shareholder that actually gets listened to (i.e., a very, very large one), there is little you can do to impact the nation's biggest companies.

As for the world's geopolitical picture? Well, we certainly have no influence over that. Protest all you like. In the coming years, wars may well rattle the markets. They may cause prices of home heating oil and gasoline to rise, or lead to increases in unemployment. Those are macro issues.

But You Can Control a Lot

Particularly during years when the factors that we can't control take us for a wild ride—and the past few years have been a fine example—it's easy to forget that there is just as much—if not more—about your money that is within your control. The AA serenity prayer got it right: *Grant me the serenity to accept the things I cannot change, the courage to change the things I can, and the wisdom to know the difference.*

For instance? While you can't control the markets, you can control how much you invest in the markets, and what sort of investments you make. While you can't control America's corporations, you can choose to sell your shares in those companies with results, behaviors, or news that you don't like. While you can't control whether or not our country goes to war, you can choose to drive cars that don't guzzle gas. And you can opt to stash away enough of a cash cushion that if your industry is hit by layoffs as a result of a protracted conflict overseas, you can still pay your mortgage and get a good night's sleep.

And that's not all. You choose how much debt you take on. The extent of the financial precautions you take to protect yourself and your loved ones is up to you. You control how organized you are about your finances—whether or not you choose to put a system in place to deal with the onslaught of mail and other paperwork, or whether you run your money matters by the seat of your pants. You do or fail to do all of those things (and if you're not doing them today, you can tomorrow). As a result, you can have a substantial impact on your own feelings of comfort, security, and happiness.

How Much Control Do You Have Right Now?

When it comes to the tactical business of managing your money, you're typically on one side of the equation or the other. You're left-brained or right-brained. You're a fairly organized individual who has found some sort of financial system that makes enough sense to work in everyday practice for you. Or . . . you're not.

If you're left-brained and at least quasi-organized, the business of running your financial life probably doesn't bog you down much or get in your way. You don't pop out of bed in the middle of the night because you suddenly remember you forgot to pay the Visa bill or cancel cable. You don't start with $100 in your wallet on Monday morning and by five o'clock Tuesday afternoon have little idea where it's gone. You manage the flow of your money into your various accounts to an acceptable degree, have a pretty good sense that you're getting the best deals on interest rates and large purchases, and can see a steady, upward trend in your net worth.

If you've got the control issue licked, you have my permission to skim the rest of this chapter. Unfortunately, chances are you're not that left-brained, quasi-organized individual. Chances are, you're the right-brained, quasi-scattered alternative. (And even if you look perfectly organized—clean desk, clean closets, clean wallet—but, if asked, couldn't put your finger on, say, last month's cable bill, you qualify.) Why is this an issue? Because it costs you.

It costs you time. It costs you money. And it costs you mental energy.

How? Think about the last time you couldn't find a certain financial document. Let's say it's the week of Thanksgiving. You come home from a hectic week at the office, trying to wrap up all the odds and ends before you fly out early Wednesday morning—to your parents' home in sunny Boca!—hoping to get a jump on the travel rush. Then it hits you. If you don't file the paperwork for next year's flexible spending account before you leave, by the time you get back, November will be over and it will be too late. Oops!

There's some real money on the table here: You can save a few grand by paying for day camp, braces, and your ob/gyn (the one you love because she delivered your kids, but is no longer on your health plan) with pretax dollars. That would pay for yet another jaunt to Boca in midwinter, just when you need it most.

There's hope. You could fax in the form tonight. The benefits people will be in tomorrow morning. But where did you put it? Did you bring it home? Is it in the mail pile? Your briefcase? Your tote bag? Did you fold it up and stick it in your Filofax, figuring you'd see it every day and eventually take care of it? Or is it hidden under the stack of trade journals in your in box? Think. *Think.* Do you have to run back to the office or can you take care of this from home?

Let's decode what happened here. You certainly lost time—at least a half hour thinking about the problem and searching for the elusive paperwork at home. If you had to run back to the office, tack on another sixty minutes. You got unnecessarily stressed out, frustrated for not dealing with the form when you first received it (after all, it would have taken all of five minutes). Now you're stuck packing until all hours of the night, which simply builds on your anxiety. And finally, if it turns out you *can't* find the paper, *can't* solve the problem (although you could likely get another copy of the form in the morning by e-mail or fax, even if you had to do it from the Laptop Lane in the airport)—or if you throw up your hands in frustration and decide it isn't worth the hassle—you've lost some serious cash.

None of this was necessary.

One aspect of being content with your finances—and therefore your life—is the near absence of this sort of stressful situation. Notice the word *near*. I'm not saying that once you get your act together you're never going to lose anything. You will, once in a while, misplace something. Even organized people occasionally draw a blank. But if you have a system in place for handling the chaos of financial paperwork and e-mails, you will certainly face that sort of problem less frequently. And that'll boost your happiness overall. The first thing you need to know is where you stand.

Money and Happiness Results: Part 3

1. How much do you agree or disagree with each of the following statements? Use a scale ranging from 1 to 7, where 1 means you completely disagree with the statement, 7 means you completely agree with the statement, and the other numbers represent levels in between.

a. I spend a lot of time and energy managing my finances and making financial decisions.

b. Managing money is too complicated and time-consuming.

About your responses: There is no question we live in a time-starved society. But is lack of time the reason we fall behind when it comes to managing our money? Our research says no. Only one-fifth of Americans say their finances take a lot of time and energy. Even fewer people think managing their money is "too complicated and time-consuming."

Additionally—and I think surprisingly—spending a lot of time and energy managing your finances is not necessarily a good thing. People who spend a lot of time managing their money aren't any happier—or less happy—overall. They do not have more—or less—control over their finances or any other aspect of their lives. They do not feel more—or less—financially secure.

All that time doesn't even translate into more money. The average income of people who spend a lot of time and energy managing their money is $58,300; the average of those who do not is $54,900. (What they do have is substantially more debt. The average credit card debt of people who spend tons of time focusing on their finances is $5,300, 30 percent more than people who don't spend much time at all.)

In addition, people who spend a lot of time managing their money tend to feel more restless, stressed, and hopeless than people who do not. These same folks are also less likely to say they have enough money to purchase the things they need or want, or to go out and have a good time.

Clearly, the problem is not a matter of how much time you do or do not spend on your finances. It's how you use that time that determines your money management success. And getting organized is the key.

2. Choose the statement that comes closer to your own personal behavior.

a. My finances are somewhat disorganized and I have to scramble to find what I need.

b. My finances are pretty well organized and I can find what I need quickly.

About your response: People who feel that their finances are pretty well organized—organized at least enough so they don't have to waste precious time finding what they need—are much better off in general. Take a look at this profile of the "pretty well organized." (The disorganized person's profile is in parentheses.)

- *72 are financially secure (23 percent)*
- *56 percent worry about their finances (86 percent)*
- *24 percent are knowledgeable investors (7 percent)*
- *61 percent are good money managers (28 percent)*
- *73 percent are in control of their finances (42 percent)*

What does it take to get organized? In fact, a few small steps—like balancing your checkbook regularly and paying your bills as they come in rather than stockpiling them for a once-a-month check-writing marathon—seem to go a very long way. And of course, some sort of filing system never hurts.

3. How much do you agree or disagree with the following statement? Use a scale ranging from 1 to 7, where 1 means you completely disagree with the statement, 7 means you completely agree with the statement, and the other numbers represent levels in between.

I balance my checkbook at least once a month.

About your response: I've long found it curious that checkbook math isn't part of the required curriculum in every junior high and middle school. I remember learning to balance a checkbook in Ms. Haun's eighth-grade math class in Bloomington, Indiana. It wasn't complicated. In fact, at the time it seemed like a vacation from the algebra that was bogging down my brain. In retrospect, it was probably the most important skill I learned all year.

Our research shows that two-thirds of Americans balance their checkbooks at least once a month. Those who do are likely to have more control of their finances, be less worried about their money, and feel more secure financially. It's a small step, yes. It takes a half hour to an hour at most (less if you use a computer) yet the payoff shouldn't be brushed off.

From a financial point of view, the profile of a checkbook balancer is one of a very healthy, happy individual. Checkbook balancers tend to be:

- *Planners. They do their research before making a purchase, stick to the amount they decided to pull out of the ATM, and are less likely to be surprised by the amount they put on their credit cards each month. They also have a firm grip on their family's future. Checkbook balancers are significantly more likely to have written wills, and to have purchased life and disability insurance.*
- *Savers. Two-thirds are currently saving or investing. One-third have enough to weather a financial hardship, which may not be a majority but is 50 percent greater than the number of nonbalancers who do.*
- *Satisfied. Checkbook balancers are less likely to be frustrated that they don't have as much as others, and more likely to say they have enough to make their mortgage or rent payments, purchase the things they need, purchase the things they want, have a good time, and donate to causes they believe in.*

The point? If you're among the one-third of Americans who don't balance their checkbook—perhaps like a lot of people you brush it off as passé because the ATM machine gives you your balance on your receipt—you may want to reconsider.

4. Choose the statement that comes closer to your own personal behavior.

a. I pay my bills as they come in.
b. I wait until all my bills have come in for the month and then I pay them all at once.

About your response: When you pay your bills is a defining characteristic as far as personal finances are concerned. You'd think that people who pay their bills at the end of the month would be more organized, because they know enough about their cash flow to write all their checks in a single sitting. But that's not the case at all. People who pay their bills as they come in—rather than waiting until the end of the month—are much more in *control of their financial situations. They have less credit card debt (an average $3,500 compared to the $5,000 of end-of-the-month bill payers), are more likely to be saving and investing, and have enough of a stash to weather a financial hardship and save adequately for retirement.*

As-they-come-in bill payers are also better planners. They're not surprised by the amount they've put on their credit cards. They're more likely to have planned for their family's future by writing a will and buying life insurance.

Perhaps as a result, people who pay their bills as they come in are more satisfied with the money they have. They feel they have enough to buy the things they want as well as the things they need. They feel as if they have enough both to have a good time and to support the causes they believe in. And they're less likely to feel frustrated that they're not keeping up with their friends and neighbors.

All of this is true despite the fact that people who pay their bills as they come in do not have more money than those who pay bills once a month. This is not an offshoot of income. It's an offshoot of the fact that they've taken control. And that's very good news, because it means that if you replicate this behavior, feelings of control, satisfaction, and well-being will likely follow.

5. How much do you agree or disagree with the following statement? Use a scale ranging from 1 to 7, where 1 means you completely disagree with the statement, 7 means you completely agree with the statement, and the other numbers represent levels in between.

Sometimes, frankly, I forget to pay my bills on time.

About your response: One of the pleasant repercussions of paying bills as they come in is that you're less likely to "forget" to pay those bills on time. That's something 13 percent of Americans fess up to doing now and then. It's not that they don't have the money. There's no income differential between people who do and don't pay their bills on time. The difference is in mind-set. But again, paying bills as they come in seems to help solve the problem. It also leads to this emotional payoff: People who remember to pay their bills on time are happier and more secure with their financial situation. Their money is less likely to keep them up at night.

Conquering Your Clutter

What do these answers tell you? Two things: The control you exercise over your money has just as much (or more) to do with your financial happiness and contentment as how much money you have. And the more control you have, the less money you need to live and be content.

Those are pretty powerful realizations. But you're never going to be able to exercise that sort of control unless you can conquer your clutter.

On a physical level, clutter makes it tough to focus. It's like having a number of voices shouting at you simultaneously. Consider what happens when someone shouts at you. You either cringe or shout back. Either way, you don't accomplish anything.

Likewise, faced with clutter, I'll bet many of you do precisely what I used to do. You drop everything and straighten those cushions, file those papers, clear out those closets, organize that desk. Heck, you run out to the Container Store and buy new file folders, new Rubbermaid storage units, new matching hangers, and a year's supply of Post-its. Once the mess is gone, you can think straight enough to get on with your day.

Unfortunately, unless there's a true method to your madness, you probably find that you have to go through the exact same decluttering—the straightening, the filing, the clearing out, and the organizing—month after month after month. That makes your organizing a time-waster rather than a time-saver. And that is decidedly *not* the point.

Clutter is also distracting emotionally. If you stop to think about it, there's probably a distinct reason behind each little pile of clutter—a reason you didn't complete your interaction with that piece of paper the first time you touched it. Perhaps it was a bill you weren't sure you had the money to cover, or an invitation to a party your ex-husband (and his new girlfriend) would also be asked to attend. Or maybe you're in a relationship in which the clutter is not your own, but you're not communicating well enough to discuss whether the clutter should stay or go.

Recognizing those emotional responses—that you're not balancing your checkbook because you think you may have bounced a check—is key. But having a system can also be a big help. If you've got a method to deal with your clutter generally, and financial clutter specifically, you'll be more able to blow through these struggles and complete the job rather than have to round back a second (or third) time.

So how do you achieve that sort of control?

Feng Shui Finance

Personally, I found additional answers in a sort of feng shui finance. Now, before you turn the page thinking I've veered into some new-age territory that you'd just as soon avoid, let me explain two things. First, feng shui is not a fad like Tae-bo or tiramisu. It's been around for centuries; 3,000 years ago it was used to streamline the Chinese military. That makes it older than accounting, and you can't get more practical than accounting.

Second, I am not a new ager; I'm a pragmatist. I need to see it to believe it. So for me to even look at feng shui for answers required a substantial nudge, which came over lunch with my friends Eddie and Sydney. Sydney, who used to run the human resources department for a large advertising agency, is as practical as they come. Yet there she sat, enjoying her Caesar salad, explaining how she'd completely transformed her financial life using the principles of feng shui.

"I was totally disorganized," she remembers. "I had piles of paper and piles of bills everywhere. I was working fifteen-hour days, and I thought being so busy gave me an excuse not to balance my checkbook, not to know what was where."

What finally got Sydney to change? The realization that she was losing money. Not by investing it badly—she was literally losing it as a child might lose a mitten or a teenager a dental retainer. She'd shove bills in her purse—not knowing whether they were fives or twenties—and come home not able to remember how much she had spent and what she had spent it on. She couldn't remember which bills she'd paid and which ones she hadn't, so late fees became a problem. One day she excitedly dug a refund slip—a store credit—worth $80 out of her purse, but because it was more than a year old, it had expired. More money down the drain. Finally, the chaos started carrying over into her job, preventing her from thinking straight at the office. Deadlines started passing her by. Sydney knew she had to do something.

She'd read a couple of articles on feng shui in magazines and heard a bit about it from her sister, a professional organizer. So she picked up a little book called *Clear Your Clutter with Feng Shui* by Karen Kingston at the local Barnes & Noble and went about cleaning up her act.

Feng shui provides a set of principles by which to do this. My research shows that happier people are more likely to choose positive coping mechanisms (like exercise) to deal with their stress, while those who are unhappy opt for negative behaviors like drinking, smoking, and drugs. I'd lump feng shui in with the good choices.

Feng shui disciples believe that your house has nine different sections or areas. Wealth is one of those areas (as are career, health, family, relationships). In order to live peacefully and happily, you have to keep all of those areas balanced. If your wealth or financial life is out of balance, it will throw your family, health, and sense of well-being out of balance. If your financial life is in balance, it makes it easier— says ultrapractical Sydney—to gain a reasonable balance in your life.

Where precisely is your wealth area? Imagine your living space as a tick-tack-toe diagram. If you're standing at the front door looking in, your wealth area is in the back, left corner. This is the area where you should focus on making money, your career, your investments (but not paying bills—that's money out the door—and a task that should be performed elsewhere). Your wealth area should be organized and clutter-free. Otherwise your abilities to make money and hold on to money tend to be impaired. It should be a place that makes you feel as if you are already rich. That's where color comes in. Green says growth. Black is the color of movement. Purple is the color of richness and royalty. Those are all good. Red—the color of hemorrhaging—is to be avoided.

There are other elements as well. Fountains are good; they represent productivity. But a drippy faucet in your wealth area means money is running through your fingers. If a toilet seat is up, money is pouring down the drain. A healthy plant—particularly when that plant is lucky bamboo—is a symbol of growth.

Your positioning, when sitting at your desk in your own office, is also important. You need to place yourself in a power position. Are you visually in charge, in command, behind a desk, perhaps, but facing the door, looking out? If not—if you're sitting with your back turned toward the door and are facing the window or your computer—your back is exposed. People and things can sneak up on you and throw you off your game. If you can't turn your desk and computer around (and wiring being what it is, it's sometimes tough), get a large mirror so that you can see what's happening outside your office door. At least that way you'll be able to see opportunities as they come by.

By the way, clearing the space is something you'll want to do in all areas, not just your wealth area. Some real estate agents in California now feng shui their listings before they put them on the market. When potential buyers walk in they get a calm, soothing feeling, not a bunched-up, cluttered one. Realtors say places sell faster as a result.

Start talking to practitioners of feng shui and you'll hear a plethora of anecdotes like this one: "I have a friend who owns a business," one believer told me. "Her wealth area was where she put all her yucky leftovers. Her odds and ends. She had never done anything snazzy with it. So I asked her what money meant to her and she said, 'A dollar bill.' So we decided to redo that room in the colors of a dollar bill: black, cream, and sage. It looked fabulous. Two weeks later she called and told me she had gotten the biggest contract she had ever received."

Personally, I don't buy the energy-in-the-airwaves line of thinking. I think results are all about your intentions and your actions.

When you spend time thinking about what you want to do with your house, your finances, your career, it spurs you into taking action in your life. It's a "Field of Dreams" mentality. If you build it, he will come. If you believe it, you can become it. And if you buy into something, it works.

Some feng shui experts agree. "A lot of what I do is give people permission to make changes—not just in the color of a wall—but changes in their lives that will make them happy," says Sandra Goodall, who teaches feng shui in North Carolina. "People are fundamentally afraid of change on every level. But when they make changes to their homes, then they see they can do it in their relationships, their finances, their lives."

Getting Going

For my pal Sydney, step one was paring down. First, she tossed. She threw out old ATM receipts, catalogs, insurance policies for cars she no longer owned, benefits manuals for companies she hadn't worked for in years.

What was left, she filed. Sydney's old habit was to throw all of her papers into a big wicker basket on a kitchen counter. If and when she wanted to know what she paid for electricity last July—because this year's electric bill seemed astronomical—she'd have to dig through the basket to see if she could find it. Sometimes she was successful; other times, not. It always took longer than she anticipated.

So she set up a filing system that worked for her. She made large folders for all of her important categories: brokerage accounts, insurance policies, credit cards, etc. Then she created smaller files within. The insurance folder, for example, contained files for home, auto, health, life, disability, and liability. And each one of those had a file labeled by year.

It was extremely satisfying to put all that stuff away, but even better was getting a glimpse that her system worked. Sydney was on the East Coast for work when she needed some information from a life insurance policy circa 1993. So she picked up the phone, dialed Eddie in L.A., and gave him directions on how to find it. He did so with no difficulty, and Sydney knew she had her clutter problem licked. Sound like something you'd like to do?

Four Easy Steps

Step One: Toss. Different people have different ways of throwing out, but generally, quicker is better. Spend too much time obsessing over the fact that your brilliant kindergartner knew precisely how to color a turkey and you'll never progress to the stack of three-year-old ATM receipts. (And, yes, some of those school papers have to go.)

Don't let guilt persuade you to keep certain items. Your home is where you live. It should nurture you. You should love walking through the door—not dread it. So if you hate the sad-eyed clown Great Aunt Ethel made in ceramics class, it goes. Giving yourself permission to toss junk mail (sale flyers, catalogs, etc.) unopened can be a huge time-saver as well. (Note: Credit card solicitations can be tossed unopened, too. But it's best to shred them to protect yourself from so-called dumpster divers—identity thieves who might pull them out of your garbage.) For years I tossed freely at the office, but was unable to do it at home. Getting over this—and it took only a month of tossing the junk to convince me there weren't going to be any nasty repercussions—added an extra fifteen minutes to my day (even more during the holidays, when catalogs pile up like dirty laundry).

For some people, tossing seems wasteful, and that makes it more difficult to do. If you're among them, start small. Do a shelf at a time, asking yourself about each item, Do I love it? Did I order it? How does it make me feel? If it's a book (not a potentially valuable first edition), will I or anyone in my family ever crack it open again? If the answer is no, your mission is clear. (And by the way, tossing isn't synonymous with putting something in the garbage. If it's a book, think of your local library. If it's clothing, your local career closet or Goodwill.)

Step Two: Organize. As your papers come in, they should go in one large pile (much better than two or three small piles because no pile goes forgotten or untouched). Organizing is a matter of separating the items in that one big pile into their proper categories.

Just like phyla in your tenth-grade biology class, things have a natural order. Like belongs with like, whether it's tax returns, credit card bills, books by a particular author, or the health plan cards for your immediate family. Before you can put them away, however, you have to sort them into their proper categories.

I could give you a list of all the different categories you might need in your life, but chances are that wouldn't work. My labels might be totally off base where your life is concerned. Perhaps you run your own small business on the side, or have a child who takes music lessons three times a week. Those are two of your categories. You also wouldn't remember my categories in an emergency (you wouldn't, as Sydney did, be able to call your husband cross-country and direct him to a decade-old life insurance policy). Instead, you want to give your categories the same names you use in everyday conversation—the names that are on the tip of your tongue.

Step Three: File. Getting your paperwork organized is a little like cleaning out a closet. It has to get worse before it gets better. And if you've been taking these steps in order, right about now you feel you're sitting in a sea of papers. Trust me, you've hit bottom. It gets better from here.

Once you know what your categories are, you need a large folder for each one. If we're talking about your credit card statements, for example, you make one large credit card folder, then each card—Visa, MasterCard, AmEx—gets its own file within.

Into that file place two smaller ones, the first for your bills and statements for the current year, the second for your annual statements. Once you receive the annual for each year and are sure it's accurate, then you can toss the monthlies and start over. If we're talking about insurance policies, you need one big insurance file with separate folders for each of your policies—life, health, auto, disability, etc.

Step Four: Fifteen minutes a day. Remember the fifteen minutes you're going to save by ignoring the junk mail? Now you're going to put them to better use. That quarter hour becomes the time you give yourself to stick with this program. Every day, when the mail comes in or when you get home from work, you go through that one large pile, toss the junk, open what's necessary, and deal with it. The goal is to touch each piece of paper only once. That means keeping a checkbook and a book of stamps at the ready and paying bills as they come in.

For Sydney—and other feng shui enthusiasts—clearing the paper was only the beginning. Once you deal with your documents, don't be surprised if the urge to purge takes over. The ability to distinguish junk mail from the important stuff will give you a new outlook on your shoes, your kids' toys, your medicine cabinet. Resist the urge to solve every problem immediately. Instead tackle one area a day or one area a weekend—and by area I mean one closet, one medicine chest, not an entire bedroom or bathroom—until you've made it through the house. That way you (and your garbage collector) won't get burned out on clearing your clutter.

Paper or PDA?

I longed for a Palm Pilot for months before I actually got one. I loved the idea of replacing my bulging Filofax with a device small enough and flat enough to fit in a jacket pocket and allow me to streamline my tote. Being able to sync with my PC at home and my Mac at the office was also enticing.

The $400 sticker price was keeping me at bay, but my resolve was fading. Then in June 2000, I found myself in the waiting room of a D.C. hospital with my family as my dad had bypass surgery. I read a lousy mystery and fidgeted. My youngest brother calmly played Pac-Man on his Palm. A week later, I owned a Palm V.

I unpacked it, installed the software, and connected the cradle. Piece of cake. I mastered Graffiti—the language used to input notes

These Are the Papers You Need to Keep (and for How Long)

- ATM receipts and receipts for purchases (until you get the monthly bank and credit card statements and make sure these reconcile; then keep the monthly and throw out the individual slips)

- Bills and bank and brokerage statements, including canceled checks (until you get the year-end statement, check it over, and make sure everything reconciles; then throw out the monthlies and keep the annual)

- A list of credit cards, the account numbers, and the 800 numbers you'd use to report a loss or theft (indefinitely)

- A list of items in your safe deposit box, with a running account of what you put in and take out (indefinitely)

- Tax returns (six years, unless they include information on the purchase or sale of a home or an IRA, in which case keep them forever)

- Receipts for appliances and home improvements (until you sell the home)

- Warranties (until they expire)

- Employment records, including letters of recommendation (indefinitely)

- Receipts for large purchases (for insurance purposes in case of a fire or other home emergency)

- Year-end brokerage statements or other documents relating to buying and selling stock (indefinitely; you may need them to account for your cost basis)

- Insurance policies (as long as you own the policy)

- Deed to your home (as long as you own the home)

- Wills, trusts, and other estate planning documents (indefinitely)

- An inventory of where important documents are kept and a list of phone numbers (doctors, lawyers, accountants, neighbors, children) to be called in case of emergency (indefinitely) into the device—in under an hour. Diligently, I entered every name, address, phone number, and birthday, plus my schedule through the middle of '01. I downloaded all the must-have software. I was ready to go. Or so I thought.

Even after I'd had a month to adjust, I was still having trouble entering my appointments quickly. Worse, I started double-booking. And although I put a lot of energy into making to-do lists, I kept forgetting to flip to them. The Palm was supposed to streamline my life, but I felt less organized than ever.

Turns out, I'm not the only one.

Our world is divided into visual/tactile people and linear/digital people. When visual folks like me use a paper planner, we remember not only what we wrote, but where on the page we wrote it and what color ink we used. Those clues help us to organize our days. Linear people organize in their heads. When they see what's on tap for a particular day, they can envision the way their calls to make and things to do fit in. So PDAs like the Palm tend to be easier for linear folks to use than visual ones.

If you're a visual person who wants to give it a go—and after two years back in a Filofax, I recently dug out my Palm to try again—there are a couple of things you can do to ease the transition. First, get a program such as Datebk5 that puts your calls and to-do lists on the same page as your calendar. And second, don't feel you have to give up paper entirely. My highly organized pal Lisa habitually prints out a few days of her calendar and takes it with her wherever she goes.

Money and Happiness Evaluation: Part 4

1. Which of the following statements comes c
   regarding your financial goals? (Circle one lette.,

   a. I have not identified any financial goals for myself.
   b. I have not started to achieve any of the financial goals I have set for
      myself.
   c. I have started to achieve some of my financial goals, but I have a
      long way to go.
   d. I have been working steadily toward my financial goals and I have
      achieved about half.
   e. I have achieved most of the financial goals I set for myself.
   f. I have achieved all of the financial goals I set for myself.

2. For what purpose(s) are you saving or investing? (Circle as many
   letters as apply.)

   a. Primary residence
   b. Second or vacation home
   c. Retirement
   d. Children's education
   e. Major home renovations
   f. A rainy day

3. Do you know how much you need to save or invest to attain each
   of your goals. (Check all that apply.)

	YES	NO
a. Primary residence	❏	❏
b. Second or vacation home	❏	❏
c. Retirement	❏	❏
d. Children's education	❏	❏
e. Major home renovations	❏	❏
f. A rainy day	❏	❏

. Are you on track to achieve your goal(s) within the time frame(s) you've set? (Check all that apply.)

	YES	NO	DON'T KNOW
a. Primary residence	❏	❏	❏
b. Second or vacation home	❏	❏	❏
c. Retirement	❏	❏	❏
d. Children's education	❏	❏	❏
e. Major home renovations	❏	❏	❏
f. A rainy day	❏	❏	❏

5. How much do you agree or disagree with the following statements? Use a scale ranging from 1 to 7, where 1 means you completely disagree with the statement, 7 means you completely agree with the statement, and the other numbers represent levels in between.

a. I try not to think about how much money I will have to live on in my retirement years because it is just too depressing.

b. I really believe that if you watch the pennies, the dollars will take care of themselves.

4. What Do You *Really* Want?

The first step to getting what you want out of life is this: Decide what you want.

—Ben Stein

Meet Eve. A beautiful woman in her early thirties working in television production in the Big Apple, Eve brings home a salary in the mid-five-figure range. That's a considerable amount. But when you're a single mom paying rent in New York, even in a borough that's not Manhattan, who also has to foot the bill for day care, it goes quickly. The first few years after she and her husband split, Eve candidly admits, she wallowed in self-pity. Here she was, educated, with a job many others would kill for, but she didn't much like having to do it alone.

So Eve tried a little shopping therapy to chase her blues away. Whenever she needed an emotional lift, she'd hit J. Crew or Banana Republic. She rationalized her purchases by noting that they were for modest double-digit amounts. When she found a terrific item with a sharply reduced sale price, she'd encourage herself to buy two or three. "I would think only about how much I was *saving*, never about the fact that I was actually *spending*," she recalls. After one intense shopping season (one she attributes to the fact that after months of uncertainty, her husband finally left for good) the creditors started to call. She couldn't escape them. The phone rang at dinner. It rang at breakfast. She finally had to take it off the hook.

Eventually, this pattern made Eve take a look at her life. She looked at the four-year-old son she wanted to send to private school and at the graduate degree she wanted to pursue for herself. She looked at New York City real estate prices and realized how far away she was from being able to buy a place of her own. She thought about all the other major expenses lined up in her future: not just college and retirement, but a second wedding and honeymoon if and when she met the real man of her dreams. And, like a smoker who realizes he'd like to live to see his daughter's wedding, she decided that her goals were important enough for her to try to quit spending.

She went at it cold turkey—"Is there any other way?" she asks—and it was far from easy. "There are days when I look in the windows at the Nautica store and I think: 'I want that. I need that.' But I know I don't. What I *need* is an education for my son and for me." The urge to buy hasn't vanished, Eve admits, and she doesn't believe it ever will, much as alcoholics never stop craving a drink. But she's found a solution that works for her. Today, when Eve's feeling down, she shops creatively—in her own closet. She'll pore over the racks until she hits upon a belt, a scarf, a pair of shoes that she forgot she owned. That one item can make whatever she's wearing that day seem fresh. And she says that the satisfaction she gets from pulling together a terrific outfit from her own castoffs is just as good as the high she got from buying new. Some days, it's even better.

On the saving side of the equation, Eve also actively monitors her account balances. She makes it a point to pat herself on the back when she sees the balance on Visa heading down, and her savings and 401(k) balances heading up. By recognizing the fact that she's getting closer to her financial goals, she gets the same sort of boost a dieter gets by stepping on the scale after losing those first couple of pounds, or an exerciser for making that first mile. It's inspirational. It makes her feel as if she can do more—faster and better.

Why Goal Setting Is More Than an Exercise

Personal finance books often pay lip service to setting goals, but, in fact, there are very good reasons for going to the trouble. Think for a minute about what goals are. At the most basic level, they're wants. Not wants like "I want a Coke" or "I want to see that new Richard Gere movie," but bigger than that. They're your aspirations for the future. For my friends Don and Paige, one goal is to spend the summer of 2005 traveling—literally—around the world. My brother Dave and sister-in-law Ali have set their sights on leaving the city behind and buying a house in the suburbs. My husband and I would like to put an addition on our house (he wants a sunporch, I want a modern bathroom). Goals are bigger than wants. They're *uber*wants.

Whether you do it on a piece of paper or on a computer screen or in a conversation over dinner, setting goals explicitly helps you do a number of things. It helps you see them clearly. It helps you flesh them out. It helps you realize all the interim steps you'll have to take to accomplish them. It helps you figure out what the cost might be. And it helps you decide whether the trade-offs involved are worth it, or you'd rather pursue something else.

And—oh yes—it makes you happy. Goal setters are happier with their finances and less likely to worry about their money. Likewise, financially happy people are more knowledgeable about the amount they need to save in order to reach their goals, and are more likely to be on track to do so.

Although you could just set your sights on a distant goal and try, haphazardly, to reach it, it helps if there's a method to your madness. What's the best way to set goals and be sure you achieve them?

The Four Steps of Setting Goals

See what you want. Visualization is step number one. Sit yourself in a chair and imagine yourself—happy—five or ten or twenty-five years down the road. Be specific. Be clear. One big reason people fail to reach their goals is that those goals were amorphous to begin with. You need to understand: Where are you? What are you doing? Who are you with? How did you get there?

Setting a goal of "buying my first house soon" is too wishy-washy. Deciding you'd like to buy a three-bedroom cape on at least a half acre within thirty minutes of your workplace before the next school year begins is much more specific, therefore much better.

There's no need to be overly practical about this. Dreams don't exist in any sort of physical form. The physical form is what you create as you pursue your vision. So think big. Part of the reason people like Mother Teresa and the Dalai Lama achieved long-lasting happiness is that they had big visions to sustain them.

Once you have your vision, focus on how it makes you feel. As the research of Harvard psychologist Dan Gilbert has shown, you are likely very good at identifying the things you believe you want. But when you get those things, they often don't make you as happy as you thought they would.

To become a better forecaster of your own happiness, you have to think about how those things, people, and outcomes will make you feel if and when you do get them. What kind of emotions will they elicit? How strong will those emotions be? How long will those emotions last? Try to imagine as many aspects of the outcome as you can. Winning the lottery brings not only pleasures, but also hassles—phone calls from brokers, a new close relationship with the IRS, tension in the family.

Write your goals down. Like any good idea, goals need to be written down so that you can refer to them every now and then. You may decide to change them, or to abandon them. That's your prerogative. But in the beginning, they need to be in writing.

Why? Because if you don't write them down, you're likely to forget them. I'm not kidding. That's how your brain processes information. When you *see* something—researchers call it a visual stimulus—your brain holds on to that image for about a half second. When you *hear* something, you retain it a little longer, say three seconds. After that, you lose it. Unless, that is, you make an effort to keep that information in the forefront of your mind by repeating it to yourself over and over as if it were a phone number, or by creating a memory jogger like the ones we use to remember people's names (Mrs. Green has green eyes). You can play with it to move it from your short-term memory into your long-term memory where it will be available for you to recall it, or you can go with the easier alternative: You can write it down.

Turn your goal into an action plan. Once you've got a goal, you need to figure out what steps you'll need to take to achieve it. That means breaking it down into manageable parts. Say your goal is to save $5,000 in the next year. With all those zeros attached, it sounds daunting. But saving $100 a week for fifty weeks is not so overwhelming. Further, if you know you can come up with that much money by quitting the pricey health club you never attend anyway ($35), eating out one less time a week ($40), and refinancing your car loan ($25), your course is clear.

Understand the time involved. People are funny where time is concerned. We often overestimate how much we can accomplish in a single day, yet we generally underestimate how much we can accomplish in a year if we make just a little progress every day. That's true whether you're teaching a child to swim, turning a plot of unused land into a vegetable garden, writing a book, or—again—trying to lose ten pounds. Quick fixes rarely work. Preparing for a test by cramming the night before is almost never as effective as attending class regularly and calmly reviewing your notes.

The Six Keys to Achieving Goals

For setting goals, you get a substantial payoff. For working toward them, you get a greater one. Nearly half—48 percent—of Americans who are steadily working toward their goals (or who have achieved them) say they are *very* happy with their lives overall. That's a substantial improvement over the 31 percent who have just started to achieve their goals, and an even greater leap over the 18 percent who haven't identified or taken the first step toward theirs. People who have at least started to achieve their goals are much more likely to feel useful, content, and confident. Those who haven't even started are more likely to feel hopeless and stressed. And once you start to make steady progress, worry diminishes as well.

How can you best get there?

Begin. Once you know what your goals are, you have to act on them. Sounds like a no-brainer, I know. But many people are perpetual dreamers who hope and hope, but never implement. What do you have to do? Take the first step—whether it's opening an account at the brokerage firm where you're going to put the $50 you save each week, figuring out how much a three-bedroom house is likely to cost (and how much you'd have to put down), or saying no for the first time in a long time as the dessert trolley passes by.

Recognize the obstacles in your way. Often, as you're moving toward a goal, you can predict the obstacles that will pop up in your way. Jim Ball, founder of The Goals Institute, who helps individuals and corporations structure and meet their goals, tells of working with a group of women in Omaha. One woman, Robin, said she thought she'd feel much better about her financial future and retirement if she were just able to save $50 a month. As a group, they named the goal Robin's Nest Egg and figured out where she could come up with the money (manicures biweekly instead of weekly, double coupons). Then Ball asked her what sort of barriers stood in her way. Robin answered without a second thought: "My husband," she said. "He likes to spend money."

Ball shook his head. "That's not going to work," he explained to her. "He's going to get in your way every step. Unless he has an interest in your saving—unless he sees that there's some reward in it for him at the end of the road—you're not going to be able to save without racking up additional debt. But if you can get him to buy into the program, perhaps together you can save even more."

Likewise, once you've isolated your obstacles, it makes sense to avoid them. Manage your environment so that you have little exposure to the temptations that plague you, whether that means walking out of the path of your favorite shoe store, particularly during the winter sale, or not having dinner with the friend who believes you can't get a good bottle of wine for less than $100, but meeting her for coffee instead. Condition yourself to ignore television ads. The commercial break is the perfect time to check your e-mail, make school lunches, or return a call. Then surround yourself with healthy examples—good money managers, sound eaters, avid exercisers, or other people who embody the characteristics you desire.

Build better habits. No matter what your goals are, you've got a better chance of succeeding at them if you make habits of the life changes necessary to reach them. Most people make the mistake of looking at goals as a point in time some distance away. You're better off if, instead, you can look at goals as a series of lifelong changes you have to make to achieve those desires.

How do you initiate a habit? First, by breaking the old ones. Whether you're trying to quit smoking or stop spending frivolously, start by keeping a record of every time you have a cigarette or every time you open your wallet. What triggers you to light up? What triggers you to spend? When you look over your list, don't be surprised if a lightbulb goes on. Your brain can't see your habits. You have to show it when you're smoking. You have to show it when and what you're buying.

When Jim Ball went through SmokeEnders, the record he kept showed that he lit up after a swim. "What are you going to do after a swim when you can't have a cigarette?" his counselor asked. Ball decided he would go for a run. On the counselor's instructions, he visualized it. He repeated it in his mind: Go for a run. Go for a run. Go for a run. It wasn't until summer came around again nine months later that he got a chance to see if it worked. By then, he'd been off cigarettes for nearly six months—but he also hadn't been in the pool. And wouldn't you know it—he jumped into the pool, got out, and had an urge for a cigarette. So what did he do? "I went for a run. I laughed about the fact that I was probably programmed to want the cigarette as much as anything else," he recalls. "But I did it."

You can do the same with fiscal fitness. If you're part of a couple that eats out frequently, you can't see the impact of that on your finances. In order for that to happen, you have to quantify it. Maybe each restaurant meal runs $75. And maybe you eat out twice a week. What if you decide that instead of spending $150 a week, you'll spend $75 and invest the rest. After a year, you'll have saved $3,900. Stick with the habit, shelter the money in a tax-advantaged retirement account, and invest it in a mutual fund that returns 8 percent, and you'll have $67,877 ten years from now, $209,609 twenty years from now, and $523,611 thirty years from now when you retire. A half million dollars! Just from skipping one meal out a week. That's how you begin to process a goal.

It's important to replace your broken old habits with new and improved ones. The first time you skip that second dinner out, you may find it tough to tell your friends that you can't meet them. The second time, it won't be as difficult. By the third week, they may stop asking—unless you offer an alternative. Weekly potlucks with different international themes? A classic video or DVD night? Don't be surprised if soon those same pals are angling for an invitation.

Automate where you can. You don't have to do all the heavy lifting yourself. These days you can count on technology for a substantial boost, particularly when it comes to saving and investing. Most deposits into brokerage, savings, and retirement accounts can be scheduled. You decide how much will be deposited, which shares will be bought (specific stocks or bonds, mutual funds, or money-market funds), and when the deposit will be made. You sign on the dotted line, and the transactions happen automatically. If paying your bills on time is a problem, you can schedule those payments as well.

Set up reminders. Whenever you're working toward a goal, if you can see it—clearly and often—you'll be less likely to stray. That's why people stick pictures of Britney Spears's abs and Tina Turner's legs on their refrigerator doors. It's why resorts in the Caribbean spend a fortune on slick brochures and Web sites. And it works. Each time you see Britney in her belly shirt it's a none-too-subtle reminder that you'd like to lose ten pounds. So instead of reaching for the last piece of birthday cake, you grab a pear and do thirty crunches.

Focus on tomorrow. John Wayne once said: "Tomorrow's the most important thing in life. When it arrives and puts itself in our hands, we can only hope we learned something from yesterday." In other words, look forward, not back. Dwell on your successes, not your failures. If you fall off the wagon—spending more than you'd planned, eating more than you'd planned, looking for a job with less fervor than you'd planned—don't consider it an excuse to stop trying. Simply start again tomorrow. After all, reaching your ten-year milestone eleven years from now is much better than never reaching it at all.

Having a recent positive experience to recall helps as well. Nobel Prize winner Princeton economist Daniel Kahneman and his colleagues conducted an experiment in 1993 in which they asked one group of subjects to submerge their hands in ice water 14° C for 60 seconds. A second group of subjects was asked to submerge their hands for 90 seconds; during the first 60 seconds the water was 14° C but during the last 30 seconds it was warmed to 15°. Although the second group of subjects had their hands in the icy water for a 50 percent longer stretch, they remembered it as a less painful experience because it ended on an upswing.

It works the same way with money. Maybe you had a bad month financially. The first three weeks you weren't able to save at all because you had to fly home to see your sick grandmother and your dog needed to see the vet. But by the fourth week you'd regrouped. You were able to put away $50. It wasn't the $200 you'd hoped for, but it was something. Try to focus on the accomplishment of that.

Money and Happiness Results: Part 4

1. Which of the following statements comes closest to your position regarding your financial goals? (Circle one letter.)

a. I have not identified any financial goals for myself.

b. I have not started to achieve any of the financial goals I have set for myself.

c. I have started to achieve some of my financial goals, but I have a long way to go.

d. I have been working steadily toward my financial goals and I have achieved about half.

e. I have achieved most of the financial goals I set for myself.

f. I have achieved all of the financial goals I set for myself.

About your response: Americans are split into fairly even thirds: One third haven't identified any goals or haven't taken step one toward achieving those they have set, a second third are making progress but still have a long way to go, and a final third are working steadily and have achieved at least half of the goals they've set. Here's a complete breakdown.

I have not identified any financial goals for myself. **15%**

I have not started to achieve any of the financial goals I have set for myself. **13%**

I have started to achieve some of my financial goals, but I have a long way to go. **32%**

I have been working steadily toward my financial goals and I have achieved about half. **14%**

I have achieved most of the financial goals I set for myself. **11%**

I have achieved all of the financial goals I set for myself. **1%**

How close are Americans to their financial goals?

2. For what purpose(s) are you saving or investing? (Circle as many letters as apply.)

a. Primary residence
b. Second or vacation home
c. Retirement
d. Children's education
e. Major home renovations
f. A rainy day

About your responses: The majority of Americans—about two-thirds—say they are saving or investing, with one-quarter putting away at least 10 percent of their household income. Three-quarters of those savers are putting money away for retirement. Four out of ten savers (and six out of ten senior savers) are saving for a rainy day. Saving for college comes third on the list; while only 22 percent of the savers lists this as a goal, 58 percent of those with children under age eighteen in the house are saving for college. The complete breakdown looks like this:

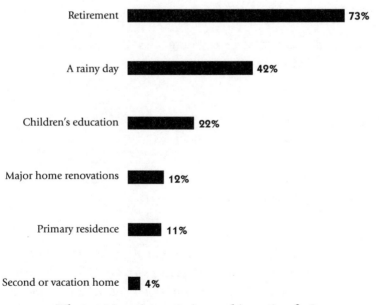

Retirement **73%**

A rainy day **42%**

Children's education **22%**

Major home renovations **12%**

Primary residence **11%**

Second or vacation home **4%**

What are Americans saving and investing for?

3. Do you know how much you need to save or invest to attain each of your goals? (Check all that apply.)

	YES	NO
a. Primary residence	❏	❏
b. Second or vacation home	❏	❏
c. Retirement	❏	❏
d. Children's education	❏	❏
e. Major home renovations	❏	❏
f. A rainy day	❏	❏

About your responses: Here's where the data start to get frightening. You may very well be saving for a particular goal, yet have no idea how much money you need to save or invest in order to get there. That's the case for some four out of ten people saving for retirement, college for their kids, or a house. Among those saving for a rainy day, half don't know what they need.

That's a problem. Saving blindly toward financial goals causes understandable unhappiness and worry. It's like hopping in the car to drive to a destination "somewhere out there," "a ways away," or "down the road a piece" but not knowing how long you're going to have to travel or whether or not you have enough gas to get there.

4. Are you on track to achieve your goal(s) within the time frame(s) you've set? (Check all that apply.)

	YES	NO	DON'T KNOW
a. Primary residence	❏	❏	❏
b. Second or vacation home	❏	❏	❏
c. Retirement	❏	❏	❏
d. Children's education	❏	❏	❏
e. Major home renovations	❏	❏	❏
f. A rainy day	❏	❏	❏

About your responses: Since most people don't know what's necessary to meet these goals, it follows that many people aren't on track, or simply don't know where they stand. This is true for all the financial goals on the list, but it's particularly problematic for retirement and college. Half of Americans saving for retirement and college say they aren't likely to hit their marks or don't know whether they will or not.

5. How much do you agree or disagree with the following statements? Use a scale ranging from 1 to 7, where 1 means you completely disagree with the statement, 7 means you completely agree with the statement, and the other numbers represent levels in between.

a. I try not to think about how much money I will have to live on in my retirement years because it is just too depressing.
b. I really believe that if you watch the pennies, the dollars will take care of themselves.

About your responses: One reason we may be unable to set goals—at least in the current economic environment—is that it's just too unhappy a subject. For the same reason that some people avoid depressing movies and others can't get near a scale, one-third of people say they try not to think about how much they'll have to live on during retirement because it's just too depressing. Women feel this way more than men, as do those whose education ended with high school (instead of continuing to college). Four out of ten people who earn less than $50,000 (per household) a year feel it's a subject they can't bear. But it's not a problem that vanishes with higher income—two out of ten individuals who earn more than $50,000 still say the thought of their retirement income gets them down.

Forty-two percent of Americans agree with the second statement. If you're one of them, chances are you're a happier person—happier not only with your finances but happier overall. People who believe in watching their pennies are less likely to worry about their finances and more likely to feel at least somewhat financially secure. They tend to be able to afford to pay off their credit cards each month, and have more money to buy the things they want, have a good time, and weather a financial hardship. And they're significantly closer to reaching their financial goals.

Attaching Numbers to Your Goals

Once you know what you want—and after going through the steps I've outlined, you should—it's time to figure out how much those goals will cost. Say you want to retire in northern California. Only when you know what it will cost to settle there can you determine how much of that cost your existing nest egg and projected Social Security are likely to cover—and how much of a gap remains. Once you know the size of the gap, you can figure out whether you'll be able to cover it by investing, say, $400 a month at a 7 percent return or whether it'll take $500 a month at a 9 percent return. For each goal you need to run a separate analysis. Once you know the total you need to sock away, you can keep it in any combination of accounts you like.

People often ask me, "How do I buy an IRA?" IRAs, like 401(k)s, 529 College Savings Plans, and Keoghs are accounts. Some are specifically for retirement, some for college, some for the self-employed. Others are open to everyone. But they're all holding pens. You don't buy them; you *open* them by filling out paperwork at your bank or brokerage firm. Then you make deposits into them much as you would into a savings or checking account (you can have those deposits made automatically/electronically, so that you don't have to do it "by hand").

Finally, you decide where you want to invest that money. The default option with most of these accounts is a no-risk money-market fund. If you don't elect to invest the money somewhere else, it will sit in the money market. You will earn a low rate of interest on that money, but you won't lose any of it either. Moving the money (some or all) out of the no-risk money market and into riskier vehicles—like lower-risk bonds and higher-risk stocks—is the only way you can earn a greater return on the money. The trade-off is that you could potentially lose more of it as well.

In the coming pages, we'll first talk about how to assess your needs for the major expenses you will face as you move through life. There are plenty of calculators on the Web that can help you run these numbers, but some people still prefer old-fashioned pencil and paper. These worksheets are for you.

How Much Do You Need to Retire?

This is my favorite worksheet for eyeballing retirement needs. It was developed by the folks at the American Savings Education Council, who—quite literally, they tell me—locked a group of actuaries in a room and wouldn't let them out until they came up with a way to compute retirement needs on a single page. I've been using it for years and have yet to see it improved upon. It's called the Ballpark Estimator. (Note: If you're married, you and your spouse should each fill out your own worksheet. Also, because the actuaries found it impossible to adjust for inflation on a one-page sheet, filling out this worksheet is something you must do once a year.)

I: Income Needs

1. How much annual income do you want in retirement? (Figure at least 70 percent of your current gross income just to maintain your standard of living. Really.) $_____
2. Subtract the income you expect to receive annually from
   - Social Security (If you make under $25,000 enter $8,000; between $25,000 and $40,000, enter $12,000; over $40,000 enter $14,500. For married couples the lower-earning spouse should enter either his or her own benefit based on income or 50 percent of the higher-earning spouse's benefit, whichever is higher.) $_____
   - Traditional employer pension—a plan that pays you a set monthly amount for life depending on salary and years of service (in today's dollars) $_____
   - Part-time income $_____
   - Other $_____

Remainder: This is how much you need to make up for each retirement year. $_____

II: Money You Need in the Bank

To estimate how much money you'll need in the bank the day you retire, the actuaries went back to work and devised this simple formula. For the record, they figure you'll realize a constant real rate of return of 3 percent after inflation, you'll live to age eighty-seven, and you'll begin to receive income from Social Security at age sixty-five. If you anticipate living longer than age eighty-seven or earning less than a 3 percent real return on your savings, you'll want to consider using a higher percentage of your current annual gross income as a goal on line 1 above.

3. To determine the amount you'll need to save, multiply the amount you need to make up by the factor below: $_____

Age you expect to retire	Your factor is
55	21.0
60	18.9
65	16.4
70	13.6

4. If you expect to retire before age sixty-five, multiply your Social Security benefit from line 2 by the factor below: $_____

Age you expect to retire	Your factor is
55	8.8
60	4.7

5. Multiply your savings to date by the factor below. Include money accumulated in 401(k), IRA, or similar retirement plans: $_____

If you want to retire in	Your factor is
10 years	1.3
15 years	1.6
20 years	1.8
25 years	2.1
30 years	2.4
35 years	2.8
40 years	3.3

Total: Additional savings needed at retirement. Add line 3 plus line 4, then subtract line 5: $_____

III. How Much Do You Need to Save?

Don't panic. Next the accountants devised another formula to show how much you need to save each year in order to reach your goal. They factored in compounding. That's where your money earns interest *and* your interest starts earning interest as well, creating a snowball effect.

6. To determine the annual amount you need to save, multiply the total in line 5 by the factor below: $_____

If you want to retire in	Your factor is
10 years	.085
15 years	.052
20 years	.036
25 years	.027
30 years	.020
35 years	.016
40 years	.013

Want to see an example? Take a thirty-five-year-old woman with two children earning $30,000 a year. She has determined she'll need 80 percent of her current income—or $24,000—to maintain her standard of living in retirement. Subtracting the $12,000 a year she expects to receive from Social Security, she's left with a shortfall of $12,000. That's how much she needs to make up for each retirement year. She expects to retire at age sixty-five, so she multiplies $12,000 by 16.4, equaling $196,799. She has already saved $2,000 in her 401(k) plan. To figure out how much that will be worth in thirty years, when she plans to retire, she multiplies $2,000 by 2.4, which equals $4,800. She subtracts that from her total, making her projected total savings needed at retirement $191,999. She then multiplies that by .020, which equals $3,839. That's the amount she needs to save this year for retirement. (Note: Remember, this worksheet doesn't account for the changing value of the dollar. That's why you need to fill it out once a year.)

How Much Do You Need to Send Your Kids to College?

These days, it's not realistic for most parents to aspire to foot the entire college bill for their kids. With tuition rising, grant money shrinking, and loans on the rise, 70 percent of families receive some form of financial aid, the vast majority of it in loans. This is not to say you shouldn't try to contribute to your child's college education. These days some students are coming out of school so debt-ridden that they put off pursuing the work they were educated for in favor of a bigger paycheck. If that doesn't immediately stick in your throat as an unfortunate and unhappy way to go through life, wait until you hit Chapter 7.

I'm not suggesting that you place college savings for your children higher on your list of financial priorities than retirement savings for yourself. After all, there is no financial aid for retirement. I am suggesting that you will feel better if you can at least make a dent in the cost, and making that dent is more than possible. It can be done in a number of ways: You can tap equity accrued in your home; you can borrow with a tax-deductible home equity loan or line of credit; or you can try to plan ahead and save a little each month for this specific purpose.

How much do you need to save?

What's College Going to Cost?
In 2002, according to the College Board, the cost of a four-year education at a public college or university was about $54,200 for state residents. The cost of four years at a private college or university was a little more than double that amount: $118,000. College costs are rising about 6 percent annually. Assuming that continues, here's what you're looking at down the road.

Year	Public	Private
2003	$57,452	$125,080
2004	$60,899	$132,584
2005	$64,553	$140,539
2006	$68,425	$148,972

2007	$72,532	$157,910
2008	$76,883	$167,385
2009	$81,496	$177,428
2010	$86,386	$188,074
2011	$91,569	$199,358
2012	$97,063	$211,320
2013	$102,887	$223,999
2014	$109,061	$237,429
2015	$115,604	$251,685
2016	$122,540	$266,786
2017	$129,893	$282,793
2018	$137,687	$299,761
2019	$145,948	$317,747
2020	$154,705	$336,812
2021	$163,987	$357,020

How Much of a Dent Can You Make?

If you open a tax-deferred account today, this is how much you'll be able to save:

Monthly Contribution	5 Years	10 Years	15 Years	20 Years
$50	$3,233	$7,704	$13,203	$20,210
$100	6,775	15,408	26,406	40,419
$150	10,163	23,112	39,609	60,629
$200	13,551	30,816	52,813	80,839

But . . . what if you don't start today? What if you wait five years? Twenty years from now that:

> $50 a month is worth only $13,203
> $100 a month is worth only $26,406
> $150 a month is worth only $39,609
> and that $200 a month is worth only $52,813

The point is, it's not just a matter of how much you're able to sock away; it's also a matter of when you start. The person who saves $100 a month for twenty years has just as much money as the person who saves $150 a month for fifteen years, even though the first person actually contributed $3,000 less. It's worth getting started now, don't you think?

How Much Can You Spend on a Home?

In order to determine what you can afford to spend on a house, you need to know how much you can borrow. The size of the mortgage you qualify for depends on your income. Lenders like to see you spend no more than 28 percent of your monthly gross income on your mortgage payment, including homeowners insurance and taxes. (That's called the housing ratio.) And they like to see no more than 36 percent of your gross go to your mortgage and other long-term debts. (That's called the total debt or total obligation ratio.) In general, that includes debts that will take more than ten months to pay off, including car loans and student loans, but not credit card debt unless it's excessive.

These numbers aren't the bottom line. Lenders, particularly in competitive environments, will often give you wiggle room, and some will give you more than others.

To the amount you can borrow, you need to add the down payment you've pulled together. The days when you had to put 20 percent down in order to get a competitive mortgage are long gone. Today, 3 percent is all you need. But if you can manage 20 percent, you won't have to buy private mortgage insurance (PMI), which adds about 1/4 percent to your interest rate. Once you reach that 20 percent threshold, PMI payments are automatically terminated.

Housing Ratio

1. Monthly gross income	$ _____
2. Multiply by .28	× .28
Total	$ _____
3. Subtract monthly real estate taxes	− _____
Total	$ _____
4. Subtract monthly homeowners insurance premium	− _____
Total = Mortgage Amount A	$ _____

Total Obligation Ratio

1. Monthly gross income $_____

2. Multiply by .36 ×.36

    Total $_____

3. Subtract monthly real estate taxes − _____

    Total $_____

4. Subtract monthly homeowners insurance
   premium − _____

    Total $_____

5. Subtract monthly installment debts − _____

    Total = Mortgage Amount B $_____

Compare Amount A to Amount B. The lower number is the one you are likely to qualify for. Now use the table on the next page to figure out how much house that will buy you at current interest rates.

How Much Can You Borrow?

After you have completed the calculations on the preceding pages, you can determine the maximum mortgage for which you can qualify using the following chart compiled by HSH.com, the country's largest publisher of mortgage rate information. Match as closely as possible your calculated A or B figure with the dollar amounts shown on the bottom line. Select the *term* (15 or 30 years) and draw a line to the top of the page between the columns. Choose an *interest rate* from the column on the left (if you're looking for a ballpark rate, check your Sunday paper) and draw a line to intersect with the dollar-amount line you drew. At the intersection, expressed in thousands, is the maximum mortgage amount you can afford to borrow. Note: When qualifying for some adjustable-rate mortgages (ARMs), lenders will usually qualify you to borrow at the *second* year's interest rate (generally the sum of the starting rate plus the per-adjustment cap).

AUTOQUAL TABLE

Rate %	15 Year	30 Year	15 Year	30 Year	15 Year	30 Year	15 Year	30 Year	15 Year	30 Year
5.000	94.8	139.7	126.5	186.2	158.0	232.8	189.6	279.4	221.2	325.9
5.125	94.0	137.7	125.4	183.6	156.7	229.5	188.1	275.4	219.4	321.4
5.250	93.2	135.8	124.3	181.0	155.4	226.3	186.5	271.6	217.6	316.9
5.375	92.5	133.9	123.3	178.5	154.2	223.2	185.0	267.8	215.9	312.5
5.500	91.7	132.0	122.3	176.1	152.9	220.1	183.5	264.1	214.1	308.2
5.625	91.0	130.2	121.3	173.7	151.7	217.1	182.0	260.5	212.5	304.0
5.750	90.3	128.5	120.4	171.3	150.5	214.1	180.6	257.0	210.7	299.8
5.875	89.5	126.7	119.4	169.0	149.3	211.3	179.1	253.5	209.0	295.8
6.000	88.8	125.0	118.5	166.7	148.1	208.4	177.7	250.1	207.3	291.8
6.125	88.1	123.4	117.5	164.5	146.9	205.7	176.3	246.8	205.7	288.0
6.250	87.4	121.8	116.6	162.4	145.7	203.0	174.9	243.6	204.1	284.2
6.375	86.7	120.2	115.7	160.2	144.6	200.3	173.5	240.4	202.4	280.6
6.500	86.0	118.6	114.7	158.2	143.4	197.7	172.1	237.3	200.8	276.8
6.625	85.4	117.1	113.8	156.1	142.3	195.2	170.8	234.2	199.3	273.3
6.750	84.7	115.6	113.0	154.1	141.2	192.7	169.5	231.2	197.7	269.8
6.875	84.0	114.1	112.1	152.2	140.1	190.2	168.1	228.3	196.2	266.3
7.000	83.4	112.7	111.2	150.3	139.0	187.8	166.8	225.4	194.6	263.0
7.125	82.7	111.3	110.3	148.4	137.9	185.5	165.5	222.6	193.1	259.7
7.250	82.1	109.9	109.5	146.5	136.9	183.2	164.3	219.8	191.7	256.5
7.375	81.5	108.5	108.7	144.7	135.8	180.9	163.0	217.1	190.2	253.3
7.500	80.9	107.2	107.8	143.0	134.8	178.7	161.8	214.5	188.7	250.2
7.625	80.2	105.9	107.0	141.2	133.8	176.6	160.5	211.9	187.3	247.2
7.750	79.6	104.6	106.2	139.5	132.7	174.4	159.3	209.3	185.9	244.2
7.875	79.0	103.4	105.4	137.9	131.7	172.3	158.1	206.8	184.5	241.3
8.000	78.4	102.2	104.6	136.2	130.8	170.3	156.9	204.4	183.1	238.4
8.125	77.8	101.0	103.8	134.6	129.8	168.3	155.7	202.0	181.7	235.6
8.250	77.3	99.8	103.0	133.1	128.8	166.3	154.6	199.6	180.3	232.9
8.375	76.7	98.6	102.3	131.5	127.8	164.4	153.5	197.3	179.0	230.2
8.500	76.1	97.5	101.5	130.0	126.9	162.5	152.3	195.0	177.7	227.5
8.625	75.5	96.4	100.7	128.5	125.9	160.7	151.1	192.8	176.3	224.9
8.750	75.0	95.3	100.0	127.1	125.0	158.8	150.0	190.6	175.0	222.4
8.875	74.4	94.2	99.3	125.6	124.1	157.1	148.9	188.5	173.8	219.9
9.000	73.9	93.2	98.5	124.2	123.2	155.3	147.8	186.4	172.5	217.4
9.125	73.4	92.1	97.8	122.9	122.3	153.6	146.8	184.3	171.2	215.0
9.250	72.8	91.1	97.1	121.5	121.4	151.9	145.7	182.3	170.0	212.7
9.375	72.3	90.1	96.4	120.2	120.5	150.2	144.6	180.3	168.8	210.3
9.500	71.8	89.1	95.7	118.9	119.7	148.6	143.6	178.3	167.5	208.1
P & I	**$750/Month**		**$1000/Month**		**$1250/Month**		**$1500/Month**		**$1750/Month**	

P = principal   *I* = interest

Rate %	15 Year	30 Year	15 Year	30 Year	15 Year	30 Year	15 Year	30 Year	15 Year	30 Year
9.625	71.3	88.2	95.0	117.6	118.8	147.0	142.6	176.4	166.3	205.8
9.750	70.7	87.2	94.3	116.3	117.9	145.4	141.4	174.5	165.1	203.6
9.875	70.2	86.3	93.7	115.1	117.5	143.9	140.5	172.7	164.0	201.5
10.000	69.7	85.4	93.0	113.9	116.3	142.4	139.5	170.9	162.8	199.4
10.125	69.2	84.5	92.3	112.7	115.4	140.9	138.5	169.1	161.6	197.3
10.250	68.8	83.6	91.7	111.5	114.6	139.4	137.6	167.3	160.5	195.2
10.375	68.3	82.8	91.1	110.4	113.8	138.0	136.6	165.6	159.4	193.2
10.500	67.8	81.9	90.4	109.3	113.0	136.6	135.6	163.9	158.3	191.3
10.625	67.3	81.1	89.8	108.2	112.2	135.2	134.7	162.3	157.2	189.3
10.750	66.9	80.3	89.2	107.1	111.5	133.9	133.8	160.6	156.1	187.4
10.875	66.4	79.5	88.5	106.0	110.7	132.5	132.8	159.0	155.0	185.5
11.000	65.9	78.7	87.9	105.0	109.9	131.2	131.9	157.5	153.9	183.7
11.125	65.5	77.9	87.3	103.9	109.2	129.9	131.0	155.9	152.9	181.9
11.250	65.0	77.2	86.7	102.9	108.4	128.6	130.1	154.4	151.8	180.1
11.375	64.6	76.4	86.1	101.9	107.7	127.4	129.2	152.9	150.8	178.4
11.500	64.2	75.7	85.6	100.9	107.0	126.2	128.4	151.4	149.8	176.7
11.625	63.7	75.0	85.0	100.0	106.2	125.0	127.5	150.0	148.7	175.0
11.750	63.3	74.3	84.4	99.0	105.5	123.8	126.6	147.2	147.7	173.3
11.875	62.9	73.6	83.8	98.1	104.8	122.6	125.8	147.2	146.7	171.7
12.000	62.4	72.9	83.3	97.2	104.1	121.5	124.9	145.8	145.8	170.1
12.125	62.0	72.2	82.7	96.3	103.4	120.3	124.1	144.4	144.8	168.5
12.250	61.6	71.5	82.2	95.4	102.7	119.2	123.3	143.1	143.8	167.0
12.375	61.2	70.9	81.6	94.5	102.0	118.1	122.5	141.8	142.9	165.4
12.500	60.8	70.2	81.1	93.6	101.4	117.1	121.7	140.5	141.9	163.9
12.625	60.4	69.6	80.6	92.8	100.7	116.0	120.9	139.2	141.0	162.4
12.750	60.0	69.0	80.0	92.0	100.0	115.0	120.1	138.0	140.1	161.0
12.875	59.6	68.4	79.5	91.2	99.4	114.0	119.3	136.8	139.2	159.6
P & I	*$750/Month*		*$1000/Month*		*$1250/Month*		*$1500/Month*		*$1750/Month*	

P = principal   *I* = interest

Rate %	15 Year	30 Year	15 Year	30 Year	15 Year	30 Year	15 Year	30 Year	15 Year	30 Year
5.000	252.9	372.5	284.5	418.1	316.1	465.7	347.7	512.2	379.3	558.8
5.125	250.8	367.3	282.1	413.2	313.5	459.1	344.9	505.0	376.2	550.9
5.250	248.7	362.1	279.8	407.4	310.9	452.7	342.0	498.0	373.1	543.2
5.375	246.7	357.1	277.6	401.8	308.4	446.4	339.3	491.0	370.1	535.7
5.500	244.7	352.2	275.3	396.2	305.9	440.3	336.5	484.3	367.1	528.3
P & I	*$2000/Month*		*$2250/Month*		*$2500/Month*		*$2750/Month*		*$3000/Month*	

P = principal   *I* = interest

AUTOQUAL TABLE (*cont.*)

Rate %	15 Year	30 Year	15 Year	30 Year	15 Year	30 Year	15 Year	30 Year	15 Year	30 Year
5.625	242.7	347.4	273.1	390.8	303.4	434.2	333.8	477.7	364.1	521.1
5.750	240.8	342.7	271.8	385.5	301.0	428.3	331.1	471.2	361.2	514.0
5.875	238.9	338.1	268.7	380.3	298.6	422.6	328.5	464.8	358.3	507.1
6.000	237.0	333.5	266.6	375.2	296.2	416.9	325.8	458.6	355.5	500.3
6.125	235.1	329.1	264.5	370.3	293.9	411.4	323.2	452.5	352.6	493.7
6.250	233.2	324.8	262.4	365.4	291.5	406.0	320.7	446.6	349.8	487.2
6.375	231.4	320.5	260.3	360.6	289.2	400.7	318.1	440.7	347.1	480.8
6.500	229.5	316.4	258.2	355.9	286.9	395.5	315.6	435.0	344.3	474.6
6.625	227.7	312.3	256.2	351.3	284.7	390.4	313.2	429.4	341.6	468.5
6.750	226.0	309.9	254.2	346.9	282.5	385.4	310.7	423.9	339.0	462.5
6.875	224.2	304.4	252.2	342.5	280.3	380.5	308.3	418.6	336.3	456.6
7.000	222.5	300.6	250.3	338.1	278.1	375.7	305.9	413.3	333.7	450.9
7.125	220.7	296.8	248.3	333.9	275.9	371.0	303.5	408.1	331.1	445.2
7.250	219.0	293.1	256.4	329.9	273.8	366.4	301.2	403.1	328.6	439.7
7.375	217.4	289.5	244.5	325.7	271.7	361.9	298.9	398.1	326.1	434.3
7.500	215.7	286.0	242.7	321.7	269.6	357.5	296.6	393.2	323.6	429.0
7.625	214.1	282.5	240.8	317.8	267.6	353.2	294.3	388.5	321.1	423.8
7.750	212.4	279.1	239.0	314.0	265.5	348.9	292.1	383.8	318.7	418.7
7.875	210.8	275.8	237.2	310.3	263.5	344.7	289.9	379.2	316.3	413.7
8.000	209.2	272.5	235.4	306.6	261.6	340.7	287.7	374.7	313.9	408.8
8.125	207.7	269.3	233.6	303.0	259.6	336.7	285.6	370.3	311.5	404.0
8.250	206.1	266.2	231.9	299.4	257.6	332.7	283.4	366.0	309.2	399.3
8.375	204.6	263.1	230.1	296.0	255.7	328.9	281.3	361.8	306.9	394.6
8.500	203.0	260.1	228.4	292.6	253.8	325.1	279.2	357.6	304.6	390.1
8.625	201.5	257.1	226.7	289.2	251.9	321.4	277.1	353.5	302.3	385.7
8.750	200.1	254.2	225.1	286.0	250.1	317.7	275.1	349.5	300.1	381.3
8.875	198.6	251.3	223.4	282.7	248.3	314.2	273.1	345.6	297.9	377.0
9.000	197.1	248.5	221.8	279.6	246.4	310.7	271.1	341.7	295.7	372.8
9.125	195.7	245.8	220.2	276.5	244.6	307.2	269.1	337.9	293.6	368.7
9.250	194.3	243.1	218.6	273.4	242.9	303.8	267.1	334.2	291.4	364.6
9.375	192.9	240.4	217.0	270.5	241.1	300.5	265.2	330.6	289.3	360.6
9.500	191.5	237.8	215.4	267.5	239.1	297.3	263.3	327.0	287.2	356.7
9.625	190.1	235.2	213.9	264.7	237.6	294.1	261.4	323.5	285.2	352.9
9.750	188.7	232.7	212.3	261.8	235.9	290.9	259.5	320.0	283.1	349.1
9.875	187.4	230.3	210.8	259.1	234.3	287.9	257.7	316.6	281.1	345.4
10.000	186.1	227.9	209.3	256.3	232.6	284.8	255.9	313.3	279.1	341.8
10.125	184.7	225.5	207.8	253.7	230.9	281.9	254.0	310.0	277.1	338.2
P & I	**$2000/Month**		**$2250/Month**		**$2500/Month**		**$2750/Month**		**$3000/Month**	

P = principal   *I* = interest

Rate %	15 Year	30 Year	15 Year	30 Year	15 Year	30 Year	15 Year	30 Year	15 Year	30 Year
10.250	183.4	223.1	206.4	251.0	229.3	278.9	252.3	306.8	275.2	334.7
10.375	182.2	220.8	204.9	248.5	227.7	276.1	250.5	303.7	273.3	331.3
10.500	180.9	218.6	203.5	245.9	226.1	273.3	248.7	300.6	271.3	327.9
10.625	179.6	216.4	202.1	243.4	224.5	270.5	247.0	297.5	269.5	324.6
10.750	178.4	214.2	200.7	241.0	223.0	267.8	245.3	294.5	267.6	321.3
10.875	177.1	212.1	199.3	238.6	221.4	265.1	243.6	291.6	265.7	318.1
11.000	175.9	210.0	197.9	236.2	219.9	262.5	241.9	288.7	263.9	315.0
11.125	174.7	207.9	196.5	233.9	218.4	259.9	240.2	285.9	262.1	311.9
11.250	173.5	205.9	195.2	231.6	216.9	257.3	238.6	283.1	260.3	308.8
11.375	172.3	203.9	193.9	229.4	215.4	254.9	237.0	280.3	258.5	305.8
11.500	171.2	201.9	192.6	227.2	214.0	252.4	235.4	277.6	256.8	302.9
11.625	170.0	200.0	191.3	225.0	212.5	250.0	233.8	275.0	255.0	300.0
11.750	168.9	198.1	190.0	222.9	211.1	247.6	232.2	272.4	253.3	297.2
11.875	167.7	196.2	188.7	220.8	209.7	245.3	230.6	269.8	251.6	294.4
12.000	166.6	194.4	187.4	218.7	208.3	243.0	229.1	267.3	249.9	291.6
12.125	165.5	192.6	186.2	216.7	206.9	240.7	227.6	264.8	248.2	288.9
12.250	164.4	190.8	184.9	214.7	205.5	238.5	226.0	262.4	246.6	286.2
12.375	163.3	189.1	183.7	212.7	204.1	236.3	224.6	260.0	245.0	283.6
12.500	162.2	187.3	182.5	210.8	202.8	234.2	223.1	257.6	243.4	281.0
12.625	161.2	185.7	181.3	208.9	201.5	232.1	221.6	255.3	241.8	278.5
12.750	160.1	184.0	180.1	207.0	200.1	230.0	220.2	253.0	240.2	276.0
12.875	159.1	182.4	178.9	205.2	198.8	228.0	218.7	250.8	238.6	273.6
P & I	*$2000/Month*		*$2250/Month*		*$2500/Month*		*$2750/Month*		*$3000/Month*	

P = principal   *I* = interest

How Much Do You Need for a Rainy Day?

If you've ever read a financial magazine, watched Power Lunch on CNBC, or sat down with a financial adviser, you've heard these words: "You need an emergency cushion." What is that? It's three to six months' worth of living expenses, stockpiled but liquid, that you could access and exist on if you lost your job, got ill, or hit some other roadblock in life where you needed a chunk of money and didn't want to put it on your credit card (and pay it off at 18 percent) or raid your retirement account (and lose 50 cents on the dollar to taxes and penalties).

The amount you need in your emergency fund is not the same as what you earn in three to six months. It's also not what you typically spend. When you're working, you spend much more freely than you would if you were just trying to get by. These are subsistence figures. Here's how to figure out how much you need.

Emergency Cushion Calculation

1. Monthly mortgage or rent $_____
2. Average utility bills $_____
3. Car payment $_____
4. Average monthly grocery bill $_____
5. Insurance premiums (including health $_____
   insurance if you had to pay COBRA)
6. Tuition bills or other mandatory $_____
   expenses for your children
7. Minimum credit card payments $_____
8. Other mandatory expenses $_____
9. Add lines 1–8 $_____
10. If you're part of a two-income couple,
    multiply by 3; if you're single or if
    your spouse doesn't work outside the
    home, multiply by 6.
    Total $_____

Dealing with the Results

Work your way through one or all of these calculations and you're likely to feel (most people do) a little behind the eight ball. But you've got to remember, simply getting a grip on your goals and what it will cost to achieve them is a huge first step in the right direction toward financial security and happiness. In the next two chapters we'll work on precisely *how* you're going to come up with that money. Don't worry. It won't be as hard as you think.

Money and Happiness Evaluation: Part 5

1. How much do you agree or disagree with each of the following statements? Use a scale ranging from 1 to 7, where 1 means you completely disagree with the statement, 7 means you completely agree with the statement, and the other numbers represent levels in between.

   a. I know how to pick a money-making stock.
   b. I know how a mutual fund works.
   c. I am a good money manager.
   d. I am a knowledgeable investor.

2. How much do you agree or disagree with the following statement? Use a scale ranging from 1 to 7, where 1 means you completely disagree with the statement, 7 means you completely agree with the statement, and the other numbers represent levels in between.

   Managing my money is too complicated and time-consuming.

5. Making It Happen

Reversion to the mean is Sir Isaac Newton's revenge on Wall Street.
—Vanguard founder John Bogle

If you've worked your way through Chapter 4, you should have a better idea of your financial goals. That should embolden you to put aside some necessary money for your future—something too few Americans are doing.

Some 25 percent of Americans still don't participate in their companies' 401(k) or other retirement plans. Less than 5 percent of Americans have Individual Retirement Accounts. And, according to a July 2002 study from Aegon Institutional Markets, some four out of ten parents are *not* saving for college for their kids. What's stopping them? In part, it's a lack of discretionary income. But it's also a result of fear—fear of a roller-coaster ride in a stock market few people can understand.

The rise of the stock market didn't translate into more actual dollars for everyone (if it had, if the majority of people had sold their winners in order to capitalize on their gains, there would have been far less griping the past couple of years). No. The paper gains in our portfolio coupled with the continuing rise of the indexes represented a symbolic assurance that the future was looking better. When we lost both simultaneously, the feeling wasn't unlike losing a job. It wasn't that we necessarily had fewer dollars in our pockets, but our future security was on the line.

It didn't help that the drop in the market shattered our perceptions of ourselves as brilliant investors and smart money managers. We wouldn't necessarily have felt this way after one good year or even two. But because the run-up lasted for nearly a decade, we became convinced investing was easy. All you had to do was buy, buy some more, hold tight, and let the rising tide of the market carry you along. It seemed like any person, regardless of age, experience, research skills, or the time to put into the task could channel Warren Buffett. Magazines, including the ones I worked for, ran stories about high schoolers whose portfolios were soaring, seniors riding the tech wave, and sports stars who were trading on the sidelines. And traders on Wall Street were sure they were going to have a banner day anytime Maria Bartiromo showed up in red.

It was no wonder 100 million Americans—half of all adults—rushed into the market to buy individual stocks. Investing was no longer just for the rich. If you earned more than $30,000 a year, chances are, you were in. Women—long left behind—invested as often as men. Democrats as often as Republicans. People on the West Coast as often as those on the East. And why not? This was money for the taking. This was the last free lunch.

Until, of course, the bubble burst. By 2002, the NASDAQ, which had hit 5,000, was reduced to just over one-quarter of that. Five trillion dollars in paper wealth—30 percent of the money in the stock market—vanished in the process. With it went people's confidence and willingness to participate in what they saw as a game. You weren't alone if you started to wonder: Is investing something I really want to do? Need to do? Have to do?

Yes. Plain and simple. Yes.

Why It Still Pays to Invest

Unless you are extremely wealthy (in which case you don't need investment-size returns), just saving your money is not enough. You need your money to work as hard as you do, to produce a return of its own, if you're going to reach the goals you set for yourself. If all you're doing is socking your money into a money-market account, in recent years you haven't been making any money at all. Taxes and inflation have gobbled up your entire return—sometimes more.

You must invest. But you don't have to do it in the aim-for-the-stars, pick-the-biggest-winners style of the 1990s. That sort of investing requires a big commitment of time and energy. It requires constant research and diligent monitoring, to say nothing of an iron stomach. And despite all of those efforts, that sort of investing— more often than not—fails.

That's right. The most compelling argument I can make against this sort of investing is that most mutual fund managers—professional investors who have research teams at their beck and call and sophisticated computer systems to do their monitoring—can't get it right. Only one mutual fund manager, Bill Miller of Legg Mason Value Trust, has beaten the market the past twelve years running.

A Marathon, Not a Sprint

There is another way. And, for most individual investors, I believe it's a better one. You don't have to take outlandish risks. You don't necessarily have to beat the market all the time either. You save as much as you can, shelter every conceivable dollar from taxes, and invest prudently.

And although you keep your eye on the ball, you do not micromanage. In 1996, Terrence Odean and Brad Barber, professors at the University of California–Davis, studied the trading habits of 35,000 discount brokerage customers. They found that women outperformed men to the tune of about 1.5 percent annually. "Is that because women are better stock pickers?" I asked Odean. "We can't say that," he acknowledged. "What we do know is that women trade less frequently. They save a significant amount of money on brokerage commissions and it boosts their returns."

And those returns don't have to be outrageous—or even double digit—to help you hit your targets. Consider:

If you earn 7 percent a year, you double your money every decade.

If you earn 8 percent a year, you double your money every nine years.

If you earn 9 percent a year, you double your money every eight years.

And if you earn 10 percent a year, you double your money every seven years.

That 10 percent a year—even after the last three dismal years—is precisely what you got over the long-term if you bought the market as a whole. Take a second to absorb what that means. It means that's what you got if you didn't make choices, if you didn't chase the hot money. That's what you got for *participating*. And yes, it is a relatively simple thing to do.

Curb Your Enthusiasm

But first you have to manage your expectations. That means understanding what an anomaly the late 1990s were. From 1995 through 1999, the S&P 500 saw average annualized gains of nearly 29 percent a year. Those were the highest gains, by a mile, of any five-year stretch in history. Unfortunately, rather than recognizing those years for the outliers they were, we adjusted. We got used to them. We grew to anticipate them, expect them, count on them. One survey of individual investors taken in December 1999 showed that investors were expecting average annualized gains of 19 percent over the next ten years.

Wrong.

Over the long term—and I'm referring to the years between 1925 and the present—the S&P 500 returned an average of just 10 to 11 percent annually. What that means is that for all those years of stellar returns, there were down years (like the last three) and others when the market stagnated. A number of investment houses believe that over the next decade, the market won't produce returns that high—but rather in the 7 to 9 percent range. You need to learn to expect that. Why? Because if you overestimate what you're going to earn on your money, you won't save enough to hit your goals.

Let's say you're a thirty-year-old and have decided you'd like to retire in 2035 on $60,000 (pretax) a year. You know from your Social Security statements (and if you aren't receiving them annually, call 1-800-772-1213) that Social Security will cover $14,000 of that nut. A small pension you have will furnish another $11,000 a year. So that leaves a $35,000 annual gap in today's dollars, which translates—at a conservative 3 percent rate of inflation—to $90,128 annually (or $7,511 monthly) in 2035 dollars. To cover that, you'll need savings of $2,348,000 (again, adjusted for inflation). Let's also imagine that you've already saved $50,000 in your 401(k). And finally, let's assume you want to know with 90 percent certainty that you'll be able to hit these numbers. (Certainty is a very helpful thing to be able to gauge. It's something you'll find if you use a calculator that runs a "Monte Carlo" analysis on the Web.)

The question is: How much do you need to save each month in order to meet those goals?

The answer is: That depends on how much you will be earning on that money.

If you earn a return of	You must save monthly
6 percent	$1,735
7 percent	$1,317
8 percent	$962
9 percent	$662
10 percent	$408

Now let's say you figure you'll be able to earn a 12 percent return. Based on that return, because you've already got that $50,000 working for you, you determine you need to save only $15 a month. But what if, instead of earning that 12 percent, you actually earn 9. While respectable, that's a far cry from what you anticipated, and as a result, at retirement you'll have a nest egg of only $914,798. Withdrawing 4 percent of that per year (an amount that comes close to guaranteeing that your money will last as long as you do) puts $36,592 in your pocket—or just over $60,000 when you add Social Security and your pension. That's a far cry from the $90,000 you were looking for, and it may make it very difficult to live the life you want, not to mention the life you planned.

Diversify, Diversify, Diversify

Being realistic in your expectations is step one. Step two is structuring your portfolio in such a way that it can handle some ups and downs. The key to this is diversification—investing in a wide range of instruments to spread out your risk so that if one particular stock or one investment class has a rough year, the other things you own will keep you afloat. The classic example of this sort of hedge is owning bonds as well as stocks. During the first three years of the new century, stocks stank to high heaven, but bonds gave their holders double-digit returns. If you held both, then you held steady (or at the very least, steadier).

Diversification is nothing new. Financial experts have been promoting the wisdom of not "putting all your eggs in one basket" for decades. And it held up for decades—until the bull market of the 1990s, which was when diversification went out of style. Investors didn't want to hear it. They wanted all tech, all the time. And financial television, investing magazines, even daily newspapers were standing by to give it to them—and benefit themselves at the same time. Personal finance magazines got nearly as fat as a February *Vogue*. And business and management tomes added (or beefed up preexisting) investing sections so they could come along for the ride.

Back then you could convince yourself you were diversified if you had eight or ten different tech stocks in your portfolio. And where did the money to buy all this technology come from? From the rest of your portfolio. Cashing out of financials, natural resources, even REITS (real estate investment trusts), made it easy to load up on tech.

We weighed down our portfolios with these one-note stocks—and abandoned bonds. Then, to make it worse, we stopped rebalancing. We forgot to sell our winners and pocket some gains. If we had we might have found our way into other sectors that didn't fall so dramatically or and so rapidly. Too many people took no profits at all.

How big a mistake is that? Huge. Look at the experience of one fifty-eight-year-old Lucent employee chronicled in *Money* magazine. This poor guy had $400,000 in his 401(k) in early 2000 and was planning to retire in 2003. His assets weren't diversified in the least—90 percent of the money was in Lucent stock, which proceeded to tumble—and tumble again. By the end of 2001, his balance had dipped into the five-figure range. And there was nothing he could do about it but keep working.

But there's plenty that you can do. You can be sure that you don't put more than 10 percent of your 401(k) in company stock.

And you can make sure you're diversified overall. Figuring out what asset mix is appropriate for you depends on a few things:

- Your time horizon. The more years you have to reach your goal, the more aggressively you can invest (and the more you can put into stocks) because you have more time to rebound from a setback in the market. The closer you are to your goal, the more conservative you want to be (and the less you want to put in stocks) because you don't want a rocky stretch in the market to deplete your assets right before you need to use them.
- Your age. This is closely tied to your time horizon. The older you are—and the closer you are to retirement—the less risk you should be taking and the less money you should have in stocks. In your younger years, you can handle more risk because—again—you have more years to rebound from a setback.
- Your risk tolerance. This isn't tied to either your time horizon or your age. Some people are just wired to be able to handle more risk and volatility. From my point of view, money has no business keeping you up at night. Only infants and illness have the right to do that. If your money is keeping you up, you should first try to better understand what's happening with your finances and then see if that calms you down. If that fails, dial down your risk by shifting 10 percent out of stocks into bonds. Then save more to make up for it.

Filling Your Baskets

There are two steps to the diversification process.

Step one is asset allocation. That's where you divide your pie into the three different asset classes and decide how much you want to put into stocks, into bonds, and into cash. Although there are exceptions, stocks are generally riskier than bonds, which are riskier than cash. And for taking the risk, you can generally expect a higher return. Since 1925 stocks have returned an average 10.7 percent, bonds 5.6 percent, and cash 3.2 percent.

When you hold stocks (or stock mutual funds) you hold pieces, called shares, of publicly traded companies. When those companies perform well—earning more and more per share on a quarterly basis—the price of the stock generally rises. There's no guarantee that will happen, but it usually works that way. That's why Wall Street analysts get paid a lot of money to tell us which companies are poised to do well.

When you hold bonds, you hold the debt of those same companies, governments, or municipalities. You are the lender, and for making those loans, you are paid interest. The riskier the bonds (corporate debt is generally riskier than government debt) the higher the interest you can expect to earn.

When you hold cash, or cash-like investments such as shares of money-market mutual funds, generally you hold debt instruments that have such short time horizons there's no risk at all. Holding cash doesn't net you a big investment return, but it has other benefits, namely safety and liquidity. With the exception of certificates of deposit (CDs), your money is much more liquid, which means you can get at it whenever you need it.

Step two is deciding which particular investments you want to hold in each of those asset classes. Stocks run the gamut from small company to large company, U.S.-based to international. They also differ by payout; you buy some stocks for growth because you expect their share price to increase rapidly and others for income because they pay a dependable (albeit slower-growing) dividend. Likewise, there are different kinds of bonds—short-term, intermediate-term, and long-term. When you buy a short-term bond, you're lending money for a shorter period so you're taking less risk than when you buy an intermediate- or long-term bond.

Stocks and bonds tend to work in opposition. When stocks have a good year, bonds have a not-so-good year, and vice versa. That's why you need both. Money manager Harold Evensky told me at the end of 2002 that his clients were down only about 2 percent on average for the year, an excellent return in a year the markets got slammed. How did Evensky maneuver that? Bonds kept him—and his clients—afloat.

Finally, when it comes to cash-like investments, you should know that choosing money funds is not a matter of tracking investment return as much as it is of expenses. Expenses account for the discrepancies in overall return. The Bank Rate monitor (www.bankrate.com) keeps a running tally of the country's best-performing money-market accounts and CDs, and IBC data (on the Web at imoneynet.com) tracks the best-performing money funds. Both are worth a look. The best money funds and CDs typically outperform the *average* money-market funds and CDs two to one and the average savings account four to one. In fact, the Consumer Federation of America reported that each American household could make an extra $400 a year by shifting money out of traditional bank savings accounts and into higher-paying money markets and CDs at the time savings rates were higher than they are today, but this sort of rate swap generally pays.

Six Sample Portfolios

Once you understand all your choices, you can begin filling the slots. Here are, with help from money manager Harold Evensky, six sample asset allocations: two for retirees in their sixties, seventies, or

	% FIXED	MMA	FIXED INCOME		DOMESTIC STOCKS			INT'L	
			SH	INT	LC CORE	L/M C VALUE	SC	GLBL	EMER MKTS
OLDER– lower risk	55%	2%	27.0%	26.0%	20.0%	3.0%	10.0%	14.0%	0.0%
OLDER– higher risk	45%	2%	22.0%	21.0%	25.0%	3.0%	11.0%	13.0%	3.0%
MID– lower risk	39%	2%	19.0%	18.0%	27.0%	4.0%	14.0%	13.0%	3.0%
MID– higher risk	28%	2%	12.0%	14.0%	33.0%	4.0%	16.0%	15.0%	4.0%
YOUNGER– lower risk	18%	2%	6.0%	10.0%	39.0%	5.0%	19.0%	15.0%	4.0%
YOUNGER– higher risk	9%	2%	3.0%	4.0%	42.0%	6.0%	21.0%	18.0%	4.0%

FIXED: Fixed Income
MMA: Money-Market Account
SH: Short-Term Bonds
INT: Intermediate-Term Bonds
LC CORE: Large Capitalization
  Stocks/Funds

L/M C VALUE: Large/Mid Capital-
  ization Value Stocks/Funds
SC: Small Capitalization Stocks/Funds
GLBL: Broad Global/International
  Fund
EMER MKTS: Emerging Markets

eighties; two for those in their forties or fifties; and two for those in their twenties or thirties.

You can fill your baskets by purchasing individual stocks (some 401[k]s offer this option; others don't) or by buying actively managed mutual funds (run by individuals trained to pick stocks and bonds that will outperform). Or you can buy index funds. These mirror the indexes (baskets of stocks) tracked by the market. And they're cheap!

Because these funds are not actively managed, the managers don't merit such high pay, so the expense ratios run a full percentage point, on average, less than those on active funds (.25 percent compared to 1.24 percent, respectively). Index funds have to echo an index that rarely changes in composition, so far less trading is involved in an index fund. That yields a big savings in terms of trading costs and capital gains taxes. Large-capitalization stock funds typically spend 2.4 percent a year in trading costs. Add that to the expense ratio and you have to make between 3.5 and 4 percent a year just to break even. Particularly in down markets, having that edge working for rather than against you can be a huge help.

Conventional wisdom has it that index funds are terrific in good markets, when they're able to go with a rising tide. But in poor markets, managers who can rely on their smarts to help you avoid debacles like Enron and Worldcom are supposed to be able to save your skin. The last few down years have shown it doesn't always work that way. Only 37 percent of actively managed funds beat the market in 1990. And from 2000 to 2002, only 46 percent of large-cap funds, 23 percent of mid-cap funds, and 28 percent of small-cap funds did the same. Overall—excluding fees—the S&P 500 (and thus S&P 500 index funds) has outperformed actively managed funds by about 1.5 percent a year on average since 1971.

The other nice thing index funds have going for them is that they're easy. If you're one of the 25 percent of people who say the fun of saving and investing is gone now that the market is no longer doing so well, indexing takes much of the work out of the equation. Besides, my feeling is that if you can do better by not trying than you can by racking your brain, there's very little point in trying at all.

"But," the devil's advocate (or Peter Lynch) might counter, "isn't it better to buy what you know?"

Not necessarily. Buying what you know is an argument against diversification and for that reason often doesn't work. Think about it this way: Most individual investors are specialists. We work for big department stores, so we know more than the rest of the population about retailing and retail stocks. We work as general contractors, so we understand the home-building sector. We work as doctors or bankers and are familiar with health care stocks or financials. But find me a banker who understands what it takes for a big retailer to make a profit. Find me a doctor who can tell me what's going on inside Bank of America or Dell.

The problem with buying what we know well is that we end up with most of our eggs in one sector's proverbial basket. Nowhere is that problem greater than with company stock. It's the Enron problem, but it's not just a problem with Enron. According to a survey from the Employee Benefits Research Institute, in 401(k) plans with a company stock option, workers in their forties and fifties keep 30 percent of their portfolios in that one stock, on average. Among

401(k) plans that match contributions in company stock, the average stake is 50 percent. You may think you know your company well and believe that nothing could possibly go wrong with it anytime soon. Now think about Martha Stewart Omnimedia. Do you think the employees—or anyone, for that matter—saw that one coming?

Money and Happiness Results: Part 5

Here's my final argument for letting the market—and a nice dose of asset allocation—guide your portfolio: the results of my research. Only one-fifth of you say you consider yourselves knowledgeable investors. Book after book after book has been written to try to turn that statistic around. If you haven't read them by now, you're not going to.

1. How much do you agree or disagree with each of the following statements? Use a scale ranging from 1 to 7, where 1 means you completely disagree with the statement, 7 means you completely agree with the statement, and the other numbers represent levels in between.

a. I know how to pick a money-making stock.
b. I know how a mutual fund works.
c. I am a good money manager.
d. I am a knowledgeable investor.

About your responses: Half of Americans consider themselves good money managers, but that's a measure of being able to handle your credit cards and pay your bills on time. When it comes to investing, we're much less sure on our feet. Although one-third say they know how a mutual fund works, only one in ten say they're knowledgeable investors or know how to pick a money-making stock.

That's disheartening news. Why? Because people who perceive themselves to be knowledgeable investors or good money managers are more in control of their finances and happier as a result. They feel less stress, they're not as likely to be restless, and they're much less likely to say they feel hopeless.

2. How much do you agree or disagree with the following statement? Use a scale ranging from 1 to 7, where 1 means you completely disagree with the statement, 7 means you completely agree with the statement, and the other numbers represent levels in between.

Managing my money is too complicated and time-consuming.

About your response: One-fifth of America says yes. And it's the one-fifth you'd probably suspect—the people who don't budget, don't pay their bills as they come in; the people who as a result feel worried, not in control, financially insecure. Unfortunately—and I don't mean to be harsh— managing your money is something you have to do even if it feels like drudgery. But I can promise you two things: One, the more you do it, the more comfortable and confident you'll feel about your abilities. That will make you enjoy it more. And two, there is an easier way.

Indexing for Fun and Profit

By the time you finish reading this chapter, you will have become—at least in this one area—a knowledgeable investor. You will know how to invest in index funds. As our research has shown, that is a very good thing. Knowledgeable investors are savers. They are planners. They are organized. They are less likely to say that managing their money is too complicated and time-consuming. And as a result, their credit card debt is much lower than, and their household assets greater than, those of people who classify themselves as not knowledgeable. And yes, they are less worried, less stressed, and happier overall.

As with anything else, there are good index investments and not-so-good index investments. How do you pick the best?

First, you need to understand there are two ways to buy indexes. You can buy index mutual funds or you can buy exchange-traded funds (ETFs). The former are run by mutual fund companies like Fidelity, T. Rowe Price, and Vanguard and sold by those companies as well as by brokerage firms. The latter, ETFs, trade like stocks on the American Stock Exchange. Some, like Spiders (ticker symbol: SPY), track the S&P 500 index; others track the NASDAQ or the Russell. You can buy the broad market in the form of the Wilshire 5000 by buying Vipers (ticker symbol: VPI).

Which are better? Returns on an index fund and the exchange-traded fund that tracks the same index are often comparable. Depending on how much and how often you plan to invest, you may have a preference. Mutual funds, including index funds, have minimum investment thresholds starting at $1,000 or so. Those minimums are sometimes waived if you enroll in automatic investment plans, programs that pull money out of your checking account each month and invest it in a menu of preselected choices. (For that reason, as well as the fact that automatic investment plans keep you on track, I find them very attractive.) But if you're starting with a few hundred dollars, ETFs are going to be the way to go.

How do you choose which, say, S&P 500 index fund to buy? Compare expense ratios. That's the amount a firm charges you for managing the fund. One of the reasons I like index investing is that these ratios are low compared to actively managed investments. Your goal is to get the lowest one you can find from a firm that offers all the different index funds you're interested in. It's quite possible to keep the expense ratio on, say, an S&P 500 index fund below .25 basis points or one-quarter of a percentage point (basis points are hundredths of a percentage point). And there's absolutely no need, on any index fund, to spend more than about 40 basis points.

There are many, many choices for filling the baskets—the categories—detailed above. Your aim in picking index funds is to cover all your bases. You can in fact do just that with four funds: a total stock market fund, a total bond market fund, an international fund, and a money-market fund. A Russell 3000 index fund captures 98 percent of the available U.S. stock market. The Wilshire 5000 captures even more, including a greater share of very small companies.

I suggest you start online or in the library, with Morningstar Reports. By looking at the index funds in each category, you'll be able to figure out which have performed most consistently—and have held their expenses low, and steady—over the longest period of time. Those are the funds you want to buy.

Rebalancing, Selling, Taking Your Profits

If I had a dollar for every time someone has said to me, "If only I had sold . . ." And they're absolutely right. People who sold Amazon, Cisco, AOL, and other highfliers when they still were, well, highfliers profited greatly from the bull market. But many, many others were so programmed to buy-and-hold that they didn't. They left a lot of money on the table. And they could have saved themselves considerable pain by rebalancing regularly.

What's rebalancing? Making sure you adhere to your asset allocations. Stocks, bonds, and indexes are all moving targets. During the bull market, for example, stocks ran up like crazy and bonds lagged. As a result, if you filled your portfolio to conform to a particular allocation and then did nothing else, a year later your mix was out of whack. You had too much money in stocks, too little in bonds, and too little in cash. On paper, that probably looked great—your returns were astronomical. But you left yourself wide open—your bond and cash holdings were your downside protection and you didn't keep them up.

You always have to keep in mind that the markets are cyclical. Stocks go up only for so long. Then they take a break and bonds do well. And cash—although you shouldn't park too many of your assets in it—never fails you. By not rebalancing, selling some stocks, buying more bonds, and putting a little cash away for safety, you abandoned your insurance policy. You didn't renew. And as a result, you lost much more than you would have otherwise.

By not rebalancing, you are, in a passive-aggressive sort of way, timing the market. You are making a bet that the market will continue to go up or that the market will continue to go down. That's a fool's game. Don't take my word for it; just ask former Treasury Secretary Bob Rubin.

In June 2002, a few months before the NASDAQ hit its lowest point in five years, I attended a lunch at which Bob Rubin was the featured speaker. Rubin was a study in contrasts. First, he made a good case that the market and the economy were coming back. Corporate earnings were expected to grow decently during the second half of the year. Stocks were oversold. Besides, he noted, housing prices had held up so spectacularly well that, despite the market's collapse, most Americans had gotten wealthier, not poorer.

Then he turned around and made just as strong a case that the market and economy would lag for quite some time. Why? Accounting scandals. Lack of confidence on the part of investors. The chance of another terrorist threat.

My point is this: If Bob Rubin doesn't know where the market is going in the short term—and quite clearly he was saying he did not—how are the rest of us supposed to figure it out?

In the long term, however, he—like me and just about every financial expert—is convinced that the markets will come back. Consider some new research compiled by SalomonSmithBarney that looks at how investors weathered the '73-'74 bear market (which bears strong similarities to this most recent one).

The study looks at two investors. Each put $100,000 into the S&P 500 at the start of 1973. By September 1974, with the market still sliding, each of their holdings was worth just over $57,000. At that point, one of the investors gave up, threw in the towel, and put his money into a safe haven with a guaranteed return of 5 percent. A decade later, he almost had his original $100,000 back. The other investor stuck with the S&P 500. Ten years later his portfolio was worth nearly $250,000.

Making Sure Your Money Lasts

So you learn these lessons. You accumulate; your money grows. And then you retire. You stop earning and have to make whatever you've stockpiled last another thirty years or so. That final piece of the money management puzzle is often forgotten or ignored. Using what you've accumulated simply isn't as exciting as accumulating it in the first place. But it's just as important, if not more so, and just as challenging.

We have long known that there are two keys to making retirement assets last as long as you do: asset allocation and managing your stream of withdrawals. New research from T. Rowe Price shows that managing withdrawals is more important.

Take a person with $600,000 in savings and a life expectancy of 25 years at retirement. If she limits her annual withdrawals to 4 percent of her portfolio ($2,000 a month to start), whether she puts 60 percent or 80 percent of her money in equities, she still has an 80 percent chance of meeting her retirement goals. But if she were to withdraw 5 percent a year ($2,500 a month to start), she'd have only a 50 percent chance of meeting those goals even if she put 90 percent of her money in equities. With more conservative investments, her chances would drop below 50 percent, and clearly that's nowhere near safe enough.

How can you increase your own chances of retirement success?

Keep a lid on withdrawals. Research shows the magic number is 4 percent. If you keep your annual withdrawals below that, your money has a good chance of outlasting you. Remember, though, that the balance is a moving target—4 percent of a $500,000 balance is $10,000 less than 4 percent of a $750,000 one.

Work longer. If 4 percent isn't enough to live on comfortably, think about working—not forever, but for a few years. According to the 2002 Retirement Confidence Survey from the American Savings Education Council, 24 percent of retirees are doing just that after they officially "retire," not only because their investments haven't met expectations but also because their expenses are higher. A few extra years in the workforce gives your portfolio added time to grow and reduces the number of years you will need to draw on that money.

Have a cushion. Two to three years' worth of living expenses in a money-market fund or short-term bonds means you won't have to sell investments when they're down.

And allocate wisely. The solution isn't ever to have 100 percent of your asset in equities, nor is it to have 100 percent in treasuries and cash. The solution, of course, lies somewhere in between.

Money and Happiness Evaluation: Part 6

1. Choose the statement that comes closer to your own personal behavior.

a. No matter how *much* money I had, I'd probably struggle to live within my means.
b. No matter how *little* money I had, I'd probably find a way to live within my means.

2. Looking specifically at aspects of your current financial situation, indicate whether or not you currently have enough money to do each of the following. (Check one box for each.)

	YES	NO	DON'T KNOW	N/A
a. Make your mortgage or rent payment every month	❏	❏	❏	❏
b. Purchase the things you *want*	❏	❏	❏	❏
c. Purchase the things you *need*	❏	❏	❏	❏
d. Have a good time	❏	❏	❏	❏
e. Weather a financial hardship (such as losing your job)	❏	❏	❏	❏
f. Completely pay off your credit cards every month	❏	❏	❏	❏
g. Save the amount you would like for retirement	❏	❏	❏	❏
h. Save the amount you would like for your children's education	❏	❏	❏	❏

3. How much do you agree or disagree with the following statement? Use a scale ranging from 1 to 7, where 1 means you completely disagree with the statement, 7 means you completely agree with the statement, and the other numbers represent levels in between.

Sometimes I hold off paying my bills until I have the money.

4–6. For each of the following sets of statements, choose the one that comes closer to your own personal behavior.

4.
a. I pay for most of my purchases using cash.
b. I pay for most of my purchases using a credit card.

5.
a. I put off making many purchases until I have the money to pay for them immediately.
b. I pay for many purchases using credit, because I know they will get paid for eventually.

6.
a. When I go to the ATM, I take out a planned amount and make it last the week.
b. I go to the ATM whenever I need cash.

7. For each of the following, indicate whether or not it is something you do. (Check one box for each.)

	YES	NO	DON'T KNOW
a. Follow a household budget that you or your spouse/partner have created	❑	❑	❑
b. Keep a record of how much you or your household spends each month	❑	❑	❑

8. If you had to be honest, which of the following, if any, are you spending more on than you can really afford? (Check all that apply.)

a. Mortgage/rent ❑
b. Food/groceries ❑
c. Entertainment/socializing/eating out ❑
d. Clothes ❑
e. Small personal expenses like coffee or magazines ❑

	YES
f. Gifts	❑
g. Hobbies	❑
h. Cars	❑
i. Vacations	❑
j. Children's activities or toys	❑
k. None of these	❑

9. For each of the following, indicate how often you or a family member regularly does this because you figure, "Why spend the money?" (Check one box for each.)

	A LOT	SOMETIMES	NOT TOO MUCH	NOT AT ALL	DON'T KNOW OR N/A
a. Mow your own lawn	❑	❑	❑	❑	❑
b. Wash your own car(s)	❑	❑	❑	❑	❑
c. Cook at home rather than eat out	❑	❑	❑	❑	❑
d. Check out books, CDs, or videos from the library rather than buy them	❑	❑	❑	❑	❑
e. Buy store-brand groceries rather than name brands	❑	❑	❑	❑	❑
f. Rent movies rather than go to the movie theater	❑	❑	❑	❑	❑
g. Buy clothes on sale rather than pay full price	❑	❑	❑	❑	❑
h. Use coupons whenever possible	❑	❑	❑	❑	❑

	A LOT	SOMETIMES	NOT TOO MUCH	NOT AT ALL	DON'T KNOW OR N/A
i. Clean your own house	❑	❑	❑	❑	❑
j. Buy things used/ secondhand	❑	❑	❑	❑	❑

10. Choose the statement that comes closer to your own personal behavior.

a. I am better at saving.
b. I am better at spending.

11. Are you currently saving or investing?

12. What percentage of your household income are you able to save or invest these days? (Circle one letter.)

a. 0 to 5 percent
b. 5 to 10 percent
c. 10 to 15 percent
d. 15 to 20 percent
e. 20 to 25 percent
f. 25 percent or more
g. Don't know

13. How much do you agree or disagree with each of the following statements? Use a scale ranging from 1 to 7, where 1 means you completely disagree with the statement, 7 means you completely agree with the statement, and the other numbers represent levels in between.

a. Money just evaporates out of my wallet and I don't know where it goes.
b. At the end of the month I am often surprised by the amount I have put on my credit card.

6. Living Within Your Means

I have enough money to last me the rest of my life . . . unless I buy something.

—Jackie Mason

You may think you're living within your means. Four out of five people do. They say no matter how little money they made they'd find a way to live within their means.

But here's the thing. Two out of those five are wrong. They're deceiving themselves, pulling the wool over their own eyes. How do I know? More than half can't afford to pay off their credit cards each month. Only one-third have enough stashed away to weather a financial hardship. Fewer still have enough to save sufficiently for college for their kids and for their own retirement.

Why the disconnect? Because many people don't understand what it is to live within their means. That phrase—and I grant you it's thrown around a lot—means that you are living on your own nut. You are able to afford the life you're living—from the house or apartment you inhabit, to the clothes you buy, the vacations you take, the restaurants you frequent—on your own. You aren't taking money from your parents, and you aren't floating your fun on a credit card.

Six out of ten Americans—singles more than couples, Xers more than seniors—don't fit that definition. They're spending more than they can afford on at least one thing and often more than one. But they often tell themselves they're living within their means because it makes them feel better. If you feel as if you're living within your means, you're more likely to feel useful, confident, content. And if you don't, you're more likely to feel restless and hopeless—not just about your finances but about your life in general.

Joe and Diane know how uncomfortable that can be. This two-career couple in Arizona racked up a huge amount of credit card and student loan debt in graduate school. A decade has passed since then, but it still bogs them down.

"Every Sunday we look at our bills and we look at what has to be paid in the next week," Diane explains. "When we figure out the bills, we really truly have nothing left. Our income covers it exactly, and that's not including our four cats. Each time one of them gets sick and needs to go to the vet, it's 'Damn—we don't have the money for that.' We had to take the car in last month. It cost two hundred dollars. We didn't have that budgeted."

"Spending Sickness"

Joe and Diane caught what a 2002 *New York* magazine cover dubbed America's "Spending Sickness." It focused on people like A.J., who had nearly $40,000 in debt, a scant $2,000 in her checking account, and no savings account. And yet—because she was living in a world where these things seemed de rigueur—she felt entitled to taxi rides, manicures, designer clothing, pricey perfume, and a few hundred dollars a week in restaurant meals.

Examples like this are everywhere. Two girls ahead of me in line to buy tickets to the Broadway show *Rent* spent thirty minutes debating which of their maxed-out MasterCards had room to hold $180 worth of tickets. Walk through a mall and you'll spot a dozen more like them. Yet we continue to spend. We spent through 2000, 2001, and 2002. We spent through the downturn in the stock market. The consumers—the White House cheered—will keep us afloat. Yes, but at what cost? Louis Rene Beres, professor of political science at Purdue University, blames our inability to control our spending on a variety of societal evils including the frail economy and a lack of individuality. He has a point.

"Me" Redux

It was Tom Wolfe—author of *Bonfire of the Vanities* and chronicler of the excesses of every recent generation—who dubbed the '70s the "me decade." In a now-famous *New York* magazine cover story, he wrote about America's newfound quest for self-awareness, self-enlightenment, self-improvement. We were jogging, getting Rolfed, and attending consciousness-raising seminars like they were going out of style. Through Wolfe's fine-tuned eyes, we watched as the country entered a new era of self-centeredness.

From a social standpoint, Wolfe was right on the money. From an economic point of view, however, he called it twenty years too soon: The 1990s were the age of financial narcissism.

Historically, during an economic boom, consumers lag behind the economy and the stock market. The market may be skyrocketing and the economy may be soaring, but consumers typically hold back. Why? Because they're still recovering from the years leading up to a flush economy, a period during which unemployment tends to be high, inflation a problem, and money tight. That was the case at the beginning of the '90s, but those worries didn't last long. The '90s were remarkable (among other reasons) for being the longest economic boom in history. Eventually, consumers caught up—and raced ahead. In 1998, for example, the economy—measured by gross national product—grew at a rate of 4 percent. Consumer spending grew 5.5 percent. And spending on consumer durables—items like cell phones, computers, and state-of-the-art appliances—grew at a rate of more than double that.

The run-up in the stock market led the way. But we also had reasonable oil prices, and falling interest rates. With things going so well for so many years, we became convinced that this extraordinary run could go on forever. And if the market, on the whole, let us down, then our investing *brilliance* would save us.

What I Saw at the Personal Finance Revolution

I was there to see it all. In 1991, I was a young fact-checker at *Forbes* magazine, a job I had worked incredibly hard to land and one that, despite nights that dragged on until 2 A.M., I inexplicably loved, when I was offered the chance to leave *Forbes* and join a new start-up called *SmartMoney*. *SmartMoney* was all about *personal* finances. It was about you and me and Mom and Pop and the different life choices we might make with the money we took home from our workaday jobs.

I was more than mulling over the offer to go. The job at *Smart-Money* was a staff writing position, which meant I could work on my own stories full-time rather than fact-checking someone else's. Truth be told, I'd half-committed to the man who would be my new boss, a *Wall Street Journal* alum named Steve Swartz. All I had left to do was resign.

That was when a parade of *Forbes* colleagues made their way into my cubicle to tell me I was ruining my life. Personal finance, they said, was a backwater. (And in fact, at *Forbes* in 1991, it was, relegated to a scant few pages in the back of each issue.) Who in their right mind would want to spend their days writing about nothing but certificates of deposit and mutual funds, when at *Forbes* they could write (albeit, after they finished the day's fact-checking) about the richest people in the world, fascinating CEOs and fast-growing corporations? At *Forbes,* they argued, I'd spent an entire weekend on the phone with Michael Milken—*while he was in jail!*—and an entire week at the trendy Chateau Marmont in L.A. helping pull together a list of the country's weathiest celebrities. Did I think *personal* finance could hold a candle to that?

Their arguments got to me. In fact I got such cold feet I picked up the phone, took a *very* deep breath, and told Steve Swartz I was having second thoughts. I didn't want to spend my days and nights writing about expense ratios and 12-b1 fees. I wanted to write about *people.*

Steve assured me that's precisely what I would be doing. And then he stuck to his word. In five years at *SmartMoney* magazine, I wrote about little other than people. I wrote about one couple tormented because they weren't granted a Body Shop franchise (they thought it was because they lacked political correctness) and another who experienced a roller coaster ride of ups and downs as they tried to adopt a baby. I wrote about people so addicted to the personal finance program Quicken that they stayed up nights entering their receipts. And people unable to retire when their IBM shares took a huge dive.

It was through stories like these—as well as ones on how to buy cars, houses, and cell phone service; choose vacations, mortgages, and credit cards, and file your taxes without getting audited—that I held a ringside seat at the personal finance revolution. The '90s, besides being a decade of spending, were the years when Americans became interested in their wallets.

However, contrary to popular belief, this was not a transformation driven by the press. It was not spurred by Bill Gates, Morningstar, or CNBC. No, the culprit behind the personal finance revolution was none other than (drumroll, please) *the 401(k)*.

The 401(k) forced individuals to take control of their money, their retirement, their *future*. Corporate America threw its collective hands up in the air and said, "We can no longer be your guarantor. We can't survive—or thrive—if we have to fund your future. You have to do it yourselves." And as long we were able to ride the coattails of the longest period of economic expansion—and the longest bull market—in history, we were happy to take on that challenge. A corporate pension may have been able to ensure that we'd live a comfortable life. A 401(k), self-invested in tech funds chock-full of Cisco, Lucent, and Dell, would ensure we'd live a lavish one.

So in we dove. We took to heart the lesson of the crash of 1987. The Dow may have lost more than 500 points in a single session, but we quickly understood (thanks to the media beating it into our heads) that if we hadn't cashed out—if we'd held our shares or, better yet, bought more—we came out way ahead. So we bought on every market correction. We bought and we held. And then, as we amassed the sort of paper riches we didn't think we'd see until we were octogenarians, we started to spend.

In the beginning, we felt—well, we felt a bit guilty about it. We could drop $60 on a stress-busting shiatsu massage, but only if we'd lost our biggest client or logged extra hours shoveling snow. We could buy a new Lexus to fill the second bay in the garage, but only if we had a practical Honda in the first. Over time, though, the need for those excuses evaporated. Instead of having to convince ourselves that we needed that extra hour of me-time, we began to believe that we deserved it. Just as we deserved the Coach bag and Donna Karan sheer stockings, the Ping putter, Zegna tie, and the Palm.

A Pattern of Unconscious Consumption

How much money did you spend yesterday? Think about it. If you're like many people, you have absolutely no idea. Now stop and think about it. Go back. Dissect your day.

Remember, it was a rush from the minute you got up, twenty minutes after hitting the snooze button. You dragged yourself out of one side of the bed and hustled your husband into the shower. Quickly you threw clothes on the kids and moved them into the kitchen for breakfast. You fed the goldfish, the hamster, the dog. Did any money change hands during those early morning hours? Of course not—you think. Ahhh, but wait a minute. Remember that Suzy needed milk money for the month, so you put $3.40 in her backpack. Jesse asked for $20 so he could join the garden club. For that you scribbled a check.

Once the kids left for school, you could get off to work. You hopped into the car and headed toward the parkway, as usual grabbing coffee and a bagel for $2.75 at the Dunkin' Donuts drive-thru. The toll to cross the bridge was $4. You were running late (as usual) so you headed for the pricey garage close to your office instead of the cheaper out-of-the-way parking for half the price. And before rushing into the elevator you bought a second coffee—a day like that one called for extra caffeine, you rationalized—from the vendor in the lobby: $1.25.

And so it went. You dropped $6 on the Girl Scout cookies a

friend was selling for her daughter, $8 on a take-out Caesar at lunch, and $3 plus tip because your boots desperately needed a shine. You expected parking to be pricey, but the $23 tab still provided some sticker shock. Then there was the quick in-and-out at the dry cleaners on the way home, the holiday shapshots you picked up, and the brief run into the grocery store that started with "I just need broccoli" and ended six big bags and $83 later. Add it all up and your expenses for the day ran $179. Did you plan on that? Probably not.

And that might be okay, if yesterday was a once-in-a-while occurrence. Or if you had unlimited resources. But it wasn't and you don't. And if you spent like that every single day, you'd blow through nearly $1,300 a week without even thinking twice. That's an awful lot of unconscious consumption. And if you're like many people, what you'll find is that it eventually sabotages your financial goals. It gets in the way of saving, of paying down debt, of investment, even of spending.

That's right. Spending. I am not going to sit here and tell you you shouldn't be dropping $175 on a pair of slacks or $250 on dinner and a show. It's your money and your call. Instead, I am going to encourage you to start thinking about your spending in an entirely different light. I'm going to ask you to *plan* it.

Your Spending Power

To have money is to have power. People with money have the ability to get things done. They can start companies, endorse political candidates, and fund important research. You may not be a Rockefeller, but you have that power too. It's called spending power.

Think about the last time you spent money on something you really wanted. Perhaps it was the down payment on a house or apartment or car. You put a little money away regularly for a long while and then, when you felt you were nearly there, you started to shop. You called a realtor and started wandering through postmodern colonials or two-bedroom condos. You drove your reliable but old clunker to the auto mall and test-drove the new Thunderbird or

Sienna. Finally, you lined up financing, signed on the dotted line, and wrote a really big check. And you walked out of that transaction feeling—how? Powerful. Like you'd accomplished something big. And you had. You bought something meaningful. That's spending power.

The Lost Art of Saving

In order to harness your spending power, however, you must have money to spend. And that means learning how to stop frittering money away. You have spending power only if you know how to save. Most of us don't; 54 percent of Americans say they're better spenders than savers. Only 41 percent say the opposite is true.

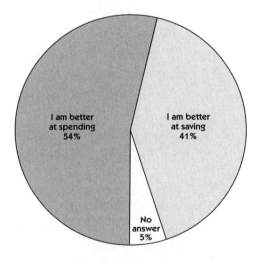

Savers vs. Spenders

What differentiates the savers from the spenders? Age, for one thing. The younger you are, the more likely you are to be a spender. That makes sense: Younger people are less likely than older folks to have dependents and responsibilities. Income plays a role as well. The less you earn, the more likely you are to say you're better at spending than saving. But even a six-figure take-home doesn't guarantee you a place in the savers' hall of fame, nor does a college education. Six-figure earners are evenly split: Half say they're better savers, but the other half say they're better spenders.

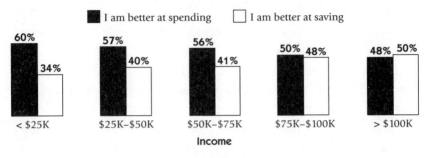

Savers vs. Spenders by Income

The differences between spenders and savers lie not so much in their demographic makeup, but in their knowledge and habits. Once you become a good manager of your own money and a knowledgeable investor, you're much more likely to say you're better at saving. Habits make a substantial difference, too. Budgeting, tracking your household expenses, balancing your checkbook, and paying your bills as they come in rather than once a month all translate into better saving.

Why bother to become a better saver? Because boosting your saving prowess can have a huge emotional payoff. Nine out of ten savers say they're "happy" with their lives. Savers are more likely than spenders to be happy with their lifestyle, self-esteem, even their weight and appearance. They're more likely to feel confident and content, less likely to feel stressed and restless. Spenders are just the opposite: They're more likely to be frustrated with their lot in life.

Living in the Margins

And the fact is: You can save only if you're living inside the margins of your take-home pay—if you're living within your means. Most people don't.

A 2002 survey from *Time* magazine found that 19 percent of Americans believe they have incomes within the top 1 percent of Americans. An additional 20 percent believe they will someday be in that top 20 percent. Of course you can spend like there's no tomorrow when tomorrow you expect to be a baby Gates or Forbes. But for 99 percent of people, and the majority of the people *Time* surveyed, it's never going to happen.

The pollsters at Yankelovich call this sort of delusion "affluent attitude." That's what takes hold when middle-income earners start to mirror the expectations and aspirations—and spending behavior—of the very wealthy. It's happening more often than you might imagine. According to a study from Automatic Data Processing, a New York–based payroll service, 42 million Americans live paycheck to paycheck. Some 60 percent of respondents said if a paycheck were late, they'd have to cut back on at least one important expense—the rent, groceries, utility bills. That's how a downward spiral starts.

You don't have to function like that. And my research shows you'll feel much better—happier, more secure, more in control—as soon as you stop.

Money and Happiness Results: Part 6

Before we get you back on track, let's see precisely where you stand—where your behaviors and attitudes are helping you, and where they're in your way.

1. Choose the statement that comes closer to your own personal behavior.
   a. No matter how *much* money I had, I'd probably struggle to live within my means.
   b. No matter how *little* money I had, I'd probably find a way to live within my means.

About your response: Most people say no matter how much money they had they'd be able to live within their means. Among people age 35 and older, 84 percent answer this way. And they're likely to be happier, not just overall, but with their finances and their lifestyle. They worry less about things—including the fact that some of their peers outearn them—and are in more control over just about every aspect of their lives.

The good news is that, more often than not, people who believe they could live within their means are taking the necessary steps to make that happen. Three-quarters balance their checkbook once a month. Six out of ten spend time researching a major purchase. But a good number of them—and you owe it to yourself to be honest about where you stand—are also living in a dream world.

The true test: Are you living within your means today?

2. Looking specifically at aspects of your current financial situation, indicate whether or not you currently have enough money to do each of the following. (Check one box for each.)

	YES	NO	DON'T KNOW	N/A
a. Make your mortgage or rent payment every month	❏	❏	❏	❏
b. Purchase the things you *want*	❏	❏	❏	❏
c. Purchase the things you *need*	❏	❏	❏	❏
d. Have a good time	❏	❏	❏	❏
e. Weather a financial hardship (such as losing your job)	❏	❏	❏	❏
f. Completely pay off your credit cards every month	❏	❏	❏	❏
g. Save the amount you would like for retirement	❏	❏	❏	❏
h. Save the amount you would like for your children's education	❏	❏	❏	❏

About your responses: Here's what the results look like graphically.

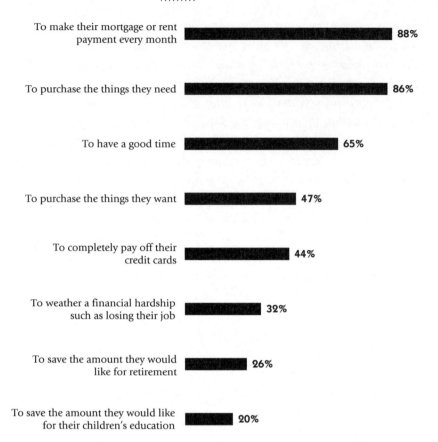

To make their mortgage or rent payment every month — 88%

To purchase the things they need — 86%

To have a good time — 65%

To purchase the things they want — 47%

To completely pay off their credit cards — 44%

To weather a financial hardship such as losing their job — 32%

To save the amount they would like for retirement — 26%

To save the amount they would like for their children's education — 20%

Graph shows percentage of respondents who say they have enough money to cover their expenses and financial obligations. [Base: Americans saying which of the statements applied to them.]

Most Americans say they have enough money to cover their expenses, to buy the things they need—and to have a good time. But that's where the gravy train ends. Only a minority have enough money for things beyond those bare essentials. Result: They don't put as much as they'd like into college funds, retirement funds, emergency cushions. And they float life on credit cards they're not able to pay off.

3. How much do you agree or disagree with the following statement? Use a scale ranging from 1 to 7, where 1 means you completely disagree with the statement, 7 means you completely agree

with the statement, and the other numbers represent levels in between.

Sometimes I have to hold off paying my bills until I have the money.

About your response: Cleopatra (Queen of Denial) may have lived in ancient Egypt, but she's got a lot of descendants in America. Three out of ten people say they sometimes have to hold off paying their bills until they have the money. Some of these—do the math—are the same folks who also say they're living within their means. And although income, not surprisingly, plays a role in who these folks are (four out of ten with household incomes less than $25,000 concur, whereas just two in ten of those with household incomes above $50,000 do), it's not the only contributing factor. In most cases, I see this as a habit that needs to be broken.

4. Choose the statement that comes closer to your own personal behavior.

a. I pay for most of my purchases using cash.
b. I pay for most of my purchases using a credit card.

About your response: Two-thirds of Americans pay for most purchases with cash, including a greater proportion of younger Americans and people earning less than $50,000 (household) per year. Although we tend to think of credit cards as a universal evil, it's interesting to note that people who rely more on plastic are happier with their lives and less worried about their finances. More credit card spenders than cash spenders say they have enough to weather a financial hardship, save for retirement, and purchase the things they want—as well as the things they need.

5. Choose the statement that comes closer to your own personal behavior.

a. I put off making many purchases until I have the money to pay for them immediately.
b. I pay for many purchases using credit, because I know they will get paid for eventually.

About your response: The answer to the previous question may sound good, but frequent credit card users are also more likely to feel they need more money to live the way they want to live, and their average credit card debt is significantly higher. The upshot? It appears that only using credit responsibly gives a sense of financial security, which leads to overall happiness. In fact, responsible spending overall has a very strong link to happiness. More Americans who are financially happy delay making purchases until they have the money to pay for them.

6. Choose the statement that comes closer to your own personal behavior.

   a. When I go to the ATM, I take out a planned amount and make it last the week.
   b. I go to the ATM whenever I need cash.

About your response: About half of Americans go to the ATM whenever they need cash. Americans who worry about their finances and those who consider themselves financially insecure are more likely to go to the ATM whenever they need cash. Americans who don't visit cash machines at will are less likely to purchase things they don't need, to agree that "splurging makes them feel good," to feel that money "evaporates out of their wallet," to spend more than they can afford on entertainment, and to think they need a lot of money to live. They also—despite the fact that pulling money out of the ATM is a different habit from randomly charging—are less likely to be surprised at the amount they've put on their credit cards at the end of the month.

7. For each of the following, indicate whether or not it is something you do. (Check one box for each.)

	YES	NO	DON'T KNOW
a. Follow a household budget that you or your spouse/partner have created	❑	❑	❑
b. Keep a record of how much you or your household spends each month	❑	❑	❑

8. If you had to be honest, which of the following, if any, are you spending more on than you can really afford? (Check all that apply.)

a. Mortgage/rent ❑

b. Food/groceries ❑

c. Entertainment/ ❑
socializing/eating out

d. Clothes ❑

e. Small personal expenses ❑
like coffee or magazines

f. Gifts ❑

g. Hobbies ❑

h. Cars ❑

i. Vacations ❑

j. Children's activities or toys ❑

k. None of these ❑

9. For each of the following, indicate how often you or a family member regularly does this because you figure, "Why spend the money?" (Check one box for each.)

	A LOT	SOMETIMES	NOT TOO MUCH	NOT AT ALL	DON'T KNOW OR N/A
a. Mow your own lawn	❑	❑	❑	❑	❑
b. Wash your own car(s)	❑	❑	❑	❑	❑
c. Cook at home rather than eat out	❑	❑	❑	❑	❑
d. Check out books, CDs, or videos from the library rather than buy them	❑	❑	❑	❑	❑
e. Buy store-brand groceries rather than name brands	❑	❑	❑	❑	
f. Rent movies rather than go to the movie theater	❑	❑	❑	❑	❑

	A LOT	SOMETIMES	NOT TOO MUCH	NOT AT ALL	DON'T KNOW OR N/A
g. Buy clothes on sale rather than pay full price	❏	❏	❏	❏	❏
h. Use coupons whenever possible	❏	❏	❏	❏	❏
i. Clean your own house	❏	❏	❏	❏	❏
j. Buy things used/ secondhand	❏	❏	❏	❏	❏

About your responses: Four in ten Americans follow a household budget they or their spouse created, about the same number of people who track their monthly spending. Women are more likely to budget than men, married people more than unmarried.

What does that mean in terms of shopping habits? How are budgeters actually different beyond the paper log they keep at home? They put off making purchases until they have the money to pay for them and are less likely to spend money on nonessentials. They save money simply because they don't see a reason to spend it. For example, they're more likely to cook at home rather than eat out, to buy clothes on sale rather than pay full price, to use coupons, wash their own cars, mow their own lawns, and borrow books from the library instead of buying them. And they're more likely to use cash instead of credit.

Adopting these habits seems to pay off. People who follow budgets and track their spending are more likely to be steadily working toward their financial goals. They're also more likely to be very happy with their overall lives, and that happiness doesn't seem to hinge on getting a shopping fix. Budgeters are less likely than nonbudgeters to shop to cope with stress. Similarly, they're less likely to say that splurging makes them feel good.

10. Choose the statement that comes closer to your own personal behavior.

    a. I am better at saving.
    b. I am better at spending.

About your response: More than half of Americans say they're better at spending. About 40 percent say they're better at saving. Five percent of people don't know where they fall. Our research shows that people who say they're better at saving actually are—they have more in the bank, more socked away for retirement and college, and less credit card debt. One thing is clear: Being able to say you're better at saving translates into being happier with your life.

11. Are you currently saving or investing?

12. What percentage of your household income are you able to save or invest these days? (Circle one letter.)

a. 0 to 5 percent
b. 5 to 10 percent
c. 10 to 15 percent
d. 15 to 20 percent
e. 20 to 25 percent
f. 25 percent or more
g. Don't know

About your responses: If you're truly living within your means, then you should be able to save something for your future. Most Americans—62 percent—say they are actively saving or investing. That's the good news. The bad is that they're not able to save much: More than 40 percent of all Americans save less than 5 percent of their annual household income. Another 16 percent save between 5 and 10 percent. Just 9 percent are able to put away more than 20 percent.

What drives these savers? Savers and investors believe they need more money to be financially secure. They won't feel sound until they have, on average, $400,000 in the bank. People who aren't saving and investing say they'd be satisfied with one-fourth less. Interestingly, though, savers and investors are less likely to pine for a bigger financial cushion than folks who are sitting on their hands. Savers and investors are much more positive when it comes to thinking about their future. Although they're realistic enough to admit that the fun has gone out of saving and investing since the *bull market ended, they're less likely to sidestep the subject of their 401(k) balance and other retirement assets because they find it "too depressing."*

Even if you can save only a little each month, it's worth trying to join the ranks of savers. Savers and investors are much less likely to say money evaporates out of their wallet and they don't know where it goes. They're not likely to be surprised by the amount on their credit card statements at the end of the month, either. And—perhaps as a result of these things— they're happier with their personal lives. They're more likely to have positive feelings about themselves and to feel they're in control of their lives and their futures, and they're much less likely to have felt hopeless of late. It also appears that saving and investing reduce the sense that you don't measure up. Only one-third of savers and investors feel frustrated that they don't have as much money as others their age; one-half of nonsavers feel this way.

13. How much do you agree or disagree with each of the following statements? Use a scale ranging from 1 to 7, where 1 means you completely disagree with the statement, 7 means you completely agree with the statement, and the other numbers represent levels in between.

   a. Money just evaporates out of my wallet and I don't know where it goes.
   b. At the end of the month I am often surprised by the amount I have charged to my credit card.

About your responses: Two out of ten Americans answer these questions af- firmatively. Interestingly, you can't group these people just based on gender, occupation, or income. The differences are habitual. People who plan what they're going to spend before they go to the store, rather than just spending whatever it takes to buy what they need, don't end up with a shockingly large Visa balance. They don't find their cash vanishes into thin air either.

How to Live Within Your Means

Meet Ellen, a 44-year-old management consultant in L.A. who makes a six-figure base salary. She's sitting pretty today, but she had a long climb up.

When Ellen first entered the working world, she earned just $24,000 a year. That's $2,000 a month, she points out, before taxes. Back then, she still managed to save $300 a month. How did she do it? She made saving her priority. She wanted to buy a car eventually, and that made money in the bank more important than a new coffee table or a day at a spa.

"The single biggest thing that I guard against is the tendency of other people to live at their gross salary, rather than their net salary. A key concept I learned coming out of college was that I wasn't really earning $2,000 a month, I was earning $1,500 a month after taxes. If my rent was $500 a month, which it was, I still needed to save so that I could eventually buy a car. So my disposable income was only what was left over after I paid all my bills *and* saved money. It wasn't a lot. But it was enough to go to the movies periodically and to go out with friends from time to time."

Did Ellen mind? Did she view it as a hardship? No. "I've always felt that saving part of my salary gave me freedom, not that I was sacrificing all this fun I could be having," she explains. "I still had a lot of fun. I see an awful lot of people who are very unhappy with their circumstances because they think they ought to have more than what they do have. I look at what I have today and where I am and I feel remarkably grateful. And that's probably what leads to my happiness."

Ellen learned early on that it's impossible to live within your means—whatever those means happen to be—if you don't know how much you have coming in each month and how much of that is already committed to covering your fixed expenses. That's where you have to start. This five-step plan will get you there.

Step One: Know what's coming in. Start with a pencil and paper (or a computer program) and your pay stubs for the last three months. Look at the net income line on your pay stubs. Your gross is meaningless; it's what you take home that matters. Add up your net income and write down the total.

Next make a tally of any other steady income (no bonuses, no tax rebates, only the checks you receive regularly) that's come in over the past three months: rents, if you own rental property; dividends from your investments; money from annuities, whatever. If taxes aren't withheld from these payments, calculate how much you'll lose to Uncle Sam and subtract that from this total.

Now add your two totals together, then divide by three. That's your average monthly income over the past three months and a fairly good representation of what you can anticipate in the months ahead.

Step Two: Track what's going out. Now you have to look at what you're spending. Start with your fixed expenses. What do you pay each month for your rent or mortgage, car, health club, insurance, utilities, phone service, cable, preexisting credit card debt, student loans, etc.? Make a list of these amounts.

Now move on to your variable expenses. Most people have no idea how much they spend each month on things like take-out food, entertainment, drinks with friends, even gasoline and groceries. So starting now, you're going to keep tabs. Every day for the next month, you're going to get a receipt for everything you buy and you're going to save those receipts, even the small ones. If you buy something online, that means printing out a record so you can account for that as well. If you shop on the phone, make a note. Then, every night when you get home, spend five minutes pulling those receipts out of your wallet and entering them into your spreadsheet or jotting them down, category by category, on your legal pad.

At the end of the month, you'll have a money map. You'll know how much you're spending, and on what. And then you'll be able to make some changes.

Step Three: Plan your future spending. Let's say your money map reveals that over the past month you spent, among other things:

    $61.87 on coffee and a buttered roll each morning
    $35.55 on magazines to read on your commute
    $20.25 on ATM fees
    $57.50 for extra minutes on your cell phone
    $89.90 on CDs
    $234.50 on clothes at Banana Republic for the coming season
    $379.23 on groceries

$348.23 on dinner-and-movie nights out
$192.00 on sitters so you could enjoy those nights out
$184.00 on gifts (for your kids' friends, your assistant, and
your sister-in-law)

When you look over your list, the first question to ask yourself is:
Where are the surprises? Perhaps you knew full well that your coffee
habit was costly—you *planned* to spend that money. But nearly $550
on weekly dates with your spouse—that was a shock. And perhaps
$15 to $20 per birthday gift for a seven-year-old is a little excessive
(especially because your seven-year-old gets invited to about twenty
parties a year).

Now ask yourself how much you want to spend on those line
items *next* month and the month after that. If you can plan where
your money is going to go, then you can increase your free cash and,
therefore, your savings. Let's look again at a few of those items.

For instance, $35.55 on magazines at the newsstand to read on
your commute. That's $426 a year—much more than necessary be-
cause magazines purchased at the newsstand are three to four times
more expensive than those purchased by subscription. That $35.55
is the cost of nine magazines at $3.95 a pop. By subscribing, you can
cut your cost to $100 to $150 a year.

Next, $20.25 on ATM fees. That adds up to $243 a year. You can
easily slash this one to zero. Switch banks so that you're patronizing
the one that has ATMs on the route you travel to and from work
every day, and you'll no longer have to pay fees at all. If you're one
of the few people for whom that won't work, check out the program
at USAA Federal Savings Bank, which will rebate to your account the
cost of ten ATM fees per month.

See how it works? Slashing expenditures in a couple of categories
means that it's okay to bust the budget in others. In fact, our research
shows that as long as you don't go crazy on more than three line
items per month, you're doing fairly well.

Step Four: Include money for saving in that plan. Unfortunately, new
habits like these aren't made overnight. As you're working on them,

you want to give yourself every possible chance of succeeding at putting some money away. The easiest way to do that is to automate your saving. Sign up for 401(k) or other payroll deduction plans at work that subtract money from your take-home pay (before you have the chance to spend it) and deposit it into savings or investment accounts. Sign up for AIPs—automatic investment plans—at your bank or brokerage firm that do the same thing by transferring money out of checking and into saving or investing accounts, again before you can fritter the money away. You can do this for just about any purpose. You can use automatic transfers to fund an IRA, fund college savings plans, buy mutual funds. This is what the financial world calls paying yourself first. Technology has made it easier than ever.

Step Five: Eliminate high-interest debt. According to new research conducted by Fair, Isaac and Co., the country's leading provider of credit scores, credit is a fact of life in most households. It's a game in good times, when you can play roulette with the half-dozen cards you carry in your wallet to rack up the most frequent flier miles and other freebies. It's a savior in bad times, when you can charge groceries or that visit to the pediatrician you just can't cover. Despite its inherent conveniences, a great many people express the desire to be debt-free.

That's because these same people understand deep down that debt, particularly high-rate credit card debt, is a savings killer. By being tardy with your payments or sending in only the minimum each month, it's quite possible to extend your credit card bills for decades. When you've finally paid a bill off, you've forked out three or four times as much in interest as you've paid in principal. And you've allowed those decades of credit card bills to get in the way of IRA contributions, 529 contributions, 401(k) contributions, buying life and disability insurance, even pulling together an emergency fund. In other words, your credit card debt has sabotaged your future.

You can't take ownership of the rest of your financial life unless you bring your relationship with your creditors under control and reap the psychological rewards that come in the bargain. So start today. How?

1. *If you find yourself in a hole, stop digging.* It's as simple as that. If you find you've borrowed so much that you have trouble making the payments, stop spending and stop borrowing. How much is too much? In general, you're in good shape if no more than 10 percent of your income goes toward paying off your consumer debts (like credit card debts and car loans) and no more than 25 percent of your income is used to pay off your mortgage. It's up to you to do whatever is necessary to make that happen—from locking your credit cards in a drawer to using a debit card or even cash. Whatever you need to do to stop charging, do it. If you're in a hole, stop digging.

2. *Lower your credit card rates.* Think about the last time you bought a major appliance. Let's say it was a dishwasher and it cost $600 to $700. Chances are you didn't just wander into your neighborhood appliance joint, point randomly, and say: "I want that one." You checked *Consumer Reports* for the best-rated dishwasher, then did a little comparison shopping to figure out which appliance store had it for the best price. Only then did you go out and actually buy it.

   But how about the last time you got a credit card? Unfortunately, many people simply sign up for one of the cards that come in the mail. That sort of nonchalance can cost you. Every extra percentage point you pay each year in interest on the average consumer's $3,500 credit card debt represents an extra $35. Pay 6 percentage points more than you have to and we're talking an extra $210.

   How do you go about lowering your rates? First check out the lowest rates at bankrate.com or in *Money* magazine. Once you know what a competitive rate is—and that you don't have one—call your card company and ask them to lower your rate. Tell them if they won't, you'll go elsewhere. And if you don't get the respect you deserve, follow through. (Note: Don't cancel your current card until you've secured another. You don't want to be without a credit card in an emergency.)

3. *Refinance to lower your other interest rates.* Your credit card interest rates aren't the only ones you can maneuver. By refinancing your

other debts—your mortgage, for example, and your car loans—you may be able to significantly lower the rates you're paying there as well, and thus reduce your out-of-pocket monthly payments.

How do you know if it's worth refinancing your mortgage? If you can find a rate half a point lower than the one you're paying now, consider it. Then it becomes a question of weighing the cost of refinancing (the closing costs and points involved in the transaction) against the savings you'd reap each month. If you think you'll be in the house long enough for the savings to exceed the cost, do the deal. If not, don't.

Refinancing to lower the interest rate you're paying on your car loan is an even simpler transaction. You hit the Internet or visit your local credit union and see if you can drum up a better rate than the one you're paying now. There are typically no closing costs and you generally don't extend your term. You simply give your business to another lender and pay less out of pocket each month. In other words, it's a no-brainer.

4. *Consolidate where possible (and wise).* Another way to lower your credit card rates is to consolidate all of your credit card debt (and sometimes your auto loans, to boot) into one big home equity loan or home equity line of credit. (What's the difference? A home equity loan is a fixed-rate sum you borrow all at once. A home equity line of credit is a variable-rate loan that usually floats with the prime rate and you draw upon as you need it.) This can be a very cost-effective way to go. Not only are the rates on home equity products typically much lower than credit card rates, but also they're tax-deductible as long as your total mortgage debt doesn't exceed $1.1 million.

The home equity approach can also be very dangerous. Why? You're putting your home on the line. Default and you could lose it. The other big problem with consolidation is that many people clear the debt off their credit cards only to charge them right back up again. If you have even the smallest doubt that a self-imposed moratorium on plastic will work for you, don't consolidate. Cut up your cards instead.

Student loans, too, can be consolidated. In this transaction, you roll all of your loans—at their varying rates—into one new, cheaper loan. Importantly, you can only do this once. But as this book goes to press, rates have just hit new all-time lows. They'll stay there through June 2004. If you have student loans, look into it.

5. *Avoid penalty rates and fees.* When banks started losing business to brokerage firms in the 1990s, they had to do something to make up their profits. They tried selling insurance and mutual funds. When that didn't work, they started hitting you with penalty fees. Go over your credit limit or send in your monthly payment late and you'll see a $25 to $35 fee attached to your bill. You may also see your interest rate jump from something close to reasonable to one that's sky-high.

   How can you stay out of harm's way? Schedule automatic debits for certain payments—your mortgage and car loan, for example—to be sure you don't miss them. As for credit card bills, many card companies will now send you e-mail reminders so that you remember to pay your bills. And it never hurts to open—and pay—your bills as they come in.

6. *Work on your credit score.* Ever since you've had credit, the country's three largest credit bureaus have been keeping tabs on how you manage it. We've already established the fact that managing it poorly can stop you in your tracks when it comes to dealing with the rest of your financial life. But a bad credit history (full of late payments, exceeding your credit limits, and applying for more credit on a regular basis) can also result in your having to pay higher interest rates than average whenever you apply to borrow. If mortgages are averaging 7½ percent, for example, and you've got a below-average credit score, you may be asked to pay 9½ percent.

   What can you do to improve your credit score? Cancel the cards in your wallet that you're not using (hold on to the ones you've had the longest, if possible), use less than 50 percent of the credit available to you, don't apply for additional credit cards in the six months before you're going to start shopping for a house and a mortgage, and—of course—pay your bills on time and without fail.

7. See number 1. It bears repeating.

To Hammer It Home, Make an "Enjoyment List"

Finally, if you want to remind yourself that it's possible to live a fun, exciting, enjoyment-filled life within your means, make a list of the things you enjoy in life. What you'll find is that many of them cost nothing at all: a hug from a grandchild; a walk with the dog; reading a great book (you could get it from the library). To get you started, here's my list.

Running at the reservoir in
    Central Park or the Rocke-
    feller Preserve
Cooking with my daughter
Having friends over for dinner
The softness of my dog's ears
Family naps on Sunday
    afternoons
Ice-skating
Knowing all the words in my
    favorite movie scenes
Riding bikes with my son
Getting a great pair of shoes
    (on sale)

Lunch with my girlfriends
Book-club meetings
Brainstorming sessions
Answering questions after a
    speech
The smell of a new baby
Singing show tunes in the car
    (loud!)
Sledding in the winter
Making a fire
Cereal for dinner
An instant message from
    my husband

Aside from that great pair of shoes (on sale, I repeat) and the cost of that lunch with my girlfriends (generally a $6 salad at our local spaghetti joint) or the cost of food to fix for my friends, these are not $1,000 line items. How little they cost was a bit of a revelation to me, as was the fact that even if I had plenty to spend on lunches at Le Cirque, they'd be pretty meaningless if I had no friends to eat with.

Money and Happiness Evaluation: Part 7

1. Are you currently employed? (Circle one letter.)

a. Yes, full-time
b. Yes, part-time
c. Yes, self-employed
d. Retired
e. Unemployed

2. What is your main occupation? (Circle one letter.)

a. Executive/professional
b. White collar
c. Blue collar
d. Retired/student/disabled/unemployed/armed forces

3. On the whole, how happy are you with your job? (Circle one letter.)

a. Very happy
b. Somewhat happy
c. Not too happy
d. Not at all happy
e. Don't know
f. N/A

4. In the past thirty days, about how often did you feel each of the following? (Check one box for each.)

	A LOT	SOMETIMES	NOT TOO MUCH	NOT AT ALL	DON'T KNOW
a. Restless	❑	❑	❑	❑	❑
b. Useful	❑	❑	❑	❑	❑
c. Stressed	❑	❑	❑	❑	❑
d. Content	❑	❑	❑	❑	❑
e. Hopeless	❑	❑	❑	❑	❑
f. Confident	❑	❑	❑	❑	❑

5. How much do you agree or disagree with each of the following statements? Use a scale ranging from 1 to 7, where 1 means you completely disagree, 7 means you completely agree, and the other numbers represent levels in between.

a. My family and friends are important to me, but frankly, when push comes to shove, my job wins out.
b. Exercise and maintaining my health are important to me, but frankly, when push comes to shove, my job wins out.

6. Choose the statement that comes closer to your own personal behavior.

a. I am happy because I am successful.
b. I am successful because I am happy.

7. How much do you agree or disagree with the following statement? Use a scale ranging from 1 to 7, where 1 means you completely disagree, 7 means you completely agree, and the other numbers represent levels in between.

I don't have enough money to support the causes I believe in.

8. How often, if at all, do you personally do any of the following? (Check one box for each.)

	A LOT	SOMETIMES	NOT TOO MUCH	NOT AT ALL	DON'T KNOW
a. Volunteer at a local school, hospital, library, shelter, etc.	❏	❏	❏	❏	❏
b. Donate money to charity	❏	❏	❏	❏	❏
c. Make non-monetary donations to charity	❏	❏	❏	❏	❏

7. Go with the "Flow"

When what we are is what we want to be, that's happiness.
—Malcolm S. Forbes

Serendipity, a 2001 John Cusack/Kate Beckinsale flick, was a so-so movie with a couple of memorable lines, one of which came from Jeremy Piven in the best-friend role he often plays (see: *The Family Man*). It comes about five minutes before the end. Cusack has just spent the past hour and a half completely upsetting his romantic life, including calling off his wedding to a beautiful woman right before walking down the aisle, because he can't stop thinking about one evening he spent with another woman years before. He doesn't really know this other woman. He just can't help himself. And Piven tries to tell him that he did the right thing by reminding him: "The ancient Greeks asked only one thing about a man when he died. 'Did he have passion?'" Piven was talking about love, but could have been talking about work.

And the answer, in the case of most Americans, would be no. According to 5,000 households surveyed by the Conference Board in 2002, only half of Americans actually like their jobs. That was a 9 percent drop since the previous survey in 1995. The reduction was seen across all regions of the country and in all income groups. It's worth noting that only a small percentage of Americans are completely dissatisfied with their jobs. Most fall somewhere in between that and love.

You can blame some of your relative satisfaction or dissatisfaction on your age. When you first enter the workforce, in your late teens and early twenties, you're thrilled to be getting a paycheck—any paycheck. And you'd do whatever it takes to bring that money in. You'd photocopy, file, answer phones, drive long distances. Whatever. You might not enjoy every moment, but having a little green in your pocket makes it all worthwhile.

As you near your twenty-fifth birthday, disillusionment sets in. You went through four years of college, and you're still collating and filing. That boss of yours who thinks she's so smart doesn't have ideas half as creative as yours. Is it fair that the guy in the next cubicle earns double what you do despite the fact that you pull a bigger load? And speaking of that cubicle, when are you going to get an actual office?

I remember well when these feelings hit me. I had a hard time hiding them. My boss at the time, clearly fed up, said she was going to assign me a piece designed to change my attitude, called: "Don't Ask What Your Company Can Do for You, Ask What You Can Do for Your Company." I quit instead. But don't worry, this I-hate-the-system stage generally lasts only about five years. Dissatisfaction peaks around age thirty; then most people grow steadily more comfortable and pleased with their jobs and careers until retirement.

When you were born also plays a role in the way you view work. Research tells us if you're a member of the World War II generation, you believe that choices have to be made—and the earlier the better. Then you follow the path you've chosen. Only rarely do you stray. Some paths lead to more money than others, but that's just the way it goes. You already made your choice.

Competitiveness is the hallmark of the baby boomer generation. Boomers were raised to believe you sink or swim at work and there's little in between. Many boomers spend every day of their working life trying to prove they're more worthy of that raise, that promotion, that corner office than the next guy. And once they get these rewards, they don't hesitate to show them off. It was a baby boomer who noted, "He who dies with the most toys wins."

For Generation Xers, experiences are better than stuff. To them, he who dies having *done* the most wins. And because of that, a job and a paycheck simply open the door to life options. The trade-off, they understand, is having a career path that may not be particularly straight—or even vertical.

And Generation Y seems to have taken a bit from all of these playbooks and slowed it down to the point where it actually makes some sense. Ys have a very strong sense of the fact that going out into the marketplace and earning money is a choice. They know from having watched their parents that some people choose to pursue careers that are lucrative, and others don't. They don't see it as luck, but as a combination of luck and skill and choice. As a result, there's less mystery about money for them. They're more matter-of-fact about the idea that they're either going to choose to go out and make a bunch of money, or they're going to choose to do something else instead. But they feel it's up to them.

To get a sense of how this plays out in practice, think back to the late 1990s. Back then, an employer's biggest problem was keeping talented people from flying out the door to Silicon Valley (or Silicon Alley) and the dotcom world.

Many people thought the flight of X and Y talent to the Internet was just another example of gold rush fever. That's only partially true. Sure, the sound of stock options had a pretty nice ring to it, but so did freedom from the traditional organization chart. The young college grads and MBAs who ditched Wall Street for the Left Coast embraced a new frontier. They were looking to explore not just a new industry but a new career path—one in which they believed they'd have more control over their schedule, their workplace, and how they got things done. And while the venture funding lasted, they did.

I visited Intuit headquarters in Palo Alto in 1992. Quicken, the company's primary product, was on its way to becoming mainstream. Back in the early '90s, its followers were more like a small cult. And few were more devoted than the employees. When I toured the developers' cubicles, it quickly became apparent why. This was no office building—it was a dorm. Complete with Nerf hoops and Foosball, futons in case you needed to crash night or day, and coffeemakers plugged in to the floor. Casual Friday was an everyday affair. These kids routinely showed up for work in shorts and sneakers. Some biked. Others propped their surfboards against their makeshift walls, in case they felt the urge to take a breather.

It's precisely because these Xers and Ys weren't just chasing big salaries that they've been able to rebound from the dot bomb better than older investors who just bought the stocks.

How did they get this way? Thank their parents. You have to remember, generation Y grew up during the 1980s, a time during which there was a sea change in parenting, with an emphasis on boosting a child's self-esteem. As a result, Ys—as a generation—have an incredibly upbeat view of themselves and the world. They feel largely impervious to the fluctuations of the outside world.

It's true, they hadn't (until recently) lived through a war, nor did they have portfolios big enough to suffer the last couple of years. We will have to wait and see how they hold up. But right now, the attitude of Ys, to quote noted X and Y expert Bruce Tulgan, is: "Whatever." They understand the world is volatile, but they believe it's their ability to customize themselves, their lives, and their experiences that's going to lead to their happiness and their affluence. And Ys believe the future is theirs to do with as they please, as the person they choose to become. We should all drink a little of that Kool-Aid.

Other factors besides age and generation play a role in how we feel about our jobs. One is the demands placed on our time.

Harvard economist Juliet Schor has described this generation of working Americans as being trapped in the cycle of "work and spend." You work hard to buy the things you want. Buying more makes you want more, so you work harder still. Then you buy more. Then you want more. And eventually, you feel you can't escape. This cycle is at least partly responsible for the fact that the number of hours we put in at the office have risen 10 percent over the past twenty-five years. Put another way, this means that each year you're putting in a month more at the office than your parents did.

And that's just time at the office. That doesn't take into account that—thanks to cell phones and Blackberries, fax machines and e-mail—we are always accessible. When I was growing up, the fact that my father was done with work for the day was made clear because he sat down with us at the dinner table. If the phone rang, no one answered it. No one had answering machines, but it didn't matter. Back then people simply assumed you were eating and called back later. Today, we check our e-mail when we get up in the morning and before we go to sleep at night. We may set our cell phones to vibrate on the weekends so that they don't disturb the diners or moviegoers around us, but when we can feel them in our pockets, we've never really left the office, never quite escaped from work.

Interestingly, having little demand on your time isn't a panacea either. Being asked to work Sundays is a no-no as far as job satisfaction is concerned. But men, in particular, are actually happier if they're asked to put in some hours on a Saturday. Why? They feel needed. They feel involved.

How Do You Feel About the Work Itself?

None of these factors weighs as heavily as how you feel about the actual work you're doing. Is it meaningful? Is it important? Does it draw you in and make you feel useful? Unfortunately, work like that is not always easy to find. Just ask William and Jo-Ann.

When Jo-Ann met William in the late 1990s, they were both in graduate school. They both had similar goals: Get the degree. Grab the big salary. Work hard. Play hard. Travel the world. And because it was still the '90s, they were able to accomplish just that in a scant few years.

Well, almost.

They tied the knot. Bought their first house. Started pouring money into their 401(k)s, paying off their student loans, and planning romantic weekends in Napa and longer vacations overseas. They didn't see each other much during the week; when they rolled into the house around 10 or 11, they were too tired, too weary, too loopy from take-out food with too much MSG to have much of a conversation. No matter. They held hands watching Leno and figured they'd regroup on the weekend.

But those weekends rarely came. She had to work. He had to

work. So they started looking forward to a nice vacation around Christmas. And maybe a week together on the beach in the summer.

Slowly but surely it started to dawn on them that they weren't happy. Every day they would come home stressed and tired. Jo-Ann despised her job. It was uncreative, overly administrative, *boring.* And when Jo-Ann didn't have something to gripe about, William did. He was working for a guy who he felt was much less intelligent than he was, and he had yet to make a real friend in the office. Lunch every day was a cardboard sandwich at his desk.

Finally, they couldn't take it anymore. They sat down and talked about how to bring a little happiness back into their lives, and they decided it all came down to finding more pleasurable work. William's dream for as long as he could remember had been to open his own restaurant. The more Jo-Ann heard and read about massage therapy, the more she felt that was the career for her.

So they quit. Both of them. Jo-Ann enrolled in school and became a licensed massage therapist, at about half her earlier salary. William has had the tougher task. Unable to afford the cost of opening his own restaurant, he got his foot in the door by waiting tables. Now he's an assistant manager for a restaurant in their small town. His salary, too, has been halved.

So how are they doing? Financially, lousy, as you might expect. They manage their finances not month by month now, but week by week. "I can't paint a picture of bliss as far as our finances are concerned," says Jo-Ann, "but on the other hand, jobs that make us happy have allowed us to put up with a lot more financial strain than we would have been able to otherwise. If we had been at our old corporate jobs and been under this financial pressure, I don't know if our marriage would have made it."

But the fact is, they are happy. Certainly happier than they were before. "It's pretty basic when you think about it," says Jo-Ann. "We don't come home and bitch about everything that happened that day. We're not bringing home the level of stress we were bringing home before."

She says she's learned that her job and her passion and her overall happiness aren't inseparable. "The one item we do have stress about now is our finances. But because it's the only area we have stress in, we're able to talk about it and deal with it. And quite honestly I think that our whole relationship works better because we're both happy with what we're doing. We both know that we made sacrifices to be where we are."

And they wouldn't go back even if they could. "When we get really bitter about the money situation, we look at each other and say, 'Would you like to go back to your corporate job?' And we both say, 'No way.'"

Going with the Flow

Aristotle called the sort of satisfaction William and Jo-Ann derive from their new jobs "*eudaimonia:* a state characterized by engagement flow and immersion in life activities." Mihaly Csikszenthimali, former chairman of the department of psychology at the University of Chicago, simplified and called it *flow.*

Flow, as he describes it, is when you're so caught up in what you're doing that you stop watching the clock. You're not overwhelmed. You're absorbed. Time sails by. You look up only when something finally distracts you and you realize that it's three hours later. You skipped your midmorning cup of coffee. You haven't bothered to check your e-mail. You even forgot to go to the bathroom. In other words, you're involved. And being involved in something you enjoy doing—where you can use your skills to accomplish a task you feel is meaningful and important—makes for a satisfying work experience.

Chances are, you find yourself in flow only occasionally. Csikszenthimali's research has shown that 15 percent of people say they've never experienced it, and 15 to 20 percent of people experience it every day (some several times). The rest are in between. The more often you can get to this place while you're working, the happier you'll be. And as we discussed in the early chapters of this book, workplace happiness is a major contributor to lifetime happiness.

How do you get there? First, you have to figure out where you are now.

Money and Happiness Results: Part 7

1. Are you currently employed? (Circle one letter.)

a. Yes, full-time
b. Yes, part-time
c. Yes, self-employed
d. Retired
e. Unemployed

About your response: Most of the Americans we surveyed work: 47 percent full-time for someone else, another 11 percent part-time for someone else. Six percent are self-employed, 19 percent are retired, and 16 percent are not working. We know from studies that the AARP has conducted that 80 percent of seniors say they're working well into "retirement." This turns out to be a positive. Why? Because Americans who are working full-time are significantly more likely to be happy with their lives than those who are retired or not currently working. (As someone who believes she won't ever want to really retire, that makes sense to me. Busyness breeds contentment.) Working people (both full- and part-time) feel more in control of their financial situation and more financially secure as well.

2. What is your main occupation? (Circle one letter.)

a. Executive/professional
b. White collar
c. Blue collar
d. Retired/student/disabled/unemployed/armed forces

About your response: The working population is fairly evenly split: About one-third are executives or professionals, another third work at white-collar jobs, and another third at blue-collar jobs. The type of job you work in seems to have little effect on happiness: White-collar workers, blue-collar workers, and professionals are similarly likely to be happy with their lives overall as well as with their jobs in particular. The big differentiator, it turns out, isn't what you do, but how much you enjoy it. See below.

3. On the whole, how happy are you with your job? (Circle one letter.)

a. Very happy
b. Somewhat happy
c. Not too happy
d. Not at all happy
e. Don't know
f. N/A

4. In the past 30 days, about how often did you feel each of the following? (Check one box for each.)

	A LOT	SOMETIMES	NOT TOO MUCH	NOT AT ALL	DON'T KNOW
a. Restless	❏	❏	❏	❏	❏
b. Useful	❏	❏	❏	❏	❏
c. Stressed	❏	❏	❏	❏	❏
d. Content	❏	❏	❏	❏	❏
e. Hopeless	❏	❏	❏	❏	❏
f. Confident	❏	❏	❏	❏	❏

About your responses: People who are happy with their jobs—and 38 percent of people say they are—are four times more likely to be very happy with their lives. Four times! You may recall that in the early chapters of this book, when we broke down the factors contributing to overall happiness, jobs weighed in high on that list—after marriage and self-esteem, but before health, finances, children, friendships, and appearance. Being happy with your job also makes you more likely to feel useful, confident, and content, and less likely to feel stressed, restless, and hopeless. Clearly, it makes sense to find an occupation that satisfies your soul as well as your wallet. Keep reading.

5. How much do you agree or disagree with each of the following statements? Use a scale ranging from 1 to 7, where 1 means you completely disagree, 7 means you completely agree, and the other numbers represent levels in between.

a. My family and friends are important to me, but frankly, when push comes to shove, my job wins out.
b. Exercise and maintaining my health are important to me, but frankly, when push comes to shove, my job wins out.

About your responses: Although the majority of Americans deny placing their job ahead of family, friends, and exercise, it's important to note that those who do admit to this behavior are significantly less satisfied with their lives. Why, then, do they do it? My theory is that they feel that working harder will result in more money in the bank, and more money in the bank is what they feel they need to achieve happiness overall. It's a cycle. A vicious one. And it doesn't work.

6. Choose the statement that comes closer to your own personal behavior.

a. I am happy because I am successful.
b. I am successful because I am happy.

About your response: Americans who say they're happy because they're successful rather than successful because they are happy are also more likely to place their jobs before their family and their health, a negative attitude, as noted above. The one-third of men (and one-fifth of women) who say their happiness is dependent on their success are less likely to be happy than people who say the reverse. They're more likely to worry about their self-esteem and—as you might expect—their jobs. Americans who say they're successful because they're happy are happier overall, happier with their lifestyle, marriage, and financial situation than those who think their success makes them happy.

7. How much do you agree or disagree with the following statement? Use a scale ranging from 1 to 7, where 1 means you completely disagree, 7 means you completely agree, and the other numbers represent levels in between.

I don't have enough money to support the causes I believe in.

About your response: About four in ten adults state that they don't have enough money to support the causes they believe in. The answer to the question is tied to income, but not as strictly tied as you might expect. One-third of people making less than $25,000 a year manage to find enough money to support their pet causes, as do four in ten people earning between $25,000 and $50,000 a year, and half of those earning more than $50,000.

8. How often, if at all, do you personally do any of the following? (Check one box for each.)

	A LOT	SOMETIMES	NOT TOO MUCH	NOT AT ALL
a. Volunteer at a local school, hospital, library, shelter, etc.	❑	❑	❑	❑
b. Donate money to charity	❑	❑	❑	❑
c. Make nonmonetary donations to charity	❑	❑	❑	❑

About your responses: Even in tough times, Americans give. Two-thirds of us give money to charity, just slightly more than the percentage who make nonmonetary donations. One in four Americans volunteers.

In general, the older you are, the more likely you are to give. Women and men are equally inclined to give money, but women are more likely to give stuff (could it be all that closet cleaning?) as well as time. And married people are one-third more likely to give than singles.

No matter how you give—and our research shows there's little difference in the effects of giving money, time, or stuff—the act of giving resonates in a positive way. Why? Because, it seems, giving makes you a happier person. Our research shows that people who make frequent donations or who volunteer are happier overall than those who don't. They're more confident and more content. They're also happier with most aspects of their lives— their friendships, marriage, children, lifestyle, financial situation, and, not surprisingly, self-esteem.

Finding Work That Fits

If your answers to the preceding questions clue you in to the fact that you're not as happy with your workaday life as you'd like to be—or that you're compromising more, perhaps, than you'd realized—the good news is that it's possible to make changes. Understand, there are three different ways to look at work. There's work for hire, otherwise known as a job. If they didn't pay you to show up, you'd quit. There's a career. That's when you're on a track and you feel a personal drive to move from point a to point b, to accomplish some of your goals. And there's a passion. That's something you'd do even if you weren't getting paid.

Getting paid for their passion is, for many people, the ultimate goal. For others, who have come to terms with the fact that no one is going to pay them to go fly-fishing (or whatever), the goal is finding a job that pays a living wage but leaves enough free time to pursue their passion. The career—the middle road—is where most of us end up.

Unfortunately, I can't describe the scenario—job, career, or passion—that's best for you. Rob, creative director at an advertising agency, knows his passion is throwing pots; he's trying to come up with a business idea sound enough to allow him to make the transition. My brother Dave, who works in accounting for a mutual fund family—a job he likes—would eventually like to support himself with his music.

I can't tell you what's right for you, but I can lead you in the right direction. The following is a list of characteristics that, when applied to just about any job or occupation, result in more happiness rather than less. (And note: Making a lot of money isn't one of them.) Perhaps over the course of your life and career, you can remember a time when you achieved some of these things. That's a good place to start.

- Job security. We feel better, more comfortable, more competent, and better able to make decisions if we're not worried about being pink-slipped on a regular basis.

- High relative income. That's not the same as high income, but earning at least as much money as colleagues and coworkers improves your satisfaction.

- Interaction with other people. A tight-knit sense of community makes a job feel more like a family. For that reason, small workplaces tend to be preferable to large, impersonal ones.

- A challenge that requires use of your skills. Busywork won't do. Csikszenthimali's research shows that only when we are forced to focus our attention and concentrate in a way that takes us out of our everyday existence do we come close to flow.

- Clear and well-defined goals. For many of the same reasons that having financial goals makes for a happier life, having work goals does as well. It's comforting to know that you have marks to meet, that your challenge is achievable, and that you're approaching the finish line. Feedback along the way plays an important role as well.

- Autonomy. Self-employed people tend to be happier because they're able to make their own decisions without being challenged. But you get the same benefits by being a supervisor in a corporate environment or by being able to work independently. Being in control of the speed at which you work—being able to meet your deadlines in your own way—is key. A supervisor dictating your every move stifles satisfaction. If you do have to agree to a timetable, better a colleague's than a boss's, and better a customer's than a colleague's.

- Small freedoms. The ability to work from home from time to time is a very nice perk (one I value highly) but even smaller liberties, such as being able to move your desk in your office or add a chair or couch that reflects your personality, enhance feelings of satisfaction. And having a short commute is a plus.

- Variety. We are happier at work if every day isn't the same in terms of where we work (a little travel is a good thing), what we do, and which skills we draw on.

- Using the skills you've spent time acquiring. It's important to be valued for the particular skills you bring to work—and to be able to use those skills—rather than just being a warm body at a desk.

- Status. How does society view your job? Is it a position of respect? If so, that's a plus. And note: This has very little to do with how much you earn. College professors have a great deal of respect. Sanitation engineers may earn just as much, but they don't have adoring students hanging on their every word.

Money Rich, Time Poor

What if despite the fact that you have all of these things, your work life doesn't satisfy. Then, chances are, the problem isn't at work but at home. Research shows that 85 percent of Americans want more time with their families. More than half of us want *much* more time. Who are the people more likely to say there's a lack of family time in their day? People in their 40s working in high-stress, high-profile jobs; more men than women; people who have pursued their material goals, reached them, and now realize there has to be more to life. If you've ever answered the question "How are you?" with "Busy," put yourself on the list.

You may have plenty of money. But you're time poor. All of America is, on average, when compared with other countries. In the U.S., we have 4.6 hours of leisure a day; in the U.K, they have 5.4. Working more and playing less isn't a problem for everyone. Being busy actually correlates positively with happiness.

But if you're one of the people for whom it doesn't, you may want to consider simplifying. Voluntary simplicity (or "vs" as devotees call it) is reorganizing your life in a way that disentangles you from the materialistic aspects, allowing you to build up the other parts—connections with family, connections with the community, personal interests that have been left behind. Simplifiers might decide, for instance, they don't want to work sixty hours a week, they want to work forty. That would give them an extra twenty hours to paint, garden, or do whatever else they choose.

On the surface, that sounds great. But that smaller paycheck may mean compromising in other areas. Deciding to live on less means you might not be able to afford the leather-upholstered minivan, 3,000-square-foot house, two-week vacation in Europe, and $150,000 Harvard diploma for your child. You'll have to make hard choices about which of those you really, really care about and which are peripheral. And although you might decide that Harvard is worth the sacrifices you'll have to make in other areas, you might also decide that four years at the highly acclaimed state college is a fine way to begin. If your child wants that Harvard degree on his wall he can get it in graduate school—and help pay for it himself. That's why making wholesale changes like these doesn't work unless you are truly disenchanted with the life you have now.

The bigger question is: Does simplifying work? Tim Kasser and Kirk Warren Brown, of Knox College in Illinois, took a look at 200 people who identified themselves as downshifters and simplifiers. You might expect them to be less happy because they have less stuff. In fact, Kasser and Brown found them to be at least as happy as people who hadn't made the same choices—and in some cases more happy.

Like Ellen, the forty-four-year-old consultant living in L.A., you may also decide that freedom is the ultimate goal. Ellen is willing to work a little harder and save a little more today so that she'll be able to downshift tomorrow—or at least in a decade or so. "I like the sense that I won't be eighty-two years old and destitute, and that I'll have choices open to me. I like the thought of being able to make career or life decisions and not feel stuck because I'm a slave to a paycheck."

One day five or ten years down the road, Ellen believes she might want to quit her high-stress, high-paid position, work in a bookstore, and write a book. Or become a low-paid teacher and write a book. Or do nothing else while she writes a book. Ellen's parents' choices, particularly her father's, have influenced her own. "My father left an international shipping career to cash in, buy a small business, and grow it over time. He wanted the personal autonomy. He wanted the sense of satisfaction of growing something," she says. "So he made the decision that he didn't need to make multiple millions of dollars. With a couple hundred thousand in the bank he could live pretty darn well."

Making Time to Do unto Others

The late Michael Argyle, a pioneering social psychologist from the U.K., once listed in rank order the group activities that result in happiness. It was a fairly long list and included endorphin-raising pursuits like playing sports and exercising and work in which you find yourself in flow. Volunteering and other charity work, he found, ranked second on the list. The only activity ranked higher was dancing. I'd say that argues heavily for doing both. But as far as figuring out a strategy to incorporate dancing in your life—and I say this as the wife of a guy who doesn't even like to dance at weddings—you're on your own. When it comes to finding a volunteer position that suits, I can help.

More than four out of every ten Americans volunteer. Two-thirds do it regularly. If you're one, or would like to be one, you need to try to make your volunteer hours fulfilling for both you and the charity. Follow these steps.

Think about your skills. There are three ways to approach volunteering. You can offer up skills you have, the same skills you use in your workaday life as a doctor, lawyer, publicist, or accountant. You can use volunteering as a way to develop new skills you'd like to put on your résumé. Or you can approach it as a way to take a break from your daily life by doing something completely different.

Consider what else you want. Think about your motives for volunteering. Yes, it's nice to do good. But what else is driving you? Do you want to meet other singles? Spend time outdoors? Be with children (or escape from them)? Or are you trying to teach the spirit of giving to your own kids? Knowing what you're looking for will help you find the right slot.

Be realistic. The average volunteer donates 3.6 hours of time each week, according to the Independent Sector. You may have more, you may have less. Both are fine. Some 85 percent of nonprofits rely on volunteers for at least some of their labor, so they need you. What they don't need are people who make commitments they can't fulfill. If a weekly stint is too much for you, participate in onetime events like a breast-cancer walk or a beach cleanup. Or look for places like soup kitchens and food banks that welcome drop-ins.

Find a good fit. Once you have a grip on what you want, call charities directly or head to a Web site like volunteermatch.org, which has filled nearly a million volunteer positions since 1998. Then attend a volunteer orientation and if you don't believe you've found the right place for you, try something else. After all, the goal is to find something that adds to your happiness—not one that robs you of it.

The Silver Lining

After I had my first child, I took a three-month maternity leave, then went back to work. Admittedly, I have always been fairly efficient. I've always been able to meet my deadlines and still go to lunch. But when I returned from maternity leave, I picked up speed. I wasn't cutting corners—I was thinking more clearly. In the past, I had reported excessively before sitting down to write a story. Now, I found, I was getting precisely the information I needed, with little overflow. My drafts were cleaner, too. I was being asked to do fewer rewrites.

The difference? There was a baby to get back to. I didn't want to be at work until 8 P.M., I wanted out of there by 5:30 or 6. My priorities had shifted, too, so I stressed less about the work. Somehow that made the work easier—and faster. And better.

And I wasn't the only one. Many of my friends noticed the same thing once they started to have children. Moreover, studies have shown that when executives feel they've reached the limits of their careers and are no longer getting promoted, they adapt. They start working fewer hours—rolling into the office a little later each morning, taking a longer lunch, and leaving in time to make dinner with their family. They spend more time with their spouse, their friends, take up new pastimes, get a little more exercise, and actually use all their vacation time. As a result, they feel better and happier. Their minds are clearer. So what happens? They get promoted.

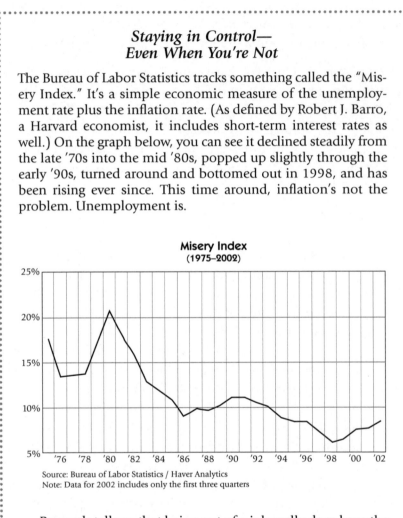

Staying in Control—
Even When You're Not

The Bureau of Labor Statistics tracks something called the "Misery Index." It's a simple economic measure of the unemployment rate plus the inflation rate. (As defined by Robert J. Barro, a Harvard economist, it includes short-term interest rates as well.) On the graph below, you can see it declined steadily from the late '70s into the mid '80s, popped up slightly through the early '90s, turned around and bottomed out in 1998, and has been rising ever since. This time around, inflation's not the problem. Unemployment is.

Misery Index
(1975–2002)

Source: Bureau of Labor Statistics / Haver Analytics
Note: Data for 2002 includes only the first three quarters

Research tells us that being out of a job really does have the ability to make us miserable. When you're unemployed, you have no control. Feeling in control of your life is a predictor of happiness. And part of feeling in control of your life is feeling in control of your income. When you have a predictable income stream, you're in control; when you're unemployed, you're not.

But it's worse than that. You not only lose control, you lose money and you lose respect. You lose direction. You thought you knew where your life was going. Even when you land that next job, which you eventually do, your outlook on life has changed. You know you're vulnerable, and that puts a damper on your happiness. It's almost like being blindsided by a divorce. The world suddenly becomes a different place.

What can you do about it? Working to find a new job in a focused, organized way tops the list. But in recent years, even people who do everything right may be looking at six to nine months out of the workforce. Importantly, Mihaly Csikszenthimali's work on flow illuminates the fact that while it may be easiest to find a skillful challenge that takes you into the flow on the job, it's certainly not the only place you can do it.

The key, when you're unemployed, is finding other activities that induce flow. They need to present a mental challenge and fulfill a need—for your family, for a charitable organization, for your future goals. In other words, you have to feel that you're doing something useful. You could volunteer, apprentice, run a half-marathon or a 10K, or take a couple of classes. You could embark on a challenge to save your family almost as much as you're not bringing in, by refinancing your mortgage and your car loan and restructuring your other debt.

The Irony of It All

Not to get overly zen about it, but there is definitely a chicken-and-egg relationship here. Not only do people who are happier in their work have slightly more money, more money comes to people who are happier in their work. If you think about it, it makes sense that it would. If you're a happier person, you have better relationships with your colleagues and superiors, and you enjoy what you're doing more. Therefore, you're likely to do better work. And when raise and bonus time rolls around, you're likely to reap the rewards.

Overcoming Unemployment

In 2001, when Kelly, a high-energy sales manager, lost her job as the East Coast representative for a big West Coast conglomerate, she put all of her skills and energy toward finding something new. She networked, took dozens of meetings, and heard from scores of people who said they'd love to hire her—if only they had an opening. But they were cutting back, downsizing. If she could be patient, they said, maybe there would be something in 2002.

Kelly knew herself well enough to know that patience wasn't her strong suit. She could have decorated her new house with abandon or joined a new gym—it wouldn't have been enough. So she quickly enrolled in school and got her real estate license. Three months later, she landed a job with the highest-profile real estate firm in her county. How? By using her well-honed sales skills to sell herself. Admittedly, with the real estate market slow, the fact that she's sold only two houses in six months has gotten her down. But she feels much better because she did something and she earned a little money. Now, when the market in her longtime field improves simultaneously with the real estate market (as she's sure it will), she has choices.

"It's better that way," she says. "Don't you think?"

Money and Happiness Evaluation: Part 8

1. Overall, how financially secure do you feel? (Circle one letter.)

a. Very secure
b. Somewhat secure
c. Not too secure
d. Not at all secure
e. Don't know

2. Looking specifically at aspects of your current financial situation, indicate whether or not you have enough money to weather a financial hardship, such as losing your job. (Circle one letter.)

a. Yes
b. No
c. Don't know

3. What amount of money do you think you would need to have in the bank to be very happy with your financial situation? Choose the minimum amount you would need. (Circle one letter.)

a. Under $50,000
b. $50,000 to $100,000
c. $100,000 to $250,000
d. $250,000 to $500,000
e. $500,000 to $1 million
f. $1 million to $2 million
g. More than $2 million
h. Don't know

4. How much do you agree or disagree with the following statement? Use a scale ranging from 1 to 7, where 1 means you completely disagree, 7 means you completely agree, and the other numbers represent levels in between.

I wish I had a bigger financial cushion.

5. How much do you agree or disagree with the following statement? Use a scale ranging from 1 to 7, where 1 means you completely disagree, 7 means you completely agree, and the other numbers represent levels in between.

   I have done what I can to provide for my family's future.

6. Indicate whether each of the following is something you have ever done. (Check one box for each.)

	YES	NO	DON'T KNOW
a. Purchased life insurance	❏	❏	❏
b. Purchased disability insurance	❏	❏	❏
c. Written a will	❏	❏	❏

7. Choose the statement that comes closer to your own personal behavior.

   a. I'd choose as a guardian for my kids a family that is financially secure (could cover all of their needs and their future education), even if the family's personal values were different from my own.

   b. I'd choose as a guardian for my kids a family that has personal values similar to my own, even if my child had to go without many of the things financial security would provide.

8. It's Not Just About the Money

I don't want expensive gifts. I don't want to be bought. I have every-thing I want. I just want someone to be there for me, to make me feel safe and secure.

—Diana, Princess of Wales

The first seven chapters of this book were primarily about money: how to handle it, think about it, find peace with it. Not this one. This chapter is about protecting the things in your life that are more important than money: your family, your dreams, your future. In a nuts-and-bolts sense it's about guaranteeing the security of your family with the help of insurance policies and legal documents. But it's not about the money, and thinking about it in terms of money is one of the biggest mistakes you can make.

Why? Because if you don't have what you consider significant as-sets, you'll say, "How much could I lose anyway?" and convince yourself that this chapter doesn't apply to you. You'd be wrong.

In February 1997, a Maryland woman was killed in a car acci-dent. Her husband, an alcoholic who'd been sober for twelve years, fell apart and started drinking. A year later he died of liver disease. They left three children, a modest house, and a $100,000 life insur-ance policy. But they had named no guardian, and they left no will.

That, I suppose, shouldn't come as a surprise. According to our research, 57 percent of people in this country don't have a will. That unfortunate statistic includes an awful lot of parents (and more of my friends than I care to count). What followed in this case, however, was wildly unusual.

With the help of an attorney, the middle child, age ten, filed for bankruptcy as a gambit to prevent foreclosure on the house. The family had no savings and no rich relatives, and until a court-appointed guardian was in place to receive a check, the life insurance company wouldn't pay. In the end, it worked, but the process was a nightmare.

You probably think something this sad and this dramatic could never happen in your family. Wrong again. If you don't take the proper steps to protect your family, immense ugliness can result: courtroom guardianship hearings, heated battles between family members, lawsuits over who gets what and why. But all of these things can be avoided with some fairly simple steps.

Protecting What's Yours

Estate planning is the umbrella term for advance steps you can take so that your death doesn't have unfortunate financial ramifications for your family. When people got married and stayed married it used to be a much simpler process. No more. Because three-quarters of American children don't have *Father Knows Best* families, issues such as who gets what (including guardianship of the children) and who gets to make health or financial decisions on your behalf are much touchier and more complicated than they used to be.

That's no excuse to avoid estate planning. If you won't do it for your spouse or your kids, do it for selfish reasons. Four out of ten Americans feel financially insecure. But among those who take some simple steps like writing a will or buying life insurance, the percentage drops precipitously. And if you're financially insecure, it's tough to be happy. In and of itself, financial security is no guarantee of happiness—it's not the only thing you need, nor the most important item on the list—but without it financial happiness is seriously difficult to achieve.

That's how Ellen feels. "I'm happy when I feel that disaster could strike yet I'd still be okay," says the L.A.–based management consultant. For example? Say a major earthquake hit the city and toppled her condo, or she got fired or became seriously ill. None of those scenarios would be welcome—she's not a masochist—but knowing that her homeowners insurance would cover her condo, that she has enough in savings to stay off the soup line, and that her health plan would allow her to see the doctors of her choice enables her to sleep at night.

Because she realized she needed that sort of security to guarantee her happiness, Ellen went to extra lengths to make it happen. She lobbied the condo board in her building to take out earthquake insurance on the overall building. Ellen already had as much personal coverage as she could buy—enough to pay off her mortgage and purchase a new place—but she felt better knowing the entire building was secure. Likewise, she's always purchased the sort of health coverage that didn't have any sort of maximum on coverage and that included an annual out-of-pocket cap. "I want my insurance to cover me in a catastrophic situation. And I'm willing to pay more money for that."

Money and Happiness Results: Part 8

1. Overall, how financially secure do you feel? (Circle one letter.)

a. Very secure
b. Somewhat secure
c. Not too secure
d. Not at all secure
e. Don't know

About your response: Six out of ten Americans feel somewhat or very financially secure. Not surprisingly, higher earners tend to feel more so as do older Americans, college grads, and those who work as professionals rather than in white- or blue-collar jobs. Married people are much more likely to feel financially secure than singles, perhaps because they have a second income (or at least the possibility of a second income) to fall back on should something untoward happen to them. But having kids under the age of eighteen in the home is a drain on financial security, perhaps because parents see those college tuition bills looming large.

2. Looking specifically at aspects of your current financial situation, indicate whether or not you have enough money to weather a financial hardship, such as losing your job. (Circle one letter.)

a. Yes
b. No
c. Don't know

About your response: Only 28 percent of Americans believe they have enough money to weather a financial storm. More than 50 percent say they don't. Women are less likely to have a sufficient cushion than men, singles less likely than couples. And while income, as you might expect, makes a substantial difference in having enough socked away to withstand tough times, it's no panacea. Only 57 percent of people earning six-figure salaries say they'd be able to weather a layoff. Particularly in these times, that percentage is clearly too low.

If, however, you can clear this hurdle and amass enough to get you through a rough period, you're likely to be happier and more secure. Our research shows that of people who have a sufficient stash, 42 percent are very happy overall (compared to 26 percent of those who don't), 35 percent are financially happy (compared to 5 percent of those who don't) and 90 percent feel financially secure (compared to 42 percent of those who don't).

3. What amount of money do you think you would need to have in the bank to be very happy with your financial situation? Choose the minimum amount you would need. (Circle one letter.)

a. Under $50,000
b. $50,000 to $100,000
c. $100,000 to $250,000
d. $250,000 to $500,000
e. $500,000 to $1 million
f. $1 million to $2 million
g. More than $2 million
h. Don't know

About your response: How much do we feel we need in dollar terms? On average, $92,000 (how's that for a nice round number?). The younger you *are, the less you feel you need. Women also feel they need much less than men.*

Here's the breakdown:

Age	Men	Women	Average
18–34	$66,000	$71,000	$69,000
35–49	$160,000	$75,000	$94,000
50–64	$234,000	$99,000	$179,000
65+	$102,000	$80,000	$90,000

My take on this: Wake up, women. Nine out of ten of you are going to have to stand on your own financial feet at some point in your life, and thanks to steady divorce rates and the fact that more people are marrying later (or not at all), there's no guarantee that day won't come sooner rather than later. It's time to focus on building a nest egg of your own.

4. How much do you agree or disagree with the following statement. Use a scale ranging from 1 to 7, where 1 means you completely disagree, 7 means you completely agree, and the other numbers represent levels in between.

I wish I had a bigger financial cushion.

About your response: Regardless of the amount you've managed to put away for a rainy day, chances are you wish you had more. Three-quarters of Americans do. Interestingly, though, the more control you have over your money, the less likely you are to be fretting about this. How do you get there? By working toward your goals. Only 63 percent of people who are at least halfway to the financial goals they set for themselves wish they had a bigger cushion; 90 percent of those who have started but have a long way to go wish they had more socked away.

5. How much do you agree or disagree with the following statement? Use a scale ranging from 1 to 7, where 1 means you completely disagree, 7 means you completely agree, and the other numbers represent levels in between.

I have done what I can to provide for my family's future.

About your response: Only half of Americans agree that they've done what they can to look after their family. As you might expect, this is a number that improves with age. Twice as many seniors (70 percent) as eighteen- to thirty-four-year olds (36 percent) agree with this statement. And while more married couples than singles have taken the necessary steps, more households without children than with children have done so. That's understandable—it's tough to find money to spend on things like life insurance when you have to buy new sneakers for your fast-growing eight-year-old four times a year. But it's also frightening. Families with children need to take these safety measures more than any others.

6. Indicate whether each of the following is something you have ever done. (Check one box for each.)

	YES	NO	DON'T KNOW
a. Purchased life insurance	❏	❏	❏
b. Purchased disability insurance	❏	❏	❏
c. Written a will	❏	❏	❏

About your responses: Again, we have a case of Americans deceiving themselves. Half of Americans say they've done what they can to provide for the safety and security of their families, yet our research shows that in at least some ways they clearly have not. Seven in ten have purchased life insurance. That's promising. But only 33 percent have purchased disability insurance, and only 41 percent have written a will.

Do the people who need these items most have them? Not always. It's encouraging that 74 percent of people with kids under age eighteen have life insurance. That's the right buy. But when it comes to disability insurance, only 18 percent of singles—arguably the group that needs it most—have coverage, while 46 percent are wasting money on life insurance that they don't need at all. Finally, when it comes to wills, my feeling is that everyone needs one. But parents need one most of all—not to move their belongings from one owner to another, but to name guardians for their kids. Only 31 percent of households with kids have gone through this process.

That means—and I want to be quite clear about this—if you and your spouse were to die together, God forbid, nearly seven out of ten of your chil-

dren would be fought for in the courts in what are typically nasty, expensive guardianship proceedings. I understand—I've been there—that choosing guardians can be a gut-wrenching experience. You avoid it like the plague because it means declaring, in writing, that you have chosen your own family over your spouse's (or vice versa), or a friend over both, to raise your kids if you are not there. But it must be done.

On pages 196–97 you'll find a list of five questions. Sit down with your spouse or your ex (or by yourself, if you're a single parent and this is your decision alone) and answer the questions. When you get to the end of the list, you'll have made a choice.

7. Choose the statement that comes closer to your own personal behavior.

a. I'd choose as a guardian for my kids a family that is financially secure (could cover all of their needs and their future education), even if the family's personal values were different from my own.

b. I'd choose as a guardian for my kids a family that has personal values similar to my own, even if my child had to go without many of the things financial security would provide.

About your response: America's answer is overwhelmingly clear. Eighty-two percent of people want guardians with values in line with their own. Distressingly, people who didn't answer the question this way—who chose money over values—seem to feel that their backs are up against a wall because they can't provide for their children themselves. They tend to be younger, single, and lower earners. They are more often worried about their finances, insecure about their money, and unhappy with their life. If that's the way you're feeling, my hope is that this book will help you get comfortable enough with your money that you can make a decision closer to your heart than your wallet.

Life with a Safety Net

Now that you've isolated your strengths and weaknesses, you should have a general idea of what you need in terms of an estate plan. Over the next few pages we'll nail down the specifics. But before we get to the insurance and legal documents that make up the bulk of this chapter, I want to return for a moment to something we discussed in Chapter 4: the emergency cushion.

Other than death, most financial emergencies are temporary. Lay-offs, disabilities, even stays in a nursing home last months, not years. Your goal ought to be to have a sufficient amount in savings—liquid assets that you can draw on if need be—to get yourself through those times. In fact, the insurance industry forces you into paying for them yourself by incorporating into its policies waiting periods before coverage kicks in. Opt for a very short waiting period (thirty days rather than ninety, for example) and you'll pay much more for coverage to begin with. These are all reasons you need to have an emergency cushion: three to six months' worth of living expenses to tide you over these times. Having such a cushion is step one of protecting your other assets because it means you don't have to borrow from your retirement plan, pilfer your cash-value life insurance policy, or take out extra debt against your home in order to get through.

Protecting Yourself with Insurance

Another way to protect yourself is with insurance. In the year following September 11, a record number of people bought life insurance—either adding to preexisting policies they owned or buying them for the first time. And do you know how they felt after they'd written the check? After they'd signed on the dotted line? I'll tell you how they felt—I know because I felt exactly the same way when I took these steps in my own life—they felt better.

Now, not every individual needs every type of insurance. There are some types of insurance—like the credit life insurance you're pitched on the bottom of your credit card statement or the accidental death insurance sold in airports—that practically no one needs. But it's important that where you do have a need for coverage, you budget the money and you go out and buy it. Why? Because insurance, like an emergency cushion, can prevent you from having to raid your future in the event of a life-threatening illness, a disability, the need to move to a nursing home, or a death in the family. If you don't have the right coverage and even one of these things happens to you or a loved one, it can mean sabotaging your future.

Who needs that?

Everyone Needs Health Insurance

We all need it. Every one of us. Hopefully you are covered by your employer or Medicare. If you are given a choice of plans—perhaps you're asked to choose between an HMO and a PPO, or maybe you're given the option of several different HMOs, some with more flexibility than others—take the time to fully understand the differences between the plans.

HMOs tend to be better for families because you get pricey physicals and vaccines gratis. PPOs are generally a little more expensive, but they also give you access to a wider range of physicians. If you're among the 10 to 15 percent of Americans who have the choice of a traditional indemnity plan that doesn't limit your selection of doctors, it's probably going to be significantly more expensive. But if it's taken you years to come up with a roster of physicians you're comfortable with and they're not in the network of any of the HMOs or PPOs you're offered, it may also be worth it.

If you're on your own—if you're self-employed, for example—getting coverage is likely to be more time-consuming (you have to shop around to find the best plan for your needs) and more costly (because no employer is absorbing even a small portion of your premiums). Do it anyway. Call local insurance brokers, check health insurance sites on the Web, and call every association you belong to, from your alumni association to professional groups, to see if you can get into a group through the back door. Group policies are generally cheaper because they spread the risk an insurer is taking among an array of premium-paying individuals. Groups don't have to be gigantic, however. Ask a local insurance broker if it's possible to form a group on your own.

Finally, if you've gone through this exercise and find you can't afford the cost of a soup-to-nuts health plan, make sure you at least have an indemnity policy that kicks in after you cover your first few thousand in health care expenses each year. By doing this you're essentially self-insuring for what will be your likely out-of-pocket expenditures. But if you really get laid up, it will protect you from a financial catastrophe. Because you're absorbing most of the risk, a policy like this is significantly cheaper.

Life Insurance: for the Living

Instead of beginning with the people who need life insurance and the myriad reasons they may want it, let's dismiss those who don't. If you're single, you generally don't need life insurance. Why? Because life insurance isn't for the dead; it's for the living who were counting on your income. If you have no one (no spouse, no kids, no parents you support) depending on you to bring home the bacon, you're done here.

If you have those dependents, however, you're on the hook. The onus is on you to figure out how much support—in dollar terms—these people would need if something happened to you, then go out and buy that coverage at the most cost-effective price from a highly rated insurer. That's a pretty complicated mandate, so let's take it step by step.

Step One: Figure out how much you need. Recently, I moderated a panel of three financial services professionals on the subject "Nurturing Your Nest Egg." When we got to talking about insurance, I asked the insurance specialist exactly that question: How do you know how much you need? She gave me the insurance industry's standard pat answer: four to six times your income. "Wrong!" I wanted to scream. "Wrong!" But sitting there as I was, in a business suit and ladylike pumps, screaming was out of the question. Instead, I challenged her politely but persistently until she was forced to agree with me: Rules of thumb like this do not work.

Why? Because the financial reality for someone who has a spouse who could return to the workforce is very different from that of someone who doesn't. And the financial reality for someone who's so close to being done with her mortgage she can smell the paper burning is very different from that of someone who just refinanced for another thirty years. And the financial reality for someone with one child is very different from that of someone who has two, let alone three or four.

To figure out how much insurance you really need to buy, you need to use pencil and paper or one of the many worksheets available on the Web and run the numbers for your particular situation. You need to know how many years of support you want to raise with the insurance payout and what big-ticket items (like the mortgage or college) you'd want to be paid off immediately. And you also have to ask yourself whether the payout is meant to be a stopgap measure for your family until your spouse or kids can support themselves, or whether it will become the income-generating annuity they live on.

Step Two: Shop around for coverage. There are two basic types of life insurance: term and cash value. Term insurance is so called because it is in effect for a specified term and then terminates. You buy a policy that stays in force typically for one, ten, or twenty years and then expires. You can buy more at that point, but because you're older it will be more expensive. When you buy term coverage, all you get is a death benefit. If you die, your beneficiary gets a payout. It's that simple. Because it's unencumbered with bells and whistles, it's relatively inexpensive. A thirty-five-year old nonsmoking man or woman in good health could buy $400,000 worth of coverage—with the premiums guaranteed for 20 years—for around $215 annually.

Term is best for two types of people: those who can't afford any other way of ensuring they'll obtain the death benefit they need, and those who believe that when the term they've selected is up, they will have amassed a net worth so large they will no longer need insurance. Buying term insurance when you're in your sixties—when you may not be in such terrific health—becomes very costly. That same $400,000 policy from a top-rated insurer for a healthy sixty-five-year-old—with the premium guaranteed for only five years—costs $1,350 a year. If you want to guarantee the premium for an additional twenty years, you're looking at a price tag upwards of $7,000 annually. That's why, if you think you'll want some sort of coverage for life, you should start either with a term policy that gives you the option to convert to cash value insurance or with cash value insurance itself (you can also buy a combination). You can shop for term insurance, by the way, on the Internet. You'll still have to go through a physical exam, but you can get a very good sense of who's offering the best prices for a person like you.

Cash value insurance—also called whole life—is a death benefit with an investment account attached. Because of that investment account, premiums are significantly higher. When you're in your twenties, for example, you can expect to pay ten times as much for cash value as you would for term. In your thirties, you'll pay five times as much. The decreasing difference isn't because the premiums on the cash value insurance go down (typically they hold steady) but because those on the term insurance rise.

That's why cash value insurance is most appropriate for people who want to guarantee they'll have insurance throughout their life—perhaps they're having children relatively late, or have a family history of deteriorating health at a relatively young age. Many people argue that you can get the same benefits by pricing both policies, buying cheaper term insurance, and investing the difference yourself (returns from insurance companies pale in comparison with average market returns over a long period of time, but unlike the market they may be guaranteed). The question is, Will you actually take the time to do that? Be honest. For many, many people the answer is no. Their intentions are good, but when it comes right down to it, they can't be bothered. Those are cash value customers.

In the world of cash value insurance there are variations, with names like universal life and variable life, and there are annuities, which are essentially the reverse of life insurance in that they pay you a benefit in the form of monthly income during retirement and give anything left over to your heirs. Picking the one that's right for you—and getting it from the right company—is a matter of shopping around for a policy that gives you the most coverage for the lowest cost with the least risk. Often when you're not dealing with a straight whole life policy but some variation, the return on the underlying investment may determine how much you'll have to pay in premiums down the road. You may prefer that to be a sure thing.

Step Three: Check the ratings—and buy. The bottom line on all of these policies is this: If you need life insurance to care for your loved ones, the most important thing is that you get enough. For the vast majority of people, the only way to do that is with term. If you can afford to do it with cash value insurance or some combination of the two, that's fine, too, as long as you've shopped wisely for your policy and know that you'll be able to make the premium payments over the long term. Far too many policies are canceled or dropped when they're just a year or two old because the policyholder decides they're no longer "worth it." When that happens you've thrown money down the drain, because in a policy's early years, it's not unusual for half— half!—of your premium dollars to go into the pocket of the insurance agent who sold it to you in the form of a commission. It's like the interest on a mortgage. Only when you've had the policy for a few years does your investment account begin to build in any meaningful way.

Before you make the actual purchase, sign on the dotted line, and go through the physical exam (typically they send a doctor to you to perform an EKG, take a little blood, and listen to your ticker—don't worry, I've done it and it's not that bad), make sure any insurer you're thinking of patronizing is on solid financial ground. That means it should have a rating of A or better from Standard & Poors, Moody's Investors Service, or Weiss Ratings. Many of the insurance search engines on the Web (like the ones at Quotesmith.com) give you the rating along with the price.

The Most Overlooked (and Necessary) Coverage

In your thirties and forties, you are eight times more likely to become disabled before you retire than you are to die, yet America still hasn't woken up to the fact that disability insurance is a necessity. Unlike life insurance, which is more important for couples and parents, disability insurance is key for singles. Why? Because if you're single you have only your own income to fall back on. If you become ill or are injured and can't work, who's going to pay your rent, make your car payment, make a dent in your student loans? Your mom and dad? Yes, if you're lucky, but they've got their own retirement to contend with. No, the load falls squarely on you. And according to our research, most of you aren't shouldering it.

What do you need to do?

Step One: Check your employer's coverage. First check and see if you have any coverage at work. The goal is to get coverage that will replicate 60 percent of your income. If you have some insurance at work, but not that much—and in many cases it won't be—call an insurance agent about buying some more. (This is sometimes called a "gap" disability policy.)

Step Two: Hammer out the details. It's best to buy "own-occupation" coverage, which will pay you as long as you can't work in your own occupation; less desirable policies will pay you only if you can't work at all, which means if you're a surgeon who can no longer operate but who could, say, work at a hardware store, you'd be out of luck. Own-occupation coverage tends to be pricey, so you'll want to cut your premiums in other ways. One is to opt for a ninety-day waiting period (also sometimes called an elimination period) before coverage kicks in. This is a pretty safe move as long as you have a three-month emergency cushion that could tide you over.

Step Three: Buy. For the record, singles aren't the only people who need disability insurance. If you're the sole wage earner for your family, it's a must, and it's strongly recommended if you're in a dual-income family in which your salary isn't just gravy. As with life insurance, you want to make certain you're buying a policy from a company that has its financial ship in order. You want a carrier rated A or better by S&P, Moody's, or A.M. Best.

Is Long-Term-Care Insurance for You?

For most Americans, long-term-care insurance is a luxury rather than a necessity. Most of the caregiving in this country is still done by family members, who take time off from work (or in many cases, work around the clock) to care for parents who are no longer able to care for themselves.

If you're one of these people who either don't have children who could care for them in old age or would prefer that their kids not have to step up to the plate either physically or financially, long-term-care insurance is a good alternative. A good policy will pay to care for you either at home or in a nursing home once you can no longer care for yourself. It's insurance that you'll be able to get the sort of care you want rather than merely the sort the state will pay for. And it guarantees that at least some of your nest egg will last long enough to be passed down.

Unfortunately, even if that description sounds appealing, the cost of long-term care may mean it's not the right product for you. It's expensive. A policy for a sixty-year-old man in good (not excellent) health with a daily benefit of $250 guaranteed for life and a ninety-day waiting period before coverage kicks in runs around $5,000 a year from an A-rated insurer. (The same policy purchased at age fifty runs one-half to one-third less, but then you'll be paying the premiums for an additional ten years.)

That's why long-term-care insurance is best for people who have assets between about $300,000 and $1.5 to $2 million. People with fewer assets will quickly exhaust them, then qualify for Medicaid. People with more could certainly afford the insurance, but don't necessarily need it. They should be able to invest their money and fund their own care. They may decide they want the coverage anyway, however, to guarantee that their wealth can be passed on to their heirs.

Long-term-care insurance is relatively new, and the kinks are still being worked out in these policies. Those written today are much improved over the ones being sold a few years ago: They're more likely to cover home health care as well as nursing homes, and the language that describes what it takes for coverage to kick in is generally easier to understand. That said, if you opt for a long-term-care policy, you want to buy it not only from a carrier that's highly rated but also through an agent who specializes in this sort of coverage and can point you in the right direction. And assuming there is no genetic history in your family that would press you to buy it earlier, the best time to make your purchase is between ages fifty and sixty, according to Weiss Ratings. Buy earlier than that and, although your annual premiums will be much lower, you'll end up spending more out of pocket because you'll be paying those premiums over so many years. Buy later than that and the annual cost of the premiums is going to skyrocket.

The Cost of Living in a Litigious Society (Thankfully, It's Low)

Just as a serious illness or extended nursing home stay could wipe you out financially, so could a lawsuit. Like it or not, we live in times in which people sue each other at the drop of a hat, so you have to protect yourself. An umbrella liability policy is a tool you'll want to use.

Your home and auto insurance policies come with some liability coverage, generally $300,000. If you have few assets beyond your car, or if your home is *very* modest, that may be enough for you. But if you've accumulated more than that, you need more coverage, particularly if your home is on a decent-size piece of property and if you own a dog. The good news is that unlike the rest of these coverages, liability insurance is cheap. You can buy a $1 million policy for several hundred dollars.

Five Documents You Shouldn't Live Without

That's the insurance side of the story. The third piece of this protection plan revolves around some basic estate planning documents. Some people believe that estate planning is for wealthy people. Others believe it's all about trying to save on taxes so that more of your money gets into the hands of your heirs than those of Uncle Sam. Both are wrong: Estate planning is for everyone.

Estate planning is for everyone who has loved ones they care for now—and want them to be cared for in perpetuity. It's for everyone who'd like to have a say in who gets their stuff, rather than let the government make the call. It's for everyone who would like to have a say in how they themselves are cared for if they become ill or disabled and can't fend for themselves. It is for everyone over the age of twenty-one.

It doesn't even have to be expensive. If you have substantial assets, you should hire a lawyer who can advise you on some of the more complicated approaches estate planning attorneys have at their disposal. But the basics of an estate plan can all be obtained in the form of cheap software, on the Internet, or at your local Staples, Office Depot, or mom-and-pop stationery store. You need:

1. *An emergency information sheet.* This is a letter, one or two pages, a road map that could take a total stranger by the hand if something happens to you and make sure the right people are contacted and the proper documents found. It should include names and phone numbers of your closest family members, friends, and neighbors, as well as of your doctors, lawyer(s), clergyman, accountant, and anyone else you rely on. It should note the location of your will and the other documents on this list. This is not a legal document, but it is a necessary part of a complete estate plan.

2. *A durable power of attorney.* This is a legal document that gives another person the right to handle your finances—your tax matters and your legal ones—if you're sick, disabled, or out of the country. As soon as you have assets in your own name, you absolutely need one of these.

3. *A living will.* This tells the management of a hospital whether or not you want life support should that be necessary. Often, you're asked to sign one of these before you check into a hospital. Often, that's too late.

4. *A health care proxy.* This goes hand in hand with a living will in that it gives another individual the right to make health-related decisions on your behalf (some people call this a durable power of attorney for health care). Again, you want to put one of these in the hands of the proper person—one who will honor your views on matters like life support—before it's necessary.

5. *A will.* This legal document tells the state where (to which people or institutions) you want your belongings to go when you die. If you're married, it is true that most states will automatically make your spouse your heir. The argument "That's what I'd want anyway" lets many people off the emotional hook that writing a will involves. Unfortunately, the argument doesn't hold up. Why not? What if you die together? If you have children, it is even more imperative that you write a will because a will is where you name a guardian for those kids. That is most certainly not a decision you want in anyone's hands but your own.

Five Steps to Choosing a Guardian

If you have children—or if you're expecting, for that matter—choosing a guardian is something you should do before you go to sleep tonight. Seriously. Stop struggling with it. Stop dancing around it. Stop avoiding it. Pull out a piece of paper, answer these five questions, and when you get to the end you'll have your decision.

1. *Who's on the shortlist?* Your brother? Your spouse's sister? If you don't have family members who you think are ready, willing, and able, which friends do you think you could call on in this type of jam?

2. *How's their health?* It's important to choose someone who will live for a good long time, who's in good mental and physical condition. Make no mistake, caring for someone else's children is a challenge. You want to be sure they're up to it. That's why—although your parents did an A-1 job with you—siblings, cousins, friends of your generation are better choices.

3. *Do they have the resources?* The person you select must have the time to take on another child. If your child won't be self-sufficient financially, they also need to have the money.
4. *Are their values in sync with yours?* You want someone who shares your views on religion, education, and other philosophies of life. One way to gauge the answer to this question is to look at how your potential guardians are parenting their own children (if they have them).
5. *Finally, are they nearby?* This comes last on the list because it's nowhere near as important as the other four. Moving a child who has just lost one or both parents is not something you want to do, as it makes a difficult time even more stressful. But if you have to do it to ensure that your child will be raised by the right person, it's the appropriate choice. (Having moved five times as an adolescent, I can attest—kids adapt.) However, if you're down to the final two names on your list and you're looking for a tiebreaker, this one is as good as any.

Once your selection is made, you need to ask if the person is willing to take on this responsibility. This is not the sort of question you spring on someone during the Super Bowl halftime show. Take the person out to dinner. Offer time to think about it and, if you're dealing with half of a married couple, time to talk about it with their spouse.

As soon as you have an affirmative response, put it in writing. Don't you feel better now?

Could You Handle a Layoff?

One true test of whether you've done adequate planning is your answer to this question. Like so much else in life, our economy is cyclical, which means that every so often—as in 1973–75, 1980–81, 1990–91 and 2002—it experiences a downturn or recession. Consumers stop spending. Corporations that had staffed up to meet the added consumer demand that goes with good times have to pare down, and layoffs begin. Think about reading your morning paper over the last few years. Every day, it seemed, there was yet another story about how conglomerate X decided 300 employees had to go in order for it to stay in business (never mind profitable) and company Y laid off even more people. These things go in cycles, and sometimes, no matter how much you plan and how well you perform on the job, you get caught in the storm. My question is: If this happens to you, if you were to lose your job with little to no notice, could you weather it?

Sure, hopefully, you'll get severance pay (employers are generally paying a week or two for every year you've been with the company) and compensation for unused vacation time. But if you find yourself looking for a job for more than a couple of months, that well could run dry if you're not amply prepared. What do you need?

Negotiating tactics to use at your company. Some severance packages are nonnegotiable, plain and simple, particularly in mass layoffs. But if you work for a small company or if you're a fairly long-term or senior staffer, you shouldn't accept the first offer. Ask for health coverage that continues after your severance runs out. Some companies will comply because it's cheaper than paying additional severance, and they figure they'll be off the hook as soon as you land another job. If you're close to vesting for your pension or stock options, see if you can get the company to keep you on the payroll—they call this "bridging"—until you get there. Request one month of outplacement services for every year you've been with the company (and be specific about what sort of outplacement services you want: retraining, counseling, an office [of course], and a phone). Get references in writing before you leave on your last day and make sure you know what the personnel office will say about you if a prospective employer calls.

Be sure your ducks are in a row as far as unemployment insurance is concerned. In order to apply for unemployment, you need to have been fired. Your company may think it's doing you a favor by calling your layoff a resignation (it does sound better, doesn't it?), but it won't wash with Uncle Sam. Make sure you have a letter from the company confirming that you can claim unemployment.

Continued adequate health insurance. If you're married and can be added to your spouse's plan—or if you have a domestic partner who has benefits available to you—that's your best and least expensive alternative. If not, as long as your company employs twenty people or more, you can "COBRA," which is shorthand for continuing your old group coverage under the Consolidated Omnibus Budget Reconciliation Act. Unfortunately, while COBRA-ing (as those who've done it often refer to it) is easy, it is almost never cheap.

To reduce what can be a hefty chunk out of your monthly budget, whether you've already been laid off or suspect you will be, consider switching to a less expensive health plan during your company's open-enrollment period. Laid-off employees have the same menu of choices as those still on the payroll. You may also decide to skip COBRA entirely and buy an individual policy, a short-term policy, or an inexpensive catastrophic health insurance policy with a high deductible.

Strategies to free up cash. Cutting back on nonessentials and other spend-less tactics are no-brainers if you've been laid off. But you'll also need to find ways to free up some cash. Look closely at your house. You may be able to convert your home equity into a cash reserve by applying for a home equity line of credit. A line of credit is better than a loan for your purpose because you don't have to draw on it all at once. Instead, it's at your disposal—like an additional checking account—for a period of ten years, typically. And you pay interest only on what you take out. The downside: A home equity line of credit is just another way to say "second mortgage." Default and you could find yourself facing foreclosure. Refinancing your mortgage and pulling out a chunk of cash (called a cash-out refi) is another way to do practically the same thing at a more attractive interest rate because the rates on first mortgages tend to be lower than those on seconds. Unfortunately, both of these are much better options while you're employed than after you've already been laid off. If times are tough and you still have a job, applying for a line of credit as an insurance policy is not a bad idea. In fact, it's a very good one.

If You're Facing Foreclosure

Hopefully, you've saved enough so that even if you do get caught in a mass layoff, you'll be able to muddle through until you find another job. But what if you can't? What if you have trimmed everywhere and anywhere and you're still having trouble making payments on your mortgage?

First, understand what could happen. Miss three payments and a "breach letter" will arrive from your lender signaling you're in violation of your contract. You then have a month to respond. Let that month go by and the lender has the right to foreclose, which means they take ownership of the house.

Letting those three months slip past is the biggest mistake homeowners in trouble make. Here are the steps you should follow instead:

Call your lender, immediately. Explain why you're having difficulty making payments, how long that difficulty will last, and what will have to happen for the problem to resolve itself. Be prepared to provide financial details, including monthly income and expenses. The goal here is to get the lender on your side and help you to solve your problem. That means, don't wait for the lender to call you. If you call them, they'll see you as a person trying to take responsibility for his or her financial life—and financial problems—and be more willing to work with you.

Refinance. If you have yet to miss a payment, refinancing can lower your payments in a number of ways. You can lower your interest rate, extend the term of your loan (thereby stretching out your payments), or convert some of the equity in your home to a cash cushion you could use to get by.

Ask for partial payments. If you have an FHA loan, your lender may be willing to allow you to make a partial payment—$700, for example, instead of the full $1,000 you owe—for a short while without changing the terms of your mortgage. You generally can't do that with a conventional Fannie Mae or Freddie Mac loan. But if you call and say you've just missed one payment, your lender will generally tell you that you can make up that payment by spreading it over the next few months.

Look at a loan modification. If you know that you're not able to continue to pay at the current rate but can pay something, your lender will generally try to work with you to come up with a payment that you can afford. This is called a loan modification and it works a bit like a refi without going through that process. You'll pay back what you owe, but you may do it over a longer period, or at a lower interest rate, or after a short break in your payment schedule to allow you to get back on your feet.

If, after you have considered all of these alternatives, staying in your house doesn't look possible, try these two fixes. Neither will protect your house, but both can protect your credit rating. The first is called a "preforeclosure sale." It will allow you to sell your property (while living there) and move on in an organized fashion. The second is called a "deed in lieu of foreclosure." That's when you give back your house to the lender and the lender disposes of it.

As you go through all of these options, you may also want to go through credit counseling to help you get back on your financial feet. That's a smart move, but note: there are plenty of disreputable counselors lurking among the helpful. The U.S. Department of Housing and Urban Development has a list of HUD-approved counseling agencies on its Web site, www.hud.gov. These are folks skilled in addressing mortgage problems, so you might want to start there.

Money and Happiness Evaluation: Part 9

1. How often would you say you and your spouse or partner have an argument about money or finances? (Circle one letter.)

a. A lot
b. Sometimes
c. Not too much
d. Not at all
e. N/A

2. When you fight with your spouse or partner about money, how often do you fight about each of the following? (Check one box for each.)

	A LOT	SOMETIMES	NOT TOO MUCH	NOT AT ALL	N/A
a. Whether to make a major purchase	❑	❑	❑	❑	❑
b. Whether to take a financial risk	❑	❑	❑	❑	❑
c. Borrowing money without notifying the other first	❑	❑	❑	❑	❑
d. Using credit to make purchases	❑	❑	❑	❑	❑
e. Spending more money on something than was agreed	❑	❑	❑	❑	❑
f. Whether or not to loan or give money to a family member	❑	❑	❑	❑	❑
g. Whether the person who makes more money should have more say in financial decisions	❑	❑	❑	❑	❑

	A LOT	SOMETIMES	NOT TOO MUCH	NOT AT ALL	N/A
h. How much money to spend on or give to the kids	❏	❏	❏	❏	❏
i. Whether to take a vacation	❏	❏	❏	❏	❏
j. Buying something without telling the other	❏	❏	❏	❏	❏

3. Indicate whether each of the following was true for your childhood. (Check one box for each.)

	YES	NO	DON'T REMEMBER
a. My parents gave me an allowance when I was a child.	❏	❏	❏
b. My parents talked to me about the importance of saving and spending wisely.	❏	❏	❏

4. Indicate whether each of the following was true for your childhood. (Check one box for each.)

	YES	NO	DON'T KNOW OR REMEMBER
a. My parents had enough money to buy the things the family needed.	❏	❏	❏
b. My parents allowed me to spend my money on things I wanted but didn't really need.	❏	❏	❏

5. Indicate whether each of the following was true for your childhood. (Check one box for each.)

	YES	NO
a. I had a job during my high school years.	❏	❏
b. I had to work my way through college.	❏	❏

6. Indicate whether the following was true for your childhood or is true now.

	YES	NO	DON'T KNOW
I received or expect to receive a substantial inheritance.	❏	❏	❏

7. When you were a child, how often was money used as each of the following? (Check one box for each.)

	A LOT	SOMETIMES	NOT TOO MUCH	NOT AT ALL	DON'T REMEMBER
a. Payment (e.g., You got an allowance for doing chores.)	❏	❏	❏	❏	❏
b. Bribe (e.g., I'll give you $10 if you take your brother or sister with you.)	❏	❏	❏	❏	❏
c. Reward (e.g., Here is $10 because you had such a great report card.)	❏	❏	❏	❏	❏
d. Punishment (e.g., You are not getting your allowance this week because of your bad behavior.)	❏	❏	❏	❏	❏

8. Now that you're a parent, how often do you use money as each of the following? (Check one box for each.)

	A LOT	SOMETIMES	NOT TOO MUCH	NOT AT ALL	N/A
a. Payment (e.g., You get an allowance for doing chores.)	❏	❏	❏	❏	❏

	A LOT	SOMETIMES	NOT TOO MUCH	NOT AT ALL	N/A
b. Bribe (e.g.: I'll give you $10 if you take your brother or sister with you.)	❏	❏	❏	❏	❏
c. Reward (e.g., Here's $10 because you had such a great report card.)	❏	❏	❏	❏	❏
d. Punishment (e.g., You are not getting your allowance this week because of your bad behavior.)	❏	❏	❏	❏	❏

9. How often, if at all, do you personally do the following?

	A LOT	SOMETIMES	NOT TOO MUCH	NOT AT ALL	N/A
Include your children in charitable activities.	❏	❏	❏	❏	❏

9. Don't Dictate, Communicate

Your children need your presence more than your presents.
　　　　　　　　　　　　　　　　　　—Jesse Jackson

A few years ago, I wrote a book called *Talking Money* that hinged on this thought: Talking about money is tougher than talking about sex. It was true then, and it's true now, perhaps more so. If anything, talking about sex has become more commonplace in recent years, thanks to *Maxim, CosmoGirl,* Monica Lewinsky, and reality TV. Talking about money hasn't budged from the closet.

You can learn to communicate about money as smoothly, as easily, as *candidly* as you do, say, about sports or politics. Note: I didn't say you should learn to talk about it as easily as you state what you thought of the movie you saw last night or what you'd like for dinner. Like sports and politics, money is an emotionally charged topic. That's precisely why it's so tough to put your thoughts and feelings on the table.

But bottling up your emotions and desires won't do, either. If you can learn to open up about money with your spouse, your path through life will be much, much smoother. And if you can then pass your newfound communication skills on to your kids, you can be sure they'll have a smoother ride.

You can do both of these things, but first you have to get a grip on how you're communicating now. Is your style bringing comfort to your relationship? Or is it exacerbating an already troubled situation? Don't be afraid to admit that you and your spouse fight about money. A full third of Americans do—with what can be disastrous results. Money is often cited as the number one cause of divorce. It's the number one cause of fights in the first year of marriage—a bigger bone of contention than in-laws and religion.

Conquer this problem, however, and it'll work to your great advantage. How? Our research shows that people who argue with their spouse about money frequently are more likely (than those who don't) to have more than $100,000 in total debt and to have more than $5,000 in credit card debt. They're also more likely to spend more than they can afford on entertainment, socializing and eating out, gifts, and cars. Are they doing this to punish each other—sabotaging their financial present to wreak havoc with their financial future? Perhaps.

By opening the door to communication in a positive way—talking about your hopes, dreams, goals, and how to achieve them—you can end this destructive streak. And allowing your children to listen in, when appropriate, will enable them to mirror your communication prowess. Those are great skills to be able to carry into adult life. But first we need to know where you stand now.

Money and Happiness Results: Part 9

1. How often would you say you and your spouse or partner have an argument about money or finances? (Circle one letter.)

a. A lot
b. Sometimes
c. Not too much
d. Not at all
e. N/A

About your response: Couples who go hand-to-hand over money are much less likely to be financially happy than those who don't. Why is that? It's because when you fight with your spouse over money, as three in ten married Americans do, you're not fighting over dollars and cents. You're fight-

ing over goals. By spending more than your spouse prefers, lending money that your spouse would rather you didn't, buying something without telling your significant other, even investing in instruments your spouse isn't comfortable with, what you're really saying is that you're not on the same page about what you want for your lives. And you're doing it in a very passive aggressive way. Is it any wonder money creates such big problems in a marriage?

2. When you fight with your spouse or partner about money, how often do you fight about each of the following? (Check one box for each.)

	A LOT	SOMETIMES	NOT TOO MUCH	NOT AT ALL	N/A
a. Whether to make a major purchase	❏	❏	❏	❏	❏
b. Whether to take a financial risk	❏	❏	❏	❏	❏
c. Borrowing money without notifying the other first	❏	❏	❏	❏	❏
d. Using credit to make purchases	❏	❏	❏	❏	❏
e. Spending more money on something than was agreed	❏	❏	❏	❏	❏
f. Whether or not to loan or give money to a family member	❏	❏	❏	❏	❏
g. Whether the person who makes more money should have more say in financial decisions	❏	❏	❏	❏	❏
h. How much money to spend on or give to the kids	❏	❏	❏	❏	❏

	A LOT	SOMETIMES	NOT TOO MUCH	NOT AT ALL	N/A
i. Whether to take a vacation	❏	❏	❏	❏	❏
j. Buying something without telling the other	❏	❏	❏	❏	❏

About your responses: What issues, specifically, are the biggest trouble spots for American couples? Here are the top five, in rank order:

1. *Spending more money on something than was agreed*
2. *Using credit to make purchases*
3. *Buying something without telling the other*
4. *Whether or not to make a major purchase*
5. *Whether or not to loan money to a family member*

These may sound like five different items. In fact, every one of them is about the same thing: communication. It's about going behind your spouse's back to do something the two of you should have talked about beforehand. Why? Because it affects both of you afterward.

3. Indicate whether each of the following was true for your child-hood. (Check one box for each.)

	YES	NO	DON'T REMEMBER
a. My parents gave me an allowance when I was a child.	❏	❏	❏
b. My parents talked to me about the importance of saving and spending wisely.	❏	❏	❏

About your responses: Six out of ten Americans say their parents spoke to them when they were kids about the importance of saving and spending wisely. More boys were spoken to than girls. It's something we seem to have gotten better at over the years. More eighteen- to thirty-four-year-olds got the "money talk" than those in older age groups.

Did it make a difference? I certainly think so. Two-thirds of people who report they're good money managers say they heard about money from their parents, while only half of poor money managers did. The same holds true for knowledgeable investors. More people who say they're better savers than spenders learned about money at home as well.

4. Indicate whether each of the following was true for your childhood. (Check one box for each.)

	YES	NO	DON'T KNOW OR REMEMBER
a. My parents had enough money to buy the things the family needed.	❑	❑	❑
b. My parents allowed me to spend my money on things I wanted but didn't really need.	❑	❑	❑

About your responses: Growing up in a family that has enough money to meet basic needs seems to result in feelings of financial well-being in adulthood. Americans who answer this question affirmatively are also more likely to say they feel in control of their finances and more secure about their money as adults.

Importantly, this does not mean children should have free rein to buy what they want when they want it. Kids need limits on spending (just as they need limits on bedtime, Internet access, and television watching) if they're going to grow into fiscally responsible adults. The proof? Kids whose parents allowed them to spend money on things they didn't really need are more likely to be spenders than savers now that they've grown up. They're less likely to have achieved their financial goals (or even to have made significant strides toward them). And—perhaps because they have trouble controlling their spending—they're more likely to say money is a cause of worry. Clearly, if you're a parent, this is a place to step in firmly.

5. Indicate whether each of the following was true for your childhood. (Check one box for each.)

	YES	NO
a. I had a job during my high school years.	❑	❑
b. I had to work my way through college.	❑	❑

About your responses: Encouraging your children to work during their high school years—perhaps by not giving them every dollar they want—seems to breed fiscally responsible adults. Those who have started to achieve (or have actually nailed) their financial goals are more likely to have worked through high school. People who worked through high school are also more knowledgeable about investing than their nonworking counterparts. Likewise, people who had to work their way through college seem to have emerged with positive money behaviors. Not surprisingly, they also emerged with higher than average credit card debt (not to mention student loans).

6. Indicate whether the following was true for your childhood or is true now.

	YES	NO	DON'T KNOW
I received or expect to receive a substantial inheritance.	❏	❏	❏

About your response: While just 9 percent of Americans say they anticipated (or received) a substantial inheritance when they were children, half of today's parents say they plan to leave a substantial inheritance to their kids. They may want to think twice—not necessarily about leaving the money, but about how they talk about and handle the transfer.

That's because inheritors' ideas about money tend to be skewed—and not in a productive way. Inheritors equate money with power and social status. They believe they need nearly three times as much money in the bank to be happy as noninheritors do. Some of their money behaviors are questionable, too. Inheritors (perhaps because they believe they don't have to) are less likely to budget. They're more likely than noninheritors to use credit. And they're more likely to say splurging makes them feel good. They'll also spend whatever it takes to get what they want when they want it.

On the flip side, it seems inheritors also know more about their money. More say they're knowledgeable investors. More have taken such safety measures as writing a will. And not only are more inheritors than noninheritors saving, but also they have more saved—$59,000 vs. $24,000, respectively, on average. However, you have to chalk at least some of that difference up to inheritances that have already arrived.

7. When you were a child how often was money used as each of the following? (Check one box for each.)

	A LOT	SOMETIMES	NOT TOO MUCH	NOT AT ALL	DON'T REMEMBER
a. Payment (e.g., You get an allowance for doing chores.)	❑	❑	❑	❑	❑
b. Bribe (e.g., I'll give you $10 if you take your brother or sister with you.)	❑	❑	❑	❑	❑
c. Reward (e.g., Here's $10 because you had such a great report card.)	❑	❑	❑	❑	❑
d. Punishment (e.g., You are not getting your allowance this week because of your bad behavior.)	❑	❑	❑	❑	❑

8. Now that you're a parent, how often do you use money as each of the following? (Check one box for each.)

	A LOT	SOMETIMES	NOT TOO MUCH	NOT AT ALL	N/A
a. Payment (e.g., You get an allowance for doing chores.)	❑	❑	❑	❑	❑
b. Bribe (e.g., I'll give you $10 if you take your brother or sister with you.)	❑	❑	❑	❑	❑
c. Reward (e.g., Here's $10 because you had such a great report card.)	❑	❑	❑	❑	❑

	A LOT	SOMETIMES	NOT TOO MUCH	NOT AT ALL	N/A
d. Punishment (e.g., You are not getting your allowance this week because of your bad behavior.)	❏	❏	❏	❏	❏

About your responses: Most Americans say money was not used as a bribe, reward, or punishment when they were children. More are using it as some sort of carrot today. That's unfortunate, because in cases where money is used in a cause-and-effect relationship, the financial happiness of those children as adults is lower.

9. How often, if at all, do you personally do the following:

	A LOT	SOMETIMES	NOT TOO MUCH	NOT AT ALL	N/A
Include your children in charitable activities.	❏	❏	❏	❏	❏

About your response: Unfortunately, only slightly more than one-quarter of Americans are including their kids in charitable activities. Being charitable—giving money, giving time, volunteering—can add a great deal to lifetime happiness. If, at an early age, children can make helping others an important enough part of their own lives enough to grasp those good feelings, chances are this habit will stay with them into adulthood.

Mixing Money and Marriage

Now that you know where you stand, let's see if we can fine-tune to get you in better shape. We'll start with communication in your marriage and move on to communication with your kids (most people operate in that order, anyway).

Whether you're married or cohabiting, you have to talk about how much is on the table, who has it, who owes it, and what you—as a team—want to accomplish with it in the end. Why? Because when you start withholding information, you poison your relationship. If one person has more information, that person has the control—not over the money, but over the marriage. And, of course, the best relationships aren't that one-sided. Whether you're deciding how much to spend on a new refrigerator or how much to sock away in your 401(k), you need to make those decisions together.

How do you do this? It helps to have a system, a method you use to make communication possible. Once you've practiced that method enough, you'll absorb it into your life and routine like any other habit. In other words, it may feel like work at the beginning, but if you stick with it, it'll get easier over time.

Make Monday night money night. Monday just sounds good; it could be Tuesday or Thursday for that matter. The important thing is that you make a regular appointment with your partner to talk about financial issues. This is when you talk about the fact that repairing the roof, which you hadn't budgeted for, has to be done immediately and will cost $3,000. Does that mean you can't take a vacation this spring? Does it mean keeping your old car another year? This is when you say that when you opened your 401(k) statement you wanted to cry. By getting issues like these onto the table, you can answer each other's questions and come up with a game plan. Handling each problem with your partner makes you feel that you're not in it alone.

Use your skills to guide your spouse. Make it a point to revel in your differences. If one of you initially knows more about investing than the other, let that person be the financial guide. If one of you is the better researcher, let that person do the legwork on cars. And if one of you has the time or yen to pay the bills and do the administrative chores, let that person take them on.

Then swap. Particularly when it comes to things that must be done month in and month out (investing, bill paying, and other essential activities) it's important that you switch roles occasionally. Let the non–bill payer write the checks for a month, for example. Let the noninvestor come up with a scenario for rebalancing the portfolio. Why? It prevents each from becoming overly dependent on the other and forces each to appreciate the other's efforts.

Nip real problems in the bud. If money becomes a real point of contention in your marriage and you find you can't talk about it without the conversation disintegrating into a brouhaha, you should know that help is available.

Many divorce mediators now offer a service called "marital mediation." This involves working out a legal agreement, on paper, that allows couples to get past the fighting and on with the marriage. Some experts call this a postnuptial agreement. According to one of the leading practitioners of marital mediation, most couples seek help because of unresolved money issues. A wife might complain, for example, that her husband doesn't give her enough time to go over their joint tax return before signing it. A mediated agreement may specify that she get two weeks for this. If he misses the deadline, the penalty could be monetary: $100 for each week he's late. Marital mediation is usually a ten-session commitment with a mediator who'll charge $150 to $225 per hour, or $1,500 to $2,250 in total. These agreements, very much like prenups, will hold up in court if properly devised. (Of course, if you go to court over one of these, you're probably headed for divorce court anyway.)

Couples counseling is another option. Psychologists, psychiatrists, and social workers believe that money problems in a marriage aren't nearly as much about money as they are about communication. They believe that how a couple talks to each other—and, even more important, listen to each other—determines whether a marriage works or not. So these practitioners teach you how to talk, among other things, about money. Typically, they do this by restricting when you're allowed to respond. You have to give your partner his or her say before you're allowed to say anything. Then they require you to paraphrase what your partner has said, to show that you've been listening. One couple and money therapist I observed even turned couples back-to-back so that their faces didn't give their emotions away.

If You're Heading to the Altar

What if you're just getting married? Merging your lives is up to you, but here are some tips for merging your money.

Start with an information exchange. Some financial advisers would have potential husbands and wives handing over more data than the IRS requires in an audit: five years of tax returns; bank, brokerage, and retirement plan statements; recent credit card statements; credit reports from all three bureaus; even employee benefits manuals. Fat chance.

But you should be as open as possible. Why? Because while you may have paid every credit card bill you ever received in full and on time, the fact that your spouse has three sixty-day late payments on his Equifax rap may put the kibosh on your mortgage. And you ought to know that before you say "I do." Likewise, if there is something in your own credit history that can one day affect your joint finances, better to voice it before the wedding so that your fiscal misstep doesn't fester into perceived deception as well. Be as forthcoming as possible and use the opportunity to build trust in each other.

Share your goals. The other sort of information you want to share is of the what-do-we-want-to-do-with-our-lives variety. It's helpful to get specific—really specific. Knowing you want to buy a second car is great, but are you talking about a new Lexus or a used Kia? And do you want to do it next week? Or next year?

Bank together and separately. Once you've nailed your goals, having at least one joint bank account will help you achieve them. Why? Because watching the balance grow together promotes the idea that you're in this race with a partner by your side. When people have only separate accounts, there is often no accountability. They don't have agreements on how they're going to spend, save, or invest. They don't talk about retirement, or how they're going to fund education for their children. Result: Five years down the road, they're not as close to buying that first house or funding that exotic anniversary fling as they might have been.

Now, this doesn't mean you have to merge every bit of your preexisting savings or put every dollar you earn into the same pot. But having at least one joint account builds fiscal unity and will help you meet your housekeeping and long-term goals. Each of you should contribute a proportionate amount of your income to that account and then use the money for joint activities, from paying the mortgage and utilities to eating out. His and hers accounts are fine to have as well, particularly if either one of you feels strongly about maintaining some financial independence.

Maintain your own credit. Divorce isn't a word you like to see when you're thinking about marriage, but it happens in nearly half of all first marriages and even more of subsequent ones. Just in case, you ought to maintain your own credit rating. You'll need it to rent an apartment, to buy a car on your own, and to be approved for credit cards—in other words, to obtain all the tools you'll need to build a new life. That's one good reason to always have at least one credit card of your own. Also, your credit rating is strongest when you can show that you're responsible with more than one type of debt. So let your spouse finance one of your family's cars in his or her name, and you finance the other in yours. Alternate the names on the utilities. And make sure both names are on the mortgage.

Rebalance your investments as a family. You won't be able to merge all of your investments. Your retirement account at work will remain in your name, as will that of your spouse. That's fine. But once a year or so, sit down and talk about the investments you hold in those accounts to make sure your assets are properly allocated as a couple. Based on your age, you'll want to hold a certain percentage of your assets in stocks, another in bonds, and another in cash. (Roughly, 100 percent minus your average age is the amount you want in stocks, with the rest split between bonds and cash.) If one of you is investing very conservatively and the other very aggressively, you could be in the ballpark on average, but if you're both chasing the latest hot stocks you could have too high a portion in equities. Worse still, you could have far too big a percentage in a particular stock or mutual fund. If you're unsure about the mix in your portfolio, spend an afternoon with a financial planner to help you sort out the specifics.

Keep an open mind. Finally, as you head into your matrimonial adventure, understand this: Just as there's no one right answer, there's no perfect timing. You don't have to combine all of your finances as soon as you say your vows. It's fine to apply for a joint credit card now, look into the money-market accounts at your bank next year, and open accounts together for the kids once (or if) you have them. You may very well want to wait until you figure out what sort of money manager your new spouse turns out to be. Why? Because while it's advisable to talk about money before you tie the knot, therapists say most just don't. This means you may end up wedded to someone who spends more than you see fit or who has problems with credit card debt. At least until you find a middle ground, keeping your own financial identity will make you feel safer and more secure. Who can argue with that?

Putting Money in Perspective for Your Kids

When it comes to teaching kids about money, America has a problem. It's not just that the majority of high school students—85 percent at last count—aren't getting any personal finance education at school. It's also that what education there is seems to be having little impact.

Take a look at the most recent survey from the JumpStart Coalition for Personal Financial Literacy, a group founded in 1997 to promote personal finance education. That year, JumpStart asked high school seniors 31 multiple-choice questions about saving, spending, insurance, investing, and credit. The average student got 57 percent right. Three years later, the average score fell to 52 percent. In 2002, the average was 50 percent. Worse—seniors who had completed a course in money management scored *lower;* they answered just 48 percent correctly.

What's wrong? I didn't know, so I went looking for answers. In 2002, I attended a JumpStart training session for high school teachers, and I came away with these theories about why our system is failing.

Personal finance education doesn't have a home in our schools. In some high schools, money management is taught in consumer economics (which is what has replaced home economics). In others, it's taught in economics or social studies; in others, math. The upshot is that not all students are included. Economics and consumer economics are often electives. And when personal finance is part of the math curriculum, it's generally taught in lower level classes, which means the more gifted students miss out. They're too busy with calculus, but unfortunately, they're also likely to be the ones struggling with student loans.

The second problem is that high school is too late. By high school, kids are being primed for standardized tests. Their hormones are raging. More important, their money management habits are already set. Research has shown that sixteen- and seventeen-year-olds spend an average $153 a week. Some have credit cards in their own names; many more have access to their parents' cards. It's not unlike trying to teach teens about sex: Research has shown that you can better mold their behavior if you reach them before they start to practice.

The only workable solution (for now at least) is that you have to teach your kids about money at home. Not just how to use it, but how to value it. If you attend church or synagogue (or other religious institution) you may get a helping hand on the values portion. But kids aren't likely to take to heart something they hear from a pastor or Sunday School teacher once a week but then isn't practiced in the home.

Emily is trying to do both. You may remember Emily. She's the television producer from the Midwest who got a handle on her finances when she was going through a divorce. Remember how happy that newfound control made her? Now, she's hoping to pass some of the same on to her two sons.

Emily herself was frugal from the get-go. Her parents were Depression babies, and they passed some of their frugality on to her. "I've always hated waste—in everything: food, time, clothes." Her own children, however, aren't like that. "My kids wouldn't be caught dead in jeans from Marshall's or T.J. Maxx," she says unhappily. But that doesn't mean she allows them to spend her money freely. When one bought a $50 pair of jeans at the Gap, Emily made him take them back. "Now they know to call and ask first."

Teach Them Tactics

In order for kids to learn about money, they need to have some of their own. That's why I believe in allowances. Your kids' weekly payout shouldn't be tied to anything—kids shouldn't get a bigger allowance for getting a better report card, making curfew, or making their bed. Helping out around the house is something they need to learn to do simply because they're part of the family. Otherwise, they're going to try to hold you up for a fiver whenever you ask them to empty the dishwasher. It's fine, I believe, to pay them extra to do the sort of things you'd pay a stranger to do—wash the car, for example, or baby-sit—but not to make their bed or clean up their room. After all, no one is going to pay them to do those things (for themselves, anyway) when they're twenty-five.

Start young. You can start talking to your kids about money as soon as they make the connection that money can buy things (I watched my children make that link between a quarter and a gumball). Maintain a running dialogue with your three-year-old as you walk the aisles of the grocery store. "We're going to buy Charmin this week because it's on sale, Joey. See these numbers? They say it's two dollars less than the other brands. And you get more—twenty-four rolls instead of twelve."

Once your child starts school, he or she should receive an allowance. Take a poll among the parents in your neighborhood to get a grip on the going rates. You don't want your children to feel ripped off at the get-go, nor do you want them to feel like the local Midas. And be sure that you're giving them enough to buy what you are no longer going to be willing to buy for them. Then make sure they get increases with age, as well as with rising expenses and—of course—the cost of living.

Decide what they'll have to buy on their own. Once children start getting an allowance, they need to be forced into deciding what's worth spending their own money on. Perhaps, in the past, you were willing to shell out for baseball cards on a weekly basis or Cheetos in the school cafeteria. You need to stop doing that. Instead, tell your kids that now that they have their own money, they can buy those things if they want them. But they can also save their money for something they consider more important.

Give them the opportunity to earn more. It's frustrating (I know, because my nine-year-old has told me) to try to buy a big-ticket item—say, a $50 video game—on an allowance of $3 a week. Even if your child saves every penny that comes in, it's still going to take a third of a year to accumulate the dough. If that's too long for your kids (and it certainly is for mine), you may want to give them a chance to earn more. The odd-jobs route works well, particularly if you pay your kids what you'd pay a stranger. In my case, the car wash (inside and out) costs $9. My son and I would both rather he had that money. You may also want to consider a pseudo-401(k) for your child, complete with matching dollars. They save a dollar, you save a dollar. The two months your child will have to wait for the video game on that schedule may still seem like a year to him or her, but not like a lifetime.

Show—and Tell

As if it weren't tough enough to raise responsible, thoughtful, caring kids these days, the subject of money is yet another hurdle to jump. We want our kids to work hard, appreciate what they have, and give to causes they believe in, yet we live in an age when Barbie has her own ATM machine. In an environment like this, how can we help our children learn how to put money in perspective? We can show them, and we can tell them.

Your actions speak for you. You are your kids' role model when it comes to everything else in life: If you love baseball, they tend to love baseball; if you eat sushi, they'll go along for the ride. Thus, it makes perfect sense that your children will mirror your money-related behaviors. If they see you whipping out your ATM card on a daily basis—and never see you making a deposit—what sort of message does it send? How do they perceive it if they notice that you go out and spend money—for fun—after you've had a particularly rough week?

The fact is, your kids—at least in their impressionable adolescent years—will value what you value. And it's up to you whether you're going to pass along the message that you value people or the message that you value things. Think about your most recent business trip. If you're like me, any period of more than a couple of days away from my kids brings on a serious dose of the guilts. The question is: What do you do about it? Do you load down your suitcase with toys and candy to try to make up for the time away? Or do you make it a point to spend some special time with your kids when you get home—perhaps doing things *they* want to do? On occasion, when business travel has gotten out of hand, I've even alternated with my kids, bringing one, then the other, along for the ride. Yes, they miss a day of school. But they also get to see a part of the country they wouldn't otherwise see, and they get to see that their mother enjoys her work (a particularly important message for my daughter, I think). And we get a solid chunk of time together.

Sometimes you need words as well. Modeling responsible money values for your kids is key, but occasionally it's not enough. When Nell and her husband, Howard, both found themselves out of work in 2001, they struggled with how to convey that message to their adolescent girls. They didn't want to scare them. But they also didn't want their daughters to think that the fact that they weren't vacationing as they used to and eating out as much was a sign of trouble in their marriage or—even worse—some sort of punishment.

Nell opted for honesty. Not honesty of the soul-baring, yikes-we-have-only-$800-the-in-checking-account variety, but honesty that was a little less detailed. She said to the girls: "It's different now. We have less money than we had a year ago. That doesn't mean we can't keep this house. It doesn't mean you have to give up your dancing classes. It doesn't mean we will not eat, or that you will not have clothing you're proud to wear. What it does mean is that we won't have two vacations this year. It means you're going to have to wear what we purchase. And it means we're not going to get new bikes every single spring."

Nell acknowledges her girls knew something was going on before she opened her mouth. "They hear what we don't say," she says. "I feel I gave them back some control over their lives—and ours—by including them in the dialogue."

Teach Them to Give

Finally, if giving is something that's important to you, it's something you want to pass along to your kids early in their lives. By age three, children are aware of other people's ideas and feelings. That's the onset of empathy. It's a great time to start modeling giving for your children—in other words, to start showing them, rather than telling them, what to do. Very young kids need to see concrete acts. They don't understand the value of a dollar, for example, but they can understand what it means to give toys they no longer play with to children who have no toys to play with at all.

By the time children are seven or eight, giving has usually found its way into your children's school, especially if they are in a religious school. It is your responsibility to make sure that what's being taught resonates within your child. If a visit to a shelter goes over your child's head or rubs your child the wrong way, it's up to you to find something that's more meaningful to him or her. Perhaps you have a family pet you could take to an old-age home to visit with the residents. Or perhaps, once a week, you could make lunch together for a hungry person.

What else do you need to do?

Stop hiding. Opening up about your own giving decisions is key to this process. As parents, we're the most powerful role models our kids have, yet many of us are reluctant to be open about our giving decisions. That's a mistake. Our kids need to understand why we feel strongly enough to send a check for $100 to a particular organization when we could do other things with that money instead—go out to dinner as a family, buy a new outfit at the Gap. So try to be open. When you're writing a check to your local symphony, explain to your kids why you enjoy it and how the group probably wouldn't be around without your support and the support of other people like you. Take your children with you when you volunteer, when you walk for breast cancer, or, if you can swing it, when you attend a board meeting, so that they can share in the good feelings you get by helping others.

Let your kids give on their own. Instead of giving your kids money each week to put in the collection plate, let them donate some of their own money. Make sure their allowances are substantial enough to support this, but don't tell them how much they have to give—or even that they have to give. Simply suggesting that they ought to try it might make them feel good; then see what happens.

That's what Claire, a mother of two in Westchester, N.Y., did. When her son, Luke, was turning eight, she suggested that rather than ask for gifts, Luke ask his friends to make donations to a charity that made playing basketball (one of Luke's passions) possible for kids in Africa. Luke embraced the idea. He got into it. And he chose to repeat the practice when he turned nine and again when he turned ten. In fact, by his tenth birthday, many of his friends had copied the concept. That year he went to a half-dozen "donation only" parties.

For years, Luke's sister Haylee did the same thing. This year, however, she had a party with two of her friends, one of whom didn't want to go the charity route. Haylee's reaction was completely level-headed. "Don't worry, Mom," Haylee said to Claire. "Just because I'm not doing it this year doesn't mean I won't do it again." In other words, charity had become a part of her life.

Finally, if your children make a donation, one way to extend the lesson is to let the reward—which is generally a thank you note for the donation—come to them in their name. Then let them open the acknowledgment when it arrives, but you may want to intercept some of the flood of solicitations that will soon come addressed to them.

10. The Ten Commandments of Financial Happiness

If you're having a bad day, if things aren't going right for you, then change your mind. Because that's where your life is. Your life isn't in what other people do to you. You are the one in control. You change your mind.

—Ann Richards, former Governor of Texas

I think that's one of the wisest thoughts I've ever heard or read. You are in charge of your destiny. As soon as you allow a boss yelling, a child screaming, a grumpy spouse to ruin your day, those people have all the power. And that's just wrong. *You* have the power over your own mind, your own life, your own destiny, and—as we've been discussing throughout these pages—your money.

Consider this chapter the piece of string you tie around your finger. In the form of a step-by-step action plan, a prescription, this chapter is a reminder of what you've learned by reading this book. Photocopy it, if you like. Tear it out and tuck it in your Filofax. Download it—from the electronic version—into your Palm. Or shrink it and tape it to your refrigerator.

The research conducted for this book taught us many things. Sure, there is a connection between income and happiness—having enough money to retire, have a good time, purchase the things you want, and weather a financial hardship makes you feel more secure, more content, and, yes, happier. To deny that relationship would be disingenuous, not to mention wrong.

But what our research also revealed is that you don't have to be a millionaire—or even close—to get there. At a household income of $50,000 a year, the happiness curve flattens out. Most American households—which, according to the Bureau of Labor Statistics, have a median income of $42,000—are almost there. Many others are there already, yet they find happiness elusive. Why is that?

It's because how much you earn, how much you have, isn't everything. Our study documents in detail that many other factors play into this equation. And what I find especially encouraging is that they're factors you can change. Some are habits you can adopt, others are information you can absorb, and still others are behaviors you can mimic. By making those changes, chances are you'll start to feel better, happier, and more in control.

That's a big deal. There is a very strong relationship between feeling in control of your finances and feeling happy with your finances, and a powerful relationship between feeling in control of your finances and feeling happy with your life. Control over your finances plays a greater role in determining your life's happiness than being in control of your job, your health, your friendships, your weight. Clearly, it's worth striving for.

So what do you have to do?

The Ten Commandments of Financial Happiness

1. **Thou shalt get "pretty" well organized.** Don't raise your eyebrows at me. I want you to understand you have a little wiggle room here. You don't have to hire a professional organizer or spend a mint at the Container Store. You just have to come up with some sort of system that you understand, so that if you have to put your fingers on an important piece of paper, you can do it quickly and without hassle. That's the key. People who say they are "pretty well organized and can find what [they] need quickly" are happier than those who aren't and those who can't. Why is that? I'd argue it's because they're not stymied on a regular basis by frustrating losses—losses of objects, losses of hours of their

time looking for those objects. They're not consumed by the banal tasks of administration. They can focus on the good stuff.

2. **Thou shalt pay bills as they come in rather than all at once.** You wouldn't think this would make a difference, as long as your bills get paid before they're overdue. But it does! People who pay their bills as they come in rather than stockpiling them to do once a month are happier. Why? My theory is that sitting down to pay the dozen or so bills all at once is pure drudgery. It eats up a chunk of time that you'd rather spend doing just about anything else. Moreover, watching that large sum of money fly out of your hands can be an emotional drain. Do it in bits and pieces, however, and it's far less overwhelming in terms of time—and your bottom line. Make it easy on yourself. Set up a bill payment center (which can be as simple as an in-and-out box) where you open the mail. Equip it with stamps, pens, your checkbook, and any other accoutrements you need, and get yourself in the habit of opening the bill, writing the check, stamping the envelope, putting the envelope in the stack of mail that goes out tomorrow, and recording the transaction in your checkbook. The bill itself goes back in the original envelope and into a stack to be filed. That you can do once a month.

3. **Thou shalt keep tabs on your cash.** If you feel that money evaporates out of your wallet and you don't know where it goes, you're more likely to be unhappy. What's the best way to prevent this from happening? Personally, I save receipts. But you can also start the day with a certain amount of cash ($20 or $40) and try to live within those limits. You can put yourself on a regular schedule of ATM withdrawals, take out a certain amount of cash for an entire week, and put only a fraction of it in your wallet each day. You can route all transactions through a single checking account, rather than pay some bills out of one account and some bills out of others. And you can balance that checkbook regularly; our research shows that people who do are happier. That will help you stay focused on where all your money is going.

4. **Thou shalt save at least 5 percent of your household income.** People who manage to save are happier. There is a pretty powerful relationship between saving and investing at all and being happy with your finances. But manage to put away at least 5 percent of your income and the strength of that relationship soars. How can you do that? The easiest way by far is to do something to get that 5 percent out of your hands before you have the opportunity to spend it. Elect to have at least 5 percent of your pre-tax income funneled into a 401(k). Or set up a series of automatic transfers that take 5 percent of your income out of checking each month and into an IRA or other tax-advantaged investment account. The bonus: Once you find you're able to save 5 percent a month, the accumulation in your account will provide some serious encouragement to do more (just as seeing those first ripples in your previously flabby abs encourages you to do more crunches each day). Go slowly. Up your contribution to 6 percent, then 7, then 8, until you reach the level that will enable you to put away enough to fund your future.

5. **Thou shalt protect your family (and yourself).** Doing all you can to shelter your family (and yourself) from financial hardship in the future is also an important part of financial happiness. Logically, why wouldn't it be? Once you've amassed an emergency cushion, written a will, and purchased life insurance, you no longer have to worry every time you get on a plane, for example (that's not a dig against the airline industry, by the way; it just happens to be my personal trigger point, and I'm on planes a lot). In fact, our research shows, once you've taken those precautions you stem the worry tide. One note: You don't get as big a happiness pop from buying disability insurance as you do from buying life insurance or writing a will. But I'd argue that's not because it's less necessary but because we don't hear as much or know as much about it. For singles, in particular, disability insurance is crucial.

6. **Thou shalt minimize credit card debt.** Interestingly, having a very low level of *total* debt (including mortgages, car loans, home

equity loans, etc.) doesn't make us happier. We understand that in today's society, affording a house, car, or home renovation means taking on debt in these forms. As long as we're not spending more than we can afford on these large items, they don't stress us out. Credit card debt, however, is a totally different animal. If you can rid your life of revolving credit card debt—that means carrying a balance on your card that you don't pay off every month—there's a good chance you'll be happier financially, and therefore happier overall. Chapter 6 outlines a plan of attack. Follow it.

7. **Thou shalt do unto others.** Forget about the "as you would have others do unto you" part of the equation. Simply doing unto others—by volunteering or donating money or even giving away old belongings—has the ability to add to your own personal happiness. Among all charitable activities, giving money to the causes you believe in has the strongest tie to personal happiness. But making nonmonetary donations (like taking your children's old toys to the local children's hospital) works as well, as does volunteering at a local school, hospital, library, shelter, or other organization.

8. **Thou shalt spend sensibly.** That double decaf skim latte may make your stomach sing as it's going down, but if you can't afford it, it'll give you a headache later. Of these ten commandments, spending only what you can afford is arguably the hardest to adopt. That's because you first need to understand the specific items sabotaging your ability to live within your means. Once you've nailed them, whether they're lattes, magazines, car payments, or birthday gifts, then—one by one—you can make changes. Need an example? Okay. Here's how I dealt with one of mine. For a few years, I spent an exorbitant amount of money on (gulp) my hair. Twice a week I'd have it professionally washed and blown straight. I justified it because these trips were relatively inexpensive ($30) when you looked at them one by one. I told my inner wallet that since I was going on TV, my hair needed to look

good. And then I added it up: $30 twice a week, 52 weeks a year, equals $3,120. Whoa! I was horrified. So I started looking for a solution. And $110 later I found it in the form of a top-of-the-line flat (straightening) iron. I use it so often I burnt the first one out after two years and had to invest in a second. But it's been worth it. I've saved more than $6,000. How? *By not spending it.*

There are many, many ways you can make these sorts of deals with yourself. You can brew Starbucks coffee at home or buy that SUV used. People who do this—if these are points of weakness in their spending patterns—are happier. Our research tells us so. Spending no more than you can really afford on your car is important to financial happiness. Spending no more than you can afford on coffee and magazines is key too. And if you can train yourself to adopt these little money-saving ways, maybe you can get into the swing with your life overall. That has the best result. Americans who spend no more than they can afford on *anything* are very likely to be financially happy.

9. **Thou shalt start working toward your goals.** Attaining happiness is not a matter of having achieved your goals, but a matter of making progress. If you're at least halfway to your goals you've got a much better shot at happiness than if you're just meandering toward your goals—or worse, if you haven't set goals at all. Being able to see consistent progress helps as well. People who are steadily working toward their goals are much closer to the happiness levels of people who are already there than those they've left in the dust. (Personally, I'm of the camp that enjoys the process *more* than the achievement. I get an endorphin rush from getting closer and closer to the finish line—and feel a little let down when I actually get there. So I try to make sure I have one or two financial benchmarks to hit at all times. You may be like me; you may not.) The encouraging bottom line according to our research is this: You don't have to hit your marks to be happy. Just making the effort to a point at which you start to notice results makes a tremendous difference.

10. **Thou shalt communicate.** Constantly fighting with your spouse or partner about money is a drain on happiness. How do you sidestep this thorny issue? Involve each other in your spending and borrowing decisions. Before you thrust that Visa toward the cashier (or slide it through the electronic slot) think: How would Joe feel about this? Should I put this $400 snowblower on hold overnight and discuss it with Gina? Borrowing money without notifying the other first (and that's precisely what you're doing when you put a purchase on a credit card) and spending more on something than was agreed upon are both highly tied to financial unhappiness. If you can communicate about these issues so that they don't become hot buttons, you're likely to live a happier financial existence.

And one for good luck: Thou shalt try not to be consumed with a desire for more. The first ten commandments are behavior-oriented. This one requires an attitude adjustment. It asks that you focus on enjoying the life you've already been able to achieve—from your family and friends to the clothes in your closet and car in your garage. Look around. Take a breath. Relax enough to laugh at the potty joke your seven-year-old came home with today. Remind yourself that wanting more doesn't breed contentment, it breeds more wanting. The Americans happiest with their financial situations roll their eyes at the statement "The more money I make, the more money I find I need." If you can live one day in their shoes, then you can live a week, a month, a year.

Does it work? You bet it does.

Remember our two American families in the Introduction. Here they are again in greater detail. Because you've worked your way through this book, you can now more fully appreciate the differences between them.

The first, you'll recall, earn less than $50,000 but are in control of their money. They're not anal with a capital *A*, but they've adopted at least four of the following six habits.

- They balance their checkbook at least once a month.
- They have some sort of filing system in place.
- They pay their bills as they come in rather than once a month.
- They don't spend more than they can afford on three or more things (though maybe they bust the budget on one or two).
- They do not often buy things they don't need.
- They don't find money evaporating out of their wallets.

The second family earns at least 50 percent more—upwards of $75,000 a year—but they're not as controlling. They're not financial fiascoes across the board, but they've picked up at least two of these six bad habits.

- They don't balance their checkbook every month.
- Their financial records and paperwork are disorganized, not systematized, so they have to scramble to find what they're looking for.
- They pay all their bills once a month rather than as those bills come in.
- They spend more than they can afford on three or more items.
- They often buy things they don't need.
- They find money evaporates out of their wallets and don't know where it has gone.

Who's happier with their finances? Neither. Roughly six out of ten families like the first will say they're financially happy. Roughly six out of ten families like the second will say they're financially happy. My conclusion: Money management—taking ownership of your money rather than letting it ride roughshod over you—made the difference.

In other words, adopting good money management habits rather than poor ones is like earning another $25,000 a year. For our first family, it's the equivalent of a 50 percent raise in pay.

And that's it. Remember, you don't have to jump on all ten of these new habits at once. People at all income levels who have managed to adopt about half of these habits are significantly happier with their finances—and therefore, their lives—than those who have adopted fewer.

Why? Because income is just a starting point. Your happiness doesn't hinge on how much you make. Your happiness hinges on how you handle it.

Good luck!

Index

Page numbers appearing in italics refer to tables and graphs.

Accomplishments, focusing on, 89
Action plans, goal setting and, 85
Advertising, effect on materialism, 38
Affluent attitude, 138
Age
  acting one's own, 55
  buying life insurance and,
    189–90
  diversifying portfolio and, 114
  feeling control and, 28
  giving to charity and, 167
  job satisfaction and, 158
  materialism and, 41
  sample portfolios for, *117*
  saving *vs.* spending and, 136
  savings needed and, 183
  work views and, 158–60
  worry and, 26
Allowances, 221
Annual income. *See also* Income
  happiness and, *18*
Aristotle, 163
Aspirations
  high school *vs.* college grad-
    uates, 35
  mirroring wealthy, 138
Asset allocation. *See* Diversification

Asset classes, 115
Assets
  lasting through retirement,
    123–24
  purchasing long-term-care insur-
    ance and, 193
ATM machines. *See* Cash machines
Attachment theory, materialism
  and, 37–38
Attitudes, evaluating, 23–29
Automation
  achieving goals with, 88
  saving and, 150
Autonomy, job satisfaction and,
  169

Baby boomer generation, work
  views of, 158
Ball, Jim, 86, 87–88
Bank Rate monitor, 116
Banking, advice for marriage,
  217–18
Bankruptcies, increase in personal, 5
Basic comforts, money providing,
  14–15
Bill paying habits, 66–67
  commandment of, 228
  delinquent, 67–68

Bonds, investing in, 115, 116
Bribe, money as, 213–14
Budgets, Americans following, 144

Calculating
    amount to spend on new home,
        100–101
    emergency cushion, 105–6
    life insurance needs, 189
    retirement income needs, 95
    savings needed at retirement, 96
    savings needed for college,
        98–100
    savings needed for retirement, 97
Cantril, Hadley, 52
Car loans, refinancing, 152
Cash
    commandment of, 228
    freeing up, after layoffs, 199
Cash/cash-like investments, 115, 116
Cash machines
    cutting fees from, 149
    money habits and, 142
Cash value insurance, 190
Causes
    ability to support, 167
    passing on to children, 224–25
Celebrities, comparing oneself to,
    40–41
Challenges, job satisfaction and,
    169
Charity. See Giving
Checkbooks, balancing, 65–66
Children
    encouraging to work, 212
    expecting inheritances, 212
    financial security and, 181
    guardianship of, 180
        importance of planning, 184–85
        steps for choosing, 196–97
    including in charity activities, 214
    lack of financial training for,
        219–20

learning about personal finance,
    210–11
money as reward/punishment
    for, 213–14
money communication skills
    and, 207
teaching about charity/causes,
    224–25
teaching personal finance to,
    221–22
    modeling behaviors for, 222–24
teaching spending limits to, 211
Clutter
    effects of, 68–69
    organizing, 72–73
    steps to, 73–75
Cohabiting. See Marriage
College
    Americans saving for, 140
    calculating savings needed for,
        98–100
College graduates
    expectations and aspirations
        of, 35
    happiness and, vs. high school
        graduates, 34
Communication
    about money, 207–8
    commandment of, 232
    creating marital system for,
        215–16
    importance of a marriage, 214–15
    preparing for marriage and,
        217–19
Comparisons
    with celebrities and fictional
        characters, 40–41
    making down vs. up, 53–54
    measuring self by, 39–40
Consolidation, 152–53
Consumer spending. See also
    Spending
    in 1990s, 131

Control. *See also* Feng shui; Organization
   accepting some lack of, 16
   clutter and, 68–69
   exercising, 61
   feeling lack of, 28
   importance of financial, 58–60
   organization and, 61–63
   over one's own life, 226
   regaining financial, 82
   unemployment and, 174–75
Corporate America, lack of control
   over, 60
Couples. *See* Marriage
Credit
   home equity line of, 152
   in marriage, 218
Credit card debt
   Americans covering, *140*
   commandment of, 229–30
   lowering interest rates of, 151
   making purchases with, 141–42
   surprise at, 146
Credit score, improving, 153
Csikszenthimali, Mihaly, 163
Culture, materialistic, 38
Cycle of "work and spend," 160

Debt. *See also* Credit card debt;
   Mortgages
   consolidating, 152–53
   continued accumulation of,
      130–31
   controlling, 61
   eliminating high-interest,
      150–53
   happiness and, 23
   increase in consumer, 5
   money communication skills
      and, 208
   refinancing and, 151–52
Demographics, financial happiness
   and, 23

Developed countries, money and
   happiness in, 15
Developing countries, money and
   happiness in, 14–15
Disability insurance
   Americans purchasing, 184–85
   purchasing, 191–92
Diversification
   importance of, 113–14
   managing retirement savings
      and, 124
   rebalancing and, 122–23
      for marriage, 218
   steps to, 115–16
   vs. "buying what you know,"
      118–19
Divorce
   credit and, 218
   money and, 19
Durable power of attorney, 195

Economic booms, 1990s, 131
Economy, post–September 11, 1–3
Emergency cushion. *See also* Rainy
      days
   Americans having, 182
   calculating, 105–6
   managing retirement savings
      and, 124
   wanting more, 183
Emergency information sheet, 195
Emotional immune system, 48–50
Emotions. *See also* Happiness;
      Unhappiness
   about wants, evaluating, 84
   fear of stock market, 108–9
Enjoyment lists, 154
Estate planning, 180–81. *See also*
      Insurance
   Americans and, 184–85
   necessary documents for, 194–96
ETFs. *See* Exchange-traded funds
   (ETFs)

Eudaimonia, 163
Evaluations. *See* Money and happiness evaluation
Exchange-traded funds (ETFs), 120–21. *See also* Index funds
vs. index mutual funds, 121
Expectations
high school *vs.* college graduates, 35
inheritances and, 212
for long-term investing, 111–13
mirroring wealthy, 138
reality *vs.*, 46
Expenses, Americans covering, 139–40
Experiences
Generation X and, 158–60
happiness and, 50–52
reliving, 54–55

Family
finding time for, 170–72
guaranteeing security of, 179–80
protecting, commandment of, 229
shifting priorities to, 173–74
valuing over money, 42–43
Fear, of stock market, 108–9
Feng shui, 69–72. *See also* Control; Organization
Fictional characters, comparing oneself to, 41
Filing, 74
important papers to keep, 76
Finances
biggest marital trouble spots of, 210
children learning about personal, 210–11
controlling, 61
happiness and, 17
importance of control over, 58–60

regaining control of, 82
teaching children about personal, 221–22
Financial decisions, more *vs.* less income and, 13
Financial happiness, Ten Commandments of, 227–32
Financial hardship. *See* Rainy days
Financial power, regaining, 6–8
Financial security, Americans feeling, 181
Financial training, lack of, for children, 219–20
Flow, 163
unemployment and, 176
Forbes, 132
Foreclosure, dealing with, 200–201
401(k) plans
impact of, 4–5
personal finance revolution and, 133
Friendships, happiness and, 17
Future, focusing on, 89

Gender
budgeting and, 144
savings needed and, 183
time demands and job satisfaction and, 160–61
Generalities, wanting in, 55
Generation X, work views of, 158–60
Generation Y, work views of, 159–60
Genetics, happiness and, 16
Gilbert, Dan, 48–49, 55
Giving
to charity, 167
commandment of, 230
including children in, 214
teaching children about, 224–25
Goals
Americans on track for, 92–93

Americans setting, 90
Americans understanding
    specifics of, 92
average American, 91
college, calculating needs for,
    98–100
commandment of, 231
difficulty setting, 93
freedom as, 171–72
home purchase calculating
    amount to spend, 100–101
job satisfaction and, 169
keys to achieving, 85–89
rainy day, saving for, 105–6
retirement
    calculating income needs for, 95
    calculating savings needs at,
    96–97
setting
    importance of, 83
    steps of, 83–85
sharing for marriage, 217
understanding specifics of,
    94–95
Guardianship, 180
    importance of planning, 184–85
    steps for choosing, 196–97

Habits
    cash machines use, 142
    evaluating, 23–29
    modeling for children, 222–24
    of overwanters, 36–37
    replacing bad with good, 87–88
    saving vs. spending, 137
    shopping, budgeting and, 144
    spending, unconscious
        consumption and, 134–35
Happiness. See also Unhappiness
    achieving goals and, 85–86
    annual income and, 18
    budgets and, 144
    changing priorities and, 173–74

defined, 22
elements of, 16–19
    in United States, 25
employment and, 164
equating with money, 35–37
estate planning and, 180–81
experience of, 50–52
financial, importance of manag-
    ing, 28–29
financial organization and, 65
financial vs. overall, 22–23
finding a good work fit and,
    168–70
finding financial, 6–8
flow and, 163
giving to charity and, 167
goal setting and, 83
high school vs. college graduates
    and, 34
money and, 1–2, 226–27
    in developing countries, 14–15
money management habits and,
    232–34
saving and, 145
simplifying and, 171
success and, 166
Ten Commandments of financial,
    227–32
    in United States, 24–25
volunteering and, 172–73
at work, 165
work success and, 174
Health
    happiness and, 18
    problems with, money and, 19
Health-care proxy, 196
Health insurance
    layoffs and, 199
    need for, 187–88
High school graduates
    expectations and aspirations of, 35
    happiness and, vs. college gradu-
        ates, 34

HMOs, 187
Home, calculating amount to
    spend on new, 100–101
Home equity line of credit, 152
Home equity loan, 152
Housing ratio, 100

Ideals, evaluating, 23–29
Impulse purchasing, increasing
    status through, 39
Income. *See also* Annual income
    adjusting to less, 12–14
    being aware of, 147–48
    calculating retirement needs, 95
    contribution to happiness in
        United States, 25
    happiness and, 18–19
    high relative, 169
    high school *vs.* college grad-
        uates, 34
    mortgages and, 100
    saving percentage of, 145–46
    saving *vs.* spending and, 136–37
    simplifying and, 171–72
    supporting causes and, 167
Index funds, 117–18
    buying, 120–21
    selecting, 121
Index mutual funds, 120. *See also*
    Index funds
    vs. exchange-traded funds, 121
Information, sharing for marriage,
    217
Inheritances, attitudes toward
    money and, 212
Insecurity
    estate planning and, 180–81
    materialism and, 37–38
Insurance
    Americans purchasing, 184–85
    disability, 191–92
    health, 187–88
        layoffs and, 199

life, 188–91
long-term-care, 193–94
protecting yourself with, 186–87
umbrella liability, 194
unemployment, 198
Internet, offering new career
    choices, 159–60
Investing
    Americans' knowledge of, 119
    "buying what you know," 118–19
    childhood money lessons and,
        210–11
    in company stock, 118–19
    fear of stock market and, 108–19
    importance of diversification
        and, 113–14
    in index funds, 117–18, 120–21
    inheriting money and, 212
    for long-term, 110–11
        returns and, 111–13
    making assets last through retire-
        ment and, 123–24
    need for, 109–10
    rebalancing and, 122–23
        for marriage, 218
    steps to diversification and,
        115–16
    in stock, 115–16

Job satisfaction, 157–58
    Americans and, 165
    flow and, 163
    happiness and, 17
    pleasure of work and, 161–63
    time demands and, 160–61
    vs. higher income, 12–14
Job security, 168

Kahneman, Daniel, 89
"Keeping up with the Joneses,"
    40–41
Knowledge, saving *vs.* spending
    and, 137

Lawsuits, financial security and, 194
Layoffs, handling, 197–99
Leisure time, 170
Liability insurance, 194
Life, control over one's own, 226
Life insurance
    Americans purchasing, 184–85
    purchasing, 188–91
Life satisfaction
    flow and, 163
    importance of family and, 42–43
    liking work and, 161–63
    living within means and, 147
    overwanting and, 46
    valuing things *vs.* relation-ships, 45
    vs. higher income, 12–14
Lifestyle, happiness and, 16
Living will, 195
Living within your means. *See*
    Means, living within
Loan consolidation, 152–53
Long-term-care insurance, 193–94

Managed funds, *vs.* index funds, 118
Marital mediation, financial prob-
    lems and, 216
Marriage
    biggest financial trouble spots in,
        210
    budgeting and, 144
    creating money communication
        system in, 215–16
    estate planning and, 184
    fights over money in, 19
    financial security and, 181
    happiness and, 16
    importance of communication
        in, 214–15
    job satisfaction and, 161–63
    merging money for, 217–19
    money arguments in, 208–9
    money communication skills
        and, 207–8

Materialism, 35. *See also* Wants
    attachment theory and, 37
    culture influencing, 38
    media/celebrity effect on, 40–41
    temporary boosts of, 48–50
    valuing purchases and, 45
"Me decade," 131
Means, living within
    Americans capable of, 138–39
    creating enjoyment lists for, 154
    defined, 129
    eliminating high-interest debt
        and, 150–53
    planning future spending and,
        148–49
    planning savings and, 149–50
    satisfaction from, 146–47
    saving and, 137–38, 145–46
    tracking spending and, 148
    understanding income and,
        147–48
    in U.S., 129–30
Media
    creating material "needs," 38
    presenting on the elastic expecta-
        tions, 40–41
Misery Index, *174*
Money
    always wanting more, 46
    attitude about inheriting, 212
    chasing, 20–21
    communicating about, 207–8
    equating with happiness,
        35–37
    false power of, 20
    happiness and, 1–2, 6–8,
        226–27
        in developing countries, 14–15
    imports of mastering, 21–22
    losing, through disorganization,
        69–70
    marital arguments about, 208–9
    merging for marriage, 217–19

Money (*cont.*)
  unhappiness and, 19–21
  "vanishing," 146
  vs. time, 170–72
  what it represents, 44
Money and happiness evaluation
  part 1, 9–11
    results, 24–29
  part 2, 31–33
    results, 43–48
  part 3, 57
    results, 63–68
  part 4, 79–80
    results, 90–93
  part 5, 107
    results, 119–20
  part 6, 125–28
    results, 138–46
  part 7, 155–56
    results, 164–67
  part 8, 177–78
    results, 181–85
  part 9, 203–6
    results, 208–14
Money counseling, marital problems and, 216
Money management, Americans' ability for, 120
Money management habits
  balancing checkbooks and, 65–66
  bill paying, 66–68
  general lack of, 64
  happiness and, 232–34
  importance of, 8
  modeling for children, 222–24
Money management skills
  average, 46
  using in marriage, 215–16
Money map
  creating, 148
  evaluating, 148–49
Money night, planning, 215

Mortgages
  Americans covering, *140*
  dealing with foreclosure, 200–201
  determining amount to borrow, 101–5
  income qualification and, 100–101
  refinancing, 152

Needs
  Americans covering, *140*
  met in childhood, 211
  vs. wants, 53
1990s
  economic boom of, 131
  personal finance revolution in, 133–34

Obstacles, to goals, 86–87
Organization. *See also* Feng shui
  balancing checkbooks and, 65–66
  commandment of, 227–28
  controlling finances and, 63
  eliminating clutter and, 72–73
  filing, 74
  happiness and, 65
  important information/papers to keep, 76
  losing money without, 69–70
  steps to, 73–75
  using PDAs *vs.* paper, 75–77
Overwanting, 35. *See also* Materialism; Wants
  commandment of, 232
  equating money with happiness and, 35–37

Palm Pilots. *See* PDAs
Paperwork, filing, 74
PDAs, organizing with, 75–77

Penalty rates/fees, avoiding, 153
Personal finance revolution,
    133–34
Personal finances. *See* Finances
Personal interaction, job satisfac-
    tion and, 169
Personal spending. *See* Consumer
    spending; Spending
Planners
    balancing checkbooks and, 66
    bill paying and, 67
Portfolios
    diversifying, 113–14
        steps to, 115–16
    samples of, 116–17
Postnuptial agreements, 216
Power of attorney, 195
PPOs, 187
Priorities
    relationships over money, 42–43
    revaluing, 52–55
Punishment, money as, 213–14
Purchases
    feelings about, 54
    valuing, 45

Rainy days. *See also* Emergency
    cushion
    Americans covering, *140*
    Americans prepared for, 182
    saving for, 105–6
Ratios
    housing, 100
    total obligation, 101
Rebalancing
    importance of, 122–23
    for marriage, 218
Refinancing, 151–52
Relationships. *See also* Marriage
    friendships, happiness and, 17
    significant personal, happiness
        and, 16
Religion, wanting and, 54

Reminders, achieving goals with, 89
Retirement
    Americans saving for, *140*
    buying company stock for,
        118–19
    calculating income needs for,
        95
    calculating savings needed at,
        96–97
    happiness and, 17
    investing for, 112–13
    401(k) plans and, 4–5
    making assets last, 123–24
    sample portfolios for, *117*
    working during, 164
Returns
    average, 111
    long-term expectations for,
        111–13
Reward, money as, 213–14
Risk
    sample portfolios and, *117*
    of various investments, 115
Risk tolerance, diversifying portfo-
    lio and, 114
Rubin, Bob, 122–23

Savers
    childhood money lessons and,
        210–11
    vs. spenders, *136*
    by income, *137*
Saving
    Americans and, 145
    commandment of, 229
    living within means and, 137–38
    as percentage of income, 145–46
    planning, 149–50
    vs. spending, 136–37
Savings. *See also* Investing
    Americans needing, 182–83
    calculating amount needed at
        retirement, 96–97

Savings (*cont.*)
 calculating amount needed for
  college, 98–100
 needed for rainy days, 105–6
School. *See also* College
 financial training in, 219–20
Self-esteem
 attachment theory and, 37
 comparing to others and, 39–40
 happiness and, 16–17
September 11, economy and, 1–3
Severance packages, negotiating, 198
Shopping. *See also* Consumer
  spending
 coping with stress and, 47–48, 81
  stopping, 82
 habits, budgeting and, 144
 increasing status through, 39
 for life insurance, 189–91
 using debt, 130–31
Simplifying, 170–72
Skills
 evaluating, 23–29
 using, job satisfaction and, 170
 volunteering and, 172
SmartMoney, 132–33
Specifics
 avoiding wanting, 55
 goal setting and, 83–84
 understanding goals, 94–95
Spenders, *vs.* savers, *136*
 by income, *137*
Spending. *See also* Consumer
  spending
 Americans and, 145
 commandment of, 230–31
 increase in, 5
 personal finance revolution and,
  133–34
 planning future, 148–49
 teaching children about, 221–22
 teaching limits to children, 211
 tracking, 148

unconscious consumption,
  134–35
 using credit card debt, 141–42
 vs. saving, 136–37
Spending power, 135–36
"Spending sickness," 130–31
Status
 buying, 38–39
 comparing to others and,
  39–40
 job satisfaction and, 170
Stock. *See also* Investing
 investing in, 115–16
 investing in company, 118–19
Stock market. *See also* Investing
 crash of 1987, 3
 fear of, 108–9
 as game, 3–4
 increase in consumer debt and, 5
 lack of control over, 60
 post–September 11, 1–3
Stress
 budgeting and, 144
 coping with by shopping,
  46–47
 credit card debt and, 229–30
 equating money with happiness
  and, 36
 happiness and, 22–23
 how Americans cope with, *47*
 money management and, 64
 organizing finances and, 62–63
 pleasure of work and, 161–63
Success
 focusing on, 89
 happiness and, 166, 174
Swartz, Steve, 132–33

Technology, offering new career
  choices, 159–60
Ten Commandments of financial
  happiness, 227–32
Term life insurance, 189–90

Things
  valuing, 45
  vs. experiences, 50–52
Throwing away, organizing
    and, 73
Time
  demands on, job satisfaction
    and, 160–61
  diversifying portfolio and, 114
  goal setting and, 85
  volunteering and, 172–73
  vs. money, 170–72
Tossing, organizing and, 73
Total obligation ratio, 101

Umbrella liability insurance, 194
Unconscious consumption, spend-
    ing habits and, 134–35
Unemployment. *See also* Layoffs
  control and, 174–75
  coping with, 176
  happiness and, 17
Unemployment insurance, 198
Unhappiness. *See also* Happiness
  money and, 7–8, 19–21
  rebounding from, 48–50
U.S. consumers, present *vs.* 1960s
    and '70s, 15

Values
  passing on to children, 223–24
  selecting guardians and, 185
Variety, job satisfaction and, 169

Visualization, goal setting and,
    83–84
Voluntary simplicity, 170–72
Volunteering, importance of, 172–73

Wanting, commandment of, 232
Wants. *See also* Goals; Materialism;
    Overwanting
  Americans covering, *140*
  decreasing, 52–55
  emotional evaluation of, 84
  vs. needs, 53
Whole life insurance, 190
Wills
  Americans preparing, 184–85
  importance of, 179–80, 196
Withdrawals, managing retirement
    savings and, 124
Work
  Americans at, 164
  for children, 222
  encouraging children to, 212
  finding a good fit with, 168–70
  generational views of, 158–60
  importance of liking, 161–63
  managing retirement savings
    and, 124
  satisfaction with, 157–58
  success at, happiness and, 174
  time demands and, 160–61
"Work and spend" cycle, 160
Working population, 164
Worry, sources of, 26, *27*